Practical Pedagogy for Library Instructors: 17 Innovative Strategies to Improve Student Learning

Douglas Cook and Ryan L. Sittler, editors

Association of College and Research Libraries
A division of the American Library Association
Chicago, 2008

The paper used in this publication meets the minimum requirements of American National Standard for Information Sciences-Permanence of Paper for Printed Library Materials, ANSI Z39.48-1992.∞

Library of Congress Cataloging-in-Publication Data

Practical pedagogy for library instructors : 17 innovative strategies to improve student learn-ing / edited by Douglas Cook and Ryan Sittler.
    p. cm.
    ISBN 978-0-8389-8458-1 (pbk. : alk. paper) 1. Library orientation for college students--Case studies. 2. Research--Methodology--Study and teaching (Higher)--Case studies. I. Cook, Douglas, 1951- II. Sittler, Ryan.

    Z711.25.C65P73 2008
    025.5'677--dc22
                            2008008219

Printed in the United States of America.

12 11 10 09 08   5 4 3 2 1

Cases Exemplifying Student-Centered Instruction

Using Dialogue

Using Simulation

Using Students' Experiences

Using Students' Experiences to Discuss Social Injustice

Table of Contents

Preface

This book is meant to be a practical guide for those of you who have not had recent training in pedagogy. Actually, even if you *have* had recent training in pedagogy, we think you will find something new and exciting here. We have tried to provide you with a bit of theory in chapter 1, but don't let that scare you away. Most of the book is full of *new ideas*—developed and used by practicing librarians—for you to try out the next time you teach a library instruction session.

Doug has been a librarian for more than thirty years (he likes to occasionally think in a philosophical fashion when he is sitting by the fire warming his arthritic body) and he feels that all pedagogy is useful. However, there are just two major pedagogical paradigms which he will be subjecting you to in chapter 1:

1. Use *Direct Instruction* strategies when you need to present information to students as efficiently and as effectively as possible.

2. Use *Student-Centered Learning* strategies when you want to stress student engagement with learning.

Ryan, who is slightly fresher from the halls of Library School, made sure that the rest of the book included lots of active, technology-based strategies for you to use to excite your students. (He also tried to make sure that the book was written in a fashion that new librarians, and even *NON*-librarians, could understand—not an easy task!)

Dear Reader, we hope that you find this book practical. We also hope that you will find our editorial comments mildly humorous, as well. (Editorial comments appear after the author's abstract and should enhance, if only slightly, your enjoyment of the chapters. It was either that, or, include a free glass of beer with every book sold… this was a little cheaper!) After you are finished unjamming the printer, answering reference questions, figuring out how the new software works, writing your self-evaluation for your yearly review, and liaisoning with classroom faculty—go hide in your Dilbert cube, and plan your next instruction session using one of the seventeen strategies in this book.

Smile, learn, and above all else, enjoy!

Your Humble Editors…
Doug Cook, Shippensburg, PA, 2008
Ryan L. Sittler, California, PA, 2008

"It's a long road to pedagogy."
Frank McCourt, *Teacher Man: A Memoir* (NY: Scribner, 2005), 9.

"Theory are as slippery as eels."
Doug Cook, *in an e-mail to a librarian named Sara* (2007). *(I can't remember who Sara is ~Doug.) (It still made me laugh ~Ryan.)*

Acknowledgements

Doug and Ryan would like to take this opportunity to thank our colleagues, at our respective Universities, for their encouragement and support throughout the creation of this book. We have spent many hours in a personal purgatory (or our cubicles, take your pick) whining and moaning about all of the work we had to do in order to get this book finished on time… everyone politely ignored us. Thank you.

We would also like to thank all of our chapter authors for their hard work, creativity, and willingness to share their unique instructional approaches with the *community of library instructors* around the globe. This book couldn't exist without you.

Finally, we would both like to thank Doug's daughter-in-law, Jess, for lending her writing talents… and acting as editor to us, your humble editors. Also, many thanks to Kathryn Deiss at ACRL. We thank her for both editorial encouragement and her enthusiasm for this project—it made the process much easier!

Now that we've patted backs, tooted horns, and stroked egos in unison… we would like to make a few personal acknowledgements…

Doug would like to thank his wife, Carolyn, for her encouragement. (Despite the fact that he was forced to edit her doctoral dissertation in the middle of this project. Congrats Dr. Mrs. Cook!)

Ryan really has too many people he would like to thank—because this book is a direct result of his interactions with so many different people. Thanks to parents, Barry and Deborah, and former mentors (Mary Ellen and Marilyn Kay) aside… Ryan would like to thank his co-editor, Doug, for being such a great guy with whom to work!

Ryan would also like to thank April Cole for reasons too numerous to even begin typing… it would add another chapter! Suffice it to say, her unwavering support—in many things—had a great impact on my ability to finish this project. Thank you.

CHAPTER 1

Why Should Librarians Care About Pedagogy?

Douglas Cook

Author's abstract: In this introductory chapter I will describe the two major philosophical orientations to instruction in use today with college students and adults—Direct Instruction and Student-Centered Learning. Each grouping of theories will be explained so that you will become conversant with these views and that you will have enough information to make informed choices regarding instructional strategies helpful to your students. Chapters 2 to 18 of this book are described as exemplars of Direct Instruction and Student-Centered Learning. An amazing chart is included which you will want to copy and hang on your bulletin board as you make decisions regarding your library instruction.

Editors' notes: *In this chapter, Doug tries to convince you, dear reader, that you should read his expertise and opinions on pedagogy—without falling asleep. (Good luck! ~Ryan) Just like vitamin C, regular check-ups at the doctor, and, flossing your teeth everyday—it will make you a better person in the long run. The rest of the book is even MORE entertaining. (Wouldn't it have to be? ~Ryan.) (Ignore him, I'm the one with a Doctorate. ~Doug)*

Introduction

Why should you, as a librarian, be concerned about educational theory and pedagogical practices? The short answer is that *how* you teach makes a difference in *what your students learn.* Slavin calls this being an "intentional teacher." He explains that "Intentional teachers are those who are constantly thinking about outcomes they want for their students and about how each decision they make moves [students] toward those outcomes."[1] And besides that, this is one of those things which they probably didn't teach you in library school.

When you get a call for a library session you need to think about what you want your students to learn. You should not begin thinking about what you want to teach or how you want to organize your presentation until you do so. What *would* you like the students in your library instruction classes to learn? Would you like to pass on to them the requisite skills they will need to be an effective database searcher? Would you like to empower them with information literacy skills? Do you have shortcuts and timesavers you would like them to remember? Would you like to work with them to sharpen their critical thinking skills? Your lesson planning and preparation will positively impact what your students walk away with at the end of the class.

After you decide what you would like your students to learn, *then* you can determine how to move your students toward your desired outcome. Understanding effective educational theories and related pedagogical practices can give you the tools you need as an instructor to assist students in reaching your intended learning outcomes. Unfortunately, no one theory or strategy works for every outcome, for every student, or in every situation. According to Phillips and Soltis, "…[A]s a professional charged with fostering the intellectual development of your students, you should be acquainted with [a] variety of theories."[2] Effective instruction demands the use of many strategies.

This introductory chapter will overview the two major philosophical orientations to learning and instruction in use today with college students and adults—Direct Instruction (or Objectivism) and Student-Centered Learning (or Constructivism). Each grouping of theories will be discussed pragmatically: to the end that you will become conversant with these views and that you will have enough information to make informed choices regarding instructional strategies helpful to your students as you plan library instruction. The remaining chapters of this book will provide you with the accounts of librarians and classroom faculty who have deliberately chosen to work within the parameters of one of these two orientations.

How Does Theory Drive Practice? A (Mostly) True Story

As I have mentioned, academic librarians usually begin with a request from a faculty member to lead an instruction session which will assist the students to work through a particular assignment. Depending upon the requirements of the classroom faculty member, and/or your particular goal for the session, you may choose various instructional strategies.

How does all this make a difference when applied to your teaching? Before we go any further into the land of pedagogical theory, let me tell you a story. Once upon a time, as I was beginning my career as a tenured academic librarian, I was subjected to (as many academic librarians are) peer evaluation of my instruction. During my first year in this position, my instructional sessions were observed on several occasions by my more experienced colleagues. One of these observed sessions prompted me to consider how my instructional goals informed the approach I took.

It was a fifty-minute session for freshmen about finding resources for a ten-page research paper in an English Composition class. My intent was to describe the various encyclopedic print resources available in the library, demonstrate finding books with our OPAC, and then finish off with a resounding introduction to full text article databases. (This was 1993. I could demonstrate but we had no computer lab at the time.) I provided a detailed handout which listed all the resources, tips, and tricks which I could come up with under each of these three format-related categories—Reference, Books, and Articles.

As is often my tendency when instructing I began by asking students questions about what they were working on, what they had found, what they wished they could have found, etc. My goal was to try to individualize my instruction as much as possible within the lecture, and to try to keep them from falling asleep.

I talked briefly about the Reference Works and pointed out valuable tomes indicated on their handout. I moved to the OPAC demonstration, again asking students if they had used an online catalog before (in 1993 dinosaurs still roamed the earth, and most high schools did not have OPACs. OPACS were *new!*) I used a search term suggested by a freshman and found several valuable book resources.

I was just winding up the OPAC demo and getting ready to swing into a demo of our full text article databases on CD-ROM, when I happened to glance at my tenured colleague observing me that day. She had her hand in the air and a very concerned look on her face. I acknowledged her and she said, "Dr Cook, you haven't told the students about Boolean logic." She then proceeded to give a brief lecture on *Anding, Oring,* and *Noting.* I accepted my untenured status and quickly demonstrated as she talked. In my remaining few minutes, I asked students if they had questions and sent them on their merry way, reminding them of course, to drop by the Reference Desk if they had questions.

Fast forward to the next day when the tenured librarian and the untenured librarian sat down to discuss my session. I was informed that there was a List of Skills which all students should learn in order to become Successful Searchers. Of course, Boolean logic was on The List. I acknowledged the importance of the items on The List, but brought Instructional Goals into the conversation. Was it not valuable to try to engage the students in the demonstration as much as possible by using their topics and by waking them up occasionally? Well possibly, but how will they know *What To Do* when they sit down at a computer if you don't tell them everything on The List?

This conversation started my exploration of pedagogical theory. Was my tenured colleague correct? Should I have passed on all the information on The List? Was I—the junior member of the library faculty—correct? Is it important to engage students in the experience of learning? I think the answer to that depends upon the situation and upon your instructional goal. If your goal is to pass on to students your best guess at the skills and knowledge they will need to successfully find information, then teaching Boolean logic is useful. On the other hand, if your goal is to engage students and to get them started searching, then tapping into students' experiences by asking them what they think is useful. Your instructional strategy springs from your educational philosophy and from your instructional goals for the class.

I now find that discussions about educational theory are like discussions about politics and religion—interesting in the presence of adult beverages, but often the discussants go away ignoring their colleague's ideas. In this light, I prefer not to think of educational theories as *wrong* or *right.* Instead I prefer to think of educational theories in terms of *useful* or *not so useful* in particular learning situations. In the next section I will try to define several pedagogical stances and will mention situations in which you may or may not find them useful. I will try to do this as succinctly as possible, but if you are already nodding off, go take a break.

Two Learning Models: Direct Instruction and Student-Centered Learning

Direct Instruction and Student-Centered Learning are based on very different assumptions about how students should learn and what students should learn. At the very basis of the difference between these two broad categories is the assumption on the part of proponents of Direct Instruction that the primary role of the teacher is to communicate information to students. Their emphasis is on shaping the presentation so that students can learn most efficiently. Students are often engaged in learning a skill or a fact, but the thing being learned is determined by the teacher.

Instructors working within the Student-Centered Learning paradigm, on the other hand, assume that learning derives from experience. Teachers cannot *teach* information. Students must find their own way by constructing knowledge. The pedagogy which derives from this stance emphasizes approaches which will allow students to *discover* information.[3]

A Brief History of Modern Educational Theory

It may help you to consider the differences between the theories of Direct Instruction and Student-Centered Learning by looking at the recent history of educational theory. Numerous pedagogical theories have been espoused over the centuries, however many are not in use today with college students or adults. John Locke, for example, developed a theory which influenced the pedagogy of higher education for many years. Locke wrote that the minds of students were *blank slates*.[4] He theorized that it was the task of the instructor to fill the student's mind with knowledge. This theory was primarily translated into instructional strategy by knowledgeable experts—faculty standing in the front of the classroom and talking. Students were required to take notes and repeat information in a written or oral exam.[5] These *Classical* educational philosophies have largely fallen out of favor, and thus will not receive other than this passing mention. However, if you took the stagecoach to library school as I did, you probably had your *blank slate* filled regularly. You need to realize that it is not necessary for you to emulate outmoded strategies. You are reading this book to find *new ideas*.

Much more useful pedagogy has come into being as a result of the Scientific Age, as educators began to use scientific methods to look at how people learn. Some of these early scientists, such as Pavlov,[6] studied the way that animals learned new behaviors. These proponents of Direct Instruction have been labeled Behaviorists. The scientist who was responsible for popularizing Behaviorism as pedagogy was Skinner. B.F. Skinner made a great effort to apply his early work on animal behavior to human learning. In particular, he wrote much about how a student's environment shaped his behavior.[7]

Building upon the work done regarding animal and human behavior, Cognitive educational theorists such as Bruner and Ausubel became interested in how people learn concepts and solve problems.[8] Ausubel, for example, felt that the learner naturally organized concepts according to hierarchical principles. For example, the broad concept of *tree* would be supported by the more specific details of *leaves, bark, roots*, etc. If broader concepts are presented before details, the student will more efficiently grasp and understand.[9]

In our discussion of Direct Instruction I will juxtapose the Behavioral and the Cognitive, as the practicality of their application to the classroom is similar. Both are based on scientific methodology and lend themselves best to an educational situation which calls for emphasis in Direct Instruction or providing information to a student in as effective a fashion as possible. Do not confuse this with Classical pedagogy where students are not active. For Direct Instruction to be effective, students must be awake and engaged.

Student-Centered Learning theory has arisen more recently, in reaction to theories of Direct Instruction. In general we can say that Student-Centered theories do not rely upon scientific methodology to derive a theoretical base. Instead, Student-Centered Learning theories draw from our current experience as part of a community. In new situations we learn how to become a member of a community by taking part in the community's activities.

Student-Centered Learning has at least two strains which are currently in use in higher and adult education—Situated Theory and Critical Theory. Situated pedagogy assumes that students and teacher together *construct* the knowledge which they need based on experience. There is no real emphasis upon passing a body of knowledge onto students. Students work with the information provided, matching it against their own experiences, and recasting it into knowledge immediately useful. So, a List of Successful Searching Skills is less important than information specific to the unique situation in which the student is currently engaged. Useful knowledge is that which helps the student to become a better citizen of his particular community.[10] The works of Russian psychologist Vygotsky have had a tremendous influence on current Situated pedagogy. He wrote that all learning occurs within a social context.[11] These Situated theories emphasize the learner learning rather than the teacher teaching.

Critical Learning Theory builds upon Situated Learning Theory by adding a global dimension to learning. Past and present knowledge is *deconstructed* to find fallacies in thinking and *reconstructed* to meet the immediate needs of the students. A discussion point of Critical Learning Theory is the inequality which exists in most human interactions.[12] One of the strongest current pedagogies in this category is Feminist theory. This stance is especially powerful at allowing the voice of those considered as minorities to be discovered.[13] Another current critical pedagogy is called Multiliteracies.[14] This educational stance pushes Critical Learning Theory into a global environment where the skills learned in a particular community are not enough to allow students to be successful. Instead students need to be able to easily adapt to a rapidly changing global economy.

An Overview

By now your head may be swimming with theoretical possibilities. Let's take a broad look at all of this. Hopefully this overview will appeal to those of you who are *forest* people. You *tree* people hang on; we'll have some juicy details for you soon. Table 1 gives you a quick overview of these theories.[15] My goal is not to be dogmatic about all of this, but to provide you with a way to think about how you might teach so that you can help your students learn what you would like them to learn. My primary emphasis is on providing a philosophical basis for you to reflect

	TABLE 1 Two Broad Categories of Pedagogy			
	Direct Instruction		**Student Centered Learning**	
	Objectivist		**Constructivist**	
	Use Direct Instruction strategies when you want to present information as efficiently and as effectively as possible		Use Student-Centered Learning strategies when you want to stress student engagement with learning	
Description: Basis	Based on scientific methodology as applied to how people learn		Based on the assumption that all learning is contextual and that knowledge cannot be taught but must be discovered	
Description: Knowledge	Knowledge is fixed and needs to be acquired		Knowledge is constantly changing and is built upon what participants contribute and construct together	
Description: Theories	Behavioral	Cognitive	Situated	Critical
Description: Sample Proponents	• Pavlov • Skinner	• Piaget • Bruner • Ausubel	• Vygotsky • Gee	• Giroux • Ellsworth • Kalantzis and Cope
Purpose: Emphasis	Behavior	Knowledge	Experience	Uncovering unheard voices
Purpose: Learning Outcome	Change in behavior	Knowledge is learned and behavior change results	Student becomes better able to participate in community	Transformation of student and society
Purpose: Best for	Skill development	Understanding concepts	• Problem solving • Critical thinking	Expansion of experience into the global community
Learning Principles	Students acquire skills which are reinforced through drill and practice	Students acquire concepts through the effective application of learning strategies	Students and teacher co-construct knowledge through dialogue and experiences	Students and teacher deconstruct and co-construct knowledge through dialogue and experiences which emphasize perspectives of other groups
Role of Teacher	Arranger of the learning environment	Arranger of the information to be presented	• Facilitator • Co-collaborator	• Facilitator • Guide

TABLE 1			
Two Broad Categories of Pedagogy			
Direct Instruction		**Student Centered Learning**	
Objectivist		**Constructivist**	
Instructional Strategies	• Lesson planning based on objectives • Modeling desired or undesired behaviors	• *Presenting Large Amounts of Information*–Using technology to enhance presentations • *Reviewing Information Presented*–Using games to review knowledge • *Presenting Complex Ideas*–Using metaphors, analogies and cooperative instruction to explain complex concepts	• *Using Dialogue*–Using dialogue, and technology to tap students' experience • *Using Simulation*–Using simulation to provide real-world experience	• *Using Students' Experiences*–Using project-based and life-based learning to provide authentic experience • *Using Students' Experiences to Discuss Social Injustice*–Using project-based research to help students to understand how groups considered in the minority perceive reality

on the type of pedagogical strategy you would like to use in a particular teaching situation.[16] I will be using Table 1 as an outline for the rest of this chapter, so put a sticky note on this page. Do not turn over the page corner to mark this table, as you will be fined $1,000 for defacing this valuable tome.

Details of Direct Instruction

Use Direct Instruction strategies when you need to present information to students as efficiently and as effectively as possible.

Let's take a closer look. As I have mentioned, Behavioral theories of learning grew out of a desire to study human behavior with scientific methodology. Although Cognitive theories of learning are more recent, they were formulated upon the same basis as Behavioral theories—the assumption that all phenomena can be measured. Behavioral theories are centered on shaping the learning environment to bring about desired behavior. Cognitive theories are centered on shaping the learning environment to help students acquire knowledge as a basis for changing behavior. Cognitive theorists have used their observation of how people acquire information to formulate theory regarding the gaining, processing, and storage of information in the brain.

The primary emphasis of these theories is behavioral change. Direct Instruction is based on the notion that humans are a product of their environment. Instructors can elicit required behaviors simply because the student is in the right behavioral environment. As such, emphasis is placed on the presentation or organization of information. Both Behavioral and Cognitive theories provide insight regarding strategies which help the instructor to more effectively and efficiently present information to students.

Purpose of Education in Direct Instruction

The basic assumption of education for those making use of Direct Instruction, then, is that student's behavior can be shaped. Looking at learning in the broader context of Direct Instruction, students learn, or unlearn, behaviors which will help them to survive in their particular environment. Behavior change is the ultimate goal of theories of Direct Instruction.

Basic Principles of Learning in Direct Instruction

Numerous learning principles have been derived from these basic premises.[17] These theories are based upon the concept that a stimulus is followed by a response. The consequences of human behavior reinforce, positively or negatively, the potential for the human to repeat a behavior. These concepts lead to the overall stance that the teacher can shape stimuli and elicit a desired response from a student. An example is modeling proper behavior.[18] Demonstration of the use of a particular database has become a staple of our library instruction repertoires. This common-sense tactic actually is a teaching strategy which stems from Behavioral principles. Modeling, or demonstrating a desired or an undesired behavior, makes excellent pedagogical sense. Modeling presents proper behaviors quickly and efficiently.

Similar principles have been tendered by Cognitive theorists. These scientists study how information enters the brain, how it is processed, and how it is retained in short-term and long-term memory. Again the overall assumption is that the teacher can indeed shape student learning by controlling the manner in which information is presented; a good example of this is the use of analogies in instruction.[19] Students are better able to understand new concepts when instructors compare them to concepts which are already familiar. An example from the library world is trying to explain the difference between free resources and licensed resources available on the Internet. This idea can be presented by discussing the differences between broadcast television and cable television programming. Just as it is necessary to pay for access to cable television programming, it is also necessary to pay for access to licensed full text article databases.

Role of the Student in Direct Instruction

As observable behavior change is the primary concern of behaviorist educators, the role of the student is less emphasized than the role of the teacher. Students are asked to be actively engaged in the instruction, but they are seen as having less control over the behavior changes elicited. A major contribution of Behavioral Theory is the use of Instructional Objectives in lesson planning. Made popular in the 1950s, planning lessons based on a particular instructional goal is still a valuable strategy.[20] And in fact, one which I am espousing as the basis of this book: planning for outcomes can make a difference in your teaching.

Cognitive theorists give a bit more importance to the need for students to be active. One application of Cognitive theory is that of learning styles.[21] This theory assumes that students learn in different fashions. Once students discover the way they learn best, they can tailor their study habits to promote retaining information in long term memory. Some students learn better by listening and others by doing. Instructors can take advantage of this by first reminding students that each may have a different learning style and then by presenting information in multiple formats to enhance student learning. A good library instruction example would be verbally explaining how to find an article and accompanying the explanation with a visual demonstration. This would provide students with visual and oral modes of learning. Allowing students to then practice the demonstrated skill will add a third opportunity for learning.

Role of the Educator in Direct Instruction
Behavioral and Cognitive theories of education place the teacher in the driver's seat. It is the responsibility of the teacher to shape the environment so that the desired behaviors are elicited. Thus the teacher can arrange the classroom environment, the method of delivering information, the curriculum, and activities undertaken. Changes in any of these circumstances will bring about a different behavior.

Types of Instructional Strategies in Direct Instruction
From a Direct Instruction point of view the instructor can choose to arrange the learning environment so that desired student behaviors are encouraged. A pragmatic way to think about the teacher's role in student learning is to think about the various pieces of the learning environment which can be changed.

Direct Instruction: Curriculum. The Association for College & Research Libraries' (ACRL) Information Literacy Competency Standards for Higher Education[22] provide a well thought out curriculum of behaviors which are easily taught and understood. The basic skills outlined in these Standards adapt themselves easily to a one-hour instructional session. Emphasizing various skills, depending upon the session's context, can encourage various behaviors as desired outcomes. For example, if your instructional goal were to teach students requisite searching skills, Standard 2.2 might become the basis for your lesson plan: "The information literate student constructs and implements effectively-designed search strategies." This standard is broken down into the following very teachable behaviors:

    a. Develops a research plan
    b. Identifies keywords and synonyms
    c. Selects controlled vocabulary specific to the discipline
    d. Constructs a search strategy
    e. Implements the search strategy
    f. Implements the search

Direct Instruction: Classroom. In the short term, we often have little control over the classrooms which we use for instruction, other than moving chairs and tables. Over the longer term, however, we often put great thought into the design of our instructional spaces. The addition of technology in classrooms has greatly assisted instructors by providing many new methods to present information. Classroom design can help or hinder group work, for example. Teaching labs with flexible seating and laptops allow for greater flexibility in instructional strategies. Classroom management software and Web 2.0 technologies such as wikis, blogs, and social software also add new potential to creating a positive virtual environment for learning.

Direct Instruction: Method of Delivering Information. Presentation techniques lend themselves to various instructional goals. The ubiquitous use of Microsoft's PowerPoint, for example, at all educational levels has aided learning by promoting the addition of visuals to explanation. Lecture, discussion, questioning, educational video, tutorials, podcasts, etc. each have unique characteristics which lend themselves to particular learning goals.

Direct Instruction: Student Learning Activities. Practice of desired skills is one of the hallmarks of Behaviorism.[23] Providing time in a session for practice can give the student opportunity to rehearse a skill which you have just modeled. Practicing helps the student to try out the skill and also gives you the opportunity to help the student to perfect that skill. Such activities can take many forms, for example, individual practice, small group engagement, demonstration to the group, etc.

Direct Instruction Examples in this Book

Most of this book is composed of examples described by librarians who have chosen one of the two models we are discussing and have created a pedagogical strategy which corresponds. Learning is so complex, that it is often impractical for the instructor to use only one single strategy during a session with students. Although these authors have promoted the use of a primary approach, they also have included other associated strategies, as well. Their chapters will further demonstrate how pedagogical stances can provide you with new ideas.

Interestingly, when we put out a call for authors I assumed that that we would receive proposals from library instructors emphasizing skills. Although some Behavioral objectives have been included in a number of these chapters, those emphasizing Direct Instruction primarily use Cognitive strategies. Strategies examined include several exciting methods to quickly and effectively pass on large amounts of information, the use of a review game, several examples of using analogies to explain complex concepts, and a very active strategy which facilitates students teaching each other. The following brief descriptions will assist you in placing chapters 2–8 in your mental schema for Direct Instruction.

Presenting Large Amounts of Information. Chapter 2. Nigel Morgan and Linda Davies, "How Cephalonia Can Conquer the World (Or At The Very Least, Your

Students!): A Library Orientation Case Study From Cardiff University." This Direct Instructional strategy promoted is centered on the Cognitive goal of assisting students to gain knowledge during a library orientation session. The Cephalonian Method was designed to be used for a one-shot instructional session to a large group. (You need to read the chapter to find out what Cephalonian means.) Nigel and Linda started with specific learning objectives tailored to the group and the situation. They then created questions based on those objectives. This deceptively simple question-and-answer presentation format using PowerPoint, color-coded question cards, and music provides a tremendously active level of engagement with students. The Cephalonian Method of instruction can be adapted to any learning situation which requires the transfer of a large amount of information to a student group.

Chapter 3. Debbie Crumb and Eric Palo, "It's Showtime: Engaging Students in Library Instruction." Debbie and Eric have successfully applied a Cognitive strategy called Universal Design for Learning (UDL) to the medium-sized library instruction classroom. These authors also started with objectives and a desire to present information in an active fashion. Based on the idea that multiple methods of instruction should be engaged in every session, UDL emphasizes a lively and engaged presentation style which makes learning enjoyable and accessible to every student. These authors recommend using lots of humor, props, graphics, hands-on manipulatives, prizes, games, and acting to teach concepts and skills. Although the authors primarily discuss English-as-a-Second-Language (ESL) students, their instructional strategies and techniques will work equally well with any audience.

Chapter 4. Christine Bombaro, "The Clicky Things Rocked: Combating Plagiarism with Audience Response System Technology." Christine makes use of an extremely popular Direct Instructional technology called Audience Response Systems (ARS) or Clickers. Clickers, at a first look, bring Behaviorist stimulus/response principles to mind. However, this chapter primarily discusses the presentation of a large amount of potentially uninteresting (at least to students) information regarding "The Seven Deadly Sins of Plagiarism" to a group of freshmen. Working with a PowerPoint presentation, ARS technology lends itself to teaching concepts which can be divided into specific objectives. Each objective can be immediately assessed by having students respond with the Clickers to a question. This chapter is also an excellent example of objective-based lesson planning for an efficient large group lecture.

Reviewing Information Presented. Chapter 5. Julie Maginn, "Daily Doubles, Final Answers, and Library Resources." Julie uses active learning to review basic concepts which have been discussed in class. She began her experiment with using games as a method of reviewing information presented in a short lecture by using a Jeopardy format. As you may remember, Jeopardy is based on answering specific questions. As in the previous three chapters, this approach requires the instructor to define specific learning objectives and to create questions based on knowledge related to the objectives. Julie quickly moved from using Jeopardy to creating a game of her own roughly based on Jeopardy and on Family Feud which she appropriately calls, The Library Research Game. Review games can be very useful in small group situations where it is important to engage the students with concepts which have been presented.

Presenting Complex Ideas. Chapter 6. Susan Avery and Jim Hahn, "Making Meaning: Using Metaphor as a Tool to Increase Student Understanding." This chapter departs a bit from the first few. Although the authors still begin with the need to present information in an effective fashion, their presentation technique is much different. They use the discussion of concepts familiar to students to explain more complex and unfamiliar library- and research-related concepts. For example, Susan and Jim make use of the well-loved-by-students, Facebook to explain the idiosyncrasies of searching library databases. Tapping into this prior knowledge to explain new concepts is a valuable Cognitive technique. They follow their discussion of searching with guided hands-on practice regarding the concepts discussed. Metaphor can be used with large or small groups.

Chapter 7. Anna Johnson, "Analogical Storytelling as a Strategy for Teaching Concept Attainment." This chapter is also primarily concerned with Cognitive explanation strategies. Anna, however, broadens the strategy from that of using specific metaphors to illustrate concepts to the use of storytelling as an instructional strategy. Anna's storytelling makes use of analogies which are wrapped in tales she tells about her own research. For example she tells the story of her Dad being featured on the cover of the journal *Physics Today*. She pulls students into the discussion by telling an interesting account which ends with them helping her to solve a research problem similar to those that they will soon face. Storytelling of this type works better with smaller groups.

The final chapter illustrating Direct Instruction strategies was written by Chapter 8. Linda Reeves, Judy McMillan, and Renata Gibson, "Keep Them Engaged: Cooperative Learning with the Jigsaw Method." The Jigsaw Method is a presentation strategy which moves away from reliance on the instructor. In fact, it is the students who become the instructors. Jigsaw also represents active Cooperative Learning which allows students to research a complex concept as a group. Each small group takes an aspect of the topic and studies it. At the end of the session students put all their pieces together like a puzzle to explain the complete concept. Linda, Judy and Renata ask small groups to use a specific database to research a topic, and in turn to present that information to the class. Research from all databases is combined at the end of the session to get a complete picture of all the resources available for a particular topic. This technique is effective for covering large amount of information with small to medium sized groups.

In summary, the first seven cases in this book (chapters 2–8) will give you numerous excellent ideas for presenting large amounts of information or for presenting complex concepts to student groups.

So, use Direct Instruction strategies when you want to present information as efficiently and as effectively as possible. However, use Student-Centered Learning strategies when you want to stress student engagement with learning.

Details of Student-Centered Learning

Student-Centered Learning theorists are not concerned with eliciting specific behaviors, as are the proponents of Direct Instruction, but instead are concerned with facilitating student engagement in learning. As far as pedagogy is concerned, proponents of Direct Instruction feel that the teacher is the primary actor in the educational environment. Proponents of Student-Centered Learning feel that students are in control of their educational experience. These theorists believe that students learn by constructing new knowledge from current experience, or in the case of classroom instruction, on the activities in which they engage.

Purpose of Education in Student-Centered Learning

Education viewed from a Student-Centered Learning viewpoint is active. There is no body of knowledge to be memorized by students. Student-Centered Learning theorists feel that learning occurs as the students and the teacher converse about a particular experiential situation. This pedagogical philosophy moves the emphasis from the teacher presenting information to the students engaging with information. The ultimate goal of Student-Centered Learning is that the knowledge gained through such learning assists the student to better participate in the classroom community, the student's larger world, and/or the global community.

Basic Principles of Learning in Student-Centered Learning

Student-Centered Learning is based upon the assumption that all learning is contextual and that knowledge cannot be taught but must be discovered. Humans learn as they work together in their environment. In particular, humans learn by interacting with other humans. Conversation and interaction become the primary fashion in which students and the teacher interact.

Many of the basic principles of Situated pedagogy have been derived from the works of Vygotsky,[24] who theorized that learning in a group allows students to learn more than they could on their own. Learners gradually acquire expertise through interaction with a more experienced peer. And learners should be challenged with complex life-related situations and then be given enough help to achieve these tasks. These guidelines suggest that group work is the preferred instructional strategy where engagement with authentic experience is the goal. One library-related example of this would be to task students with critiquing a Web site based on several evaluative principles. The use of small discussion groups would enhance this conversation.

Critical Theory expands upon Situated Theory by introducing a global component. The instructional strategies are essentially the same; however the content of the group engagement must also include an aspect of social consciousness.[25] Searching databases for information about a topic with a social justice theme, such as the urban poor, might provide a good library opportunity for Critical pedagogy. How do various databases present the plight of this group? What conclusions can we come to based on these various resources?

Role of the Student in Student-Centered Learning

Students actually co-construct their knowledge in the midst of this type of learning situation. The student must be completely engaged in the experience of learning. As students purposefully interact with each other and with the teacher, they co-construct solutions to the problems and situations under study. In this type of classroom, students are responsible for their own learning.

Role of the Educator in Student-Centered Learning

As the classroom becomes the learning environment, it is the teacher's responsibility to facilitate the experience. Typically this occurs as discussion or as group work, with emphasis placed on critical thinking and problem-solving, rather than on finding information. The teacher engages in the learning experience as a partner or as a mentor. The instructor utilizing Critical Pedagogy also guides students as they attempt to understand a situation from a perspective other than their own.

Types of Instructional Strategies in Student-Centered Learning

Unlike proponents of Direct Instruction, educators using Student-Centered Learning do not feel that they need to control the student's environment to ensure that student learning takes place. Proponents of Student-Centered Learning feel that they are facilitators of learning, providing the context of learning and then helping students to be successful. Instructional strategies are primarily group-oriented and encourage conversation and interaction. Students' and teacher's experience is important and becomes a point of discussion.

Student-Centered Curriculum. Experience in some form or another often *becomes* the curriculum in Student-Centered Learning. Case studies, engagement in the community, projects, simulations, and other authentic situations are explored as students learn critical thinking skills.

Critical pedagogy does demand a social justice slant to the curriculum. For example, rather than simply having students engage in an evaluation of research database findings regarding Hurricane Katrina's destruction of New Orleans, it would be the responsibility of the instructor to raise the consciousness of the students by helping them hear the voices of the victims of this terrible tragedy. Why were so many of these sufferers Minority persons?

Student-Centered Classroom. The classroom does not hold the importance that it does in Direct Instruction. The space should be flexible so that it can meet the immediate needs of the student, but in reality learning can occur anywhere.

Student-Centered Method of Delivering Information. Delivery methods do not have the importance to proponents of Student-Centered Learning that they do to proponents of Direct Instruction. Information provided to a student during a class becomes a part of the experiential learning process. In Student-Centered classrooms, students often need to go out and search for requisite information on their own.

Student-Centered Learning Activities. Learning activities take on a primary importance in the Student-Centered Learning classroom. Activities provide opportunity for students to engage with new information provided by comparing and contrasting it to their existing knowledge base. Cooperative Learning[26] is a good example of an activity format which promotes Student-Centered Learning. Cooperative Learning allows students to work together on a task. Their learning is enhanced, as students working in groups will often learn more than a student is able to accomplish alone. This group orientation also allows students to tackle far more complex scenarios, as the learning responsibilities are shared. An illustration of Cooperative Learning would be an upper-division Marketing class assignment which requires small groups of students to find out as much real-world information as possible about particular companies. This authentic activity requires that each group use various library resources in a very sophisticated fashion.

Student-Centered Instruction Examples in this Book

The remainder of the case studies in this book (chapters 9–18) are concerned less with the presentation of specific knowledge than they are with students learning from experience. Instructional strategies based on Situated theory take advantage of active learning in groups. These chapters represent those librarians whose learning goals include engaging students in a more complex way with information literacy. Such strategies allow students to have a greater amount of liberty during instruction. Chapters include several examples of using dialogue as an instructional strategy, examples of extending dialogue with technology, several examples of allowing students to use their experiences as a basis for learning, and finally one example of the use of Critical pedagogy. These chapter summaries will provide you with examples of Student-Centered Learning.

Using Dialogue. Chapter 9. Karla Schmit, "True and Terrifying Stories: Using Peer-Led Discussion Groups to Evaluate Information Texts." Dialogue is a powerful strategy which allows students to engage with each other and with a topic. Dialogue also lends itself to learning how to evaluate resources. In Karla's chapter students are using broad, general criteria to evaluate a non-fiction adolescent book. It is the experience of each student in reading this book and in comparing it to another of the same topic that she is trying to tap. Karla uses dialogue in the form of small-group discussion to allow students to build a rubric based on their own experience which will assist them to learn how to critically evaluate a specific genre of children's literature.

Chapter 10. Susan Frey, "Constructing Narrative to Situate Learning in Library Instruction: Counseling an Imaginary Undergraduate." Susan uses the dialogical technique of creating a fictitious new freshman who has very specific needs in regards to the library. Her approach is similar to Karla's in the previous chapter in that her goal is to allow the students to think together as a group, thus using their own experiences to situate learning in their own context. Through conversation she builds the fictitious student's personality and basic needs in the university environment. Students then determine together with the instructor, the skills and knowledge needed for this student to be a successful researcher. This particular strategy would work better with smaller groups of students.

Chapter 11. Kathleen Lowe, "Using a Personality Test to Teach Boolean Logic." If you have a difficult time teaching students about Boolean logic, you need to read this chapter. Kathleen uses conversation and a very sneaky introductory activity—an online personality test. After the students are totally engaged in working through their personality profile, she springs Boolean on them. Her goal, of course, is to help students learn and understand concepts related to information literacy, but she does this by engaging the students in a common captivating experience. She then helps students find their way through Boolean to performing good searches.

Chapter 12. Lyda Ellis, "Plagiarism Instruction Online: Beyond the Citation." Lyda uses dialogue in a similar fashion to Kathleen, Susan, and Karla—as means of assisting students to construct ideas and opinions together and then to direct those ideas toward a specific topic. Lyda puts a special spin on getting students to talk to each other: she has them chat online. She starts with each student interviewing two friends, in person, regarding their plagiarism habits. Students then report their findings online in a chat forum. This open dialogue allows the students to first define plagiarism, and secondly to pinpoint occurrences of it in their academic environment. The technology allows the discussion to occur in the forum without the mediation of an instructor.

Chapter 13. Carl DiNardo, "Web 2.0: Using a Wiki to Extend Learning Beyond the Classroom." Have you ever wished that you could keep a good conversation going among students after the class is over? Carl has discovered how to do this with technology. After experimenting with various Web 2.0 technologies, he settled on a wiki to be the most effective way to keep instructional conversations alive after students leave the classroom. In the final chapter which uses dialogue as a Student-Centered Learning strategy, Carl provides a solid rationale for introducing Web 2.0 into the classroom.

Using a Simulation. Chapter 14. Dawn Eckenrode, "An 'Amazing Race' through the Library: Reality Television Meets Problem-Based Learning." Dawn combines a number of Student-Centered Learning strategies to introduce a group of freshmen to the library. Her primary goal is not to provide specific information to the students, but instead to help them feel comfortable in the library via an active experience. She gets her students thoroughly engaged in a game show activity, which helps to familiarize them with basic library skills. Working in groups, students race to complete a series of library-related tasks. A dose of reality television adds a bit of spice.

Using Students' Experiences. Chapter 15. Will Jefferson and Eloise Long, "Electronic Portfolios as a Means of Authentic Assessment." Authentically assessing students' experience is challenging. Portfolios have come into use recently in education as a method with which to evaluate student progress. Will and Eloise use portfolios in a library science course to document the students' experience during the course. Portfolios provide authentic assessment—that is, proof of learning that includes artifacts from the learning process. Longer term situations, such as the one written about in this chapter, often use complex rubrics to gauge excellence. You will need to read this chapter to see how portfolio assessment can be applied to a one-shot library session.

Chapter 16. Li Zhu and Kathleen Zakri, "Picture This: A Snapshot of How Technology Motivates Student Research." Julie and Kathleen write about a project-based strategy to motivate students to connect with learning about the research process. Microsoft's Movie Maker is a simple-to-use software package which quickly allows students to create presentations from available graphics, video, music, and/or narration. Students engage in the research process as they gather information for their projects. The final presentation and its creation provide a unique experience which immediately absorbs the students in the practice of learning.

Chapter 17. John Hickok, "Bringing Them into the Community: Innovative Library Instructional Strategies for International and ESL Students." John's chapter takes an unusually broad approach to teaching ESL and International students about the Library. Building on his training as an English-as-a-Second-Language (ESL) instructor, he has used Situated theory to create a three-phased program. John considers the experience of the student before he begins to plan an instruction session. His Inviting, Involving, and Interfacing strategies, although created particularly for second-language learners, can effectively be leveraged for any special-needs group.

Using Students' Experiences to Discuss Social Injustice. Chapter 18. Amanda Hornby, Suzan Parker, and Kari Lerum, "Zines! Librarians and Faculty Engaging Students in Creative Scholarship". The last chapter of this book is the only chapter included which uses Critical pedagogy as a primary strategy. Amanda, Suzan and Kari worked with a group of upper-division journalism students. They used student-centered pedagogy in several ways. The active tasks of creating, editing and evaluating assist their students to use their talents and experiences to formulate a *zine*—a self-published magazine-style report. The second strategy these authors employ is Critical pedagogy which encourages students to deconstruct current stereotypes and reconstruct them from the viewpoint of another culture. The student zine examples they have included in their chapter show that Critical pedagogy can help students to move outside their own worldview.

In summary, the final ten cases in this book will give you valuable ideas for engaging students in the discovery of knowledge, primarily via discussion and project-based learning.

Conclusion—Putting it all Together

You made it to the end of this chapter! Congratulations! So, why should you, as a librarian, be concerned about educational theory and pedagogical practices? As I have pointed out, how you teach makes a difference in what your students learn. First, decide what you would like your students to learn, and then you can determine how to move your students toward your desired outcome. Learning about various educational theories and related teaching strategies can give you the tools you need as an instructor to assist students in reaching your intended learning outcomes.

Begin your lesson planning by deciding whether the learning opportunity calls for Direct Instruction or for Student-Centered Learning. Use strategies of Direct Instruction if you need to present skills and/or concepts. Use strategies of Student-Centered learning if your primary concern is that students experience a particular phenomenon.

Finally, the next time you have a discussion with a colleague about various *useful* instructional strategies, have an adult beverage for Doug Cook and another for Ryan Sittler.

Cheers!

Notes

1. Robert E. Slavin, *Educational Psychology: Theory and Practice* (Boston: Pearson, 2006), 7.
2. D.C. Phillips and Jonas F. Soltis, *Perspectives on Learning* (New York: Teachers College Press, 1985), 6.
3. Those of you who have recently taken a statistics or research methodology course understand the difference between Quantitative and Qualitative methodology. That dichotomy is similar to the one I am now discussing between Direct Instruction (Objectivism) and Student-Centered Learning (Constructivism). Quantitative methodology, which espouses an Objectivist viewpoint, assumes that all phenomena are measurable. Qualitative methodology, which espouses a Constructivist viewpoint, ignores measurement and emphasizes uncovering the essence of the human experience. Keeping this in mind may help you understand the difference between these two pedagogical stances.
4. Phillips and Soltis, *Perspectives on Learning*, 13.
5. See Phillips and Soltis, *Perspectives on Learning*, chapter 2, for a more complete discussion of Classical learning theory.
6. Anne Becker, "Pavlov and the Wolf," *Psychology Today* 36 (2003): 88.
7. B.F. Skinner, "Contingency Management in the Classroom," *Education* 90 (1969): 93.
8. Anita Woolfolk, *Educational Psychology* (New York: Allyn & Bacon, 2003), 236.
9. Joseph T. Lawton, Ruth A. Saunders, and Paul Muhs, "Theories of Piaget, Bruner, and Ausubel: Explications and Implications," *Journal of Genetic Psychology* 136 (1980): 134.
10. James Paul Gee, "Reading as Situated Language: A Sociocognitive Perspective," *Journal of Adolescent & Adult Literacy* (2001): 715.
11. Ninah Beliavsky, "Revisiting Vygotsky and Gardner: Realizing Human Potential," *The Journal of Aesthetic Education* 40 (2006): 1-11.
12. Henry A. Giroux, "Public Pedagogy and the Politics of Resistance: Notes on a Critical Theory of Educational Struggle," *Educational Philosophy & Theory* 35 (2003): 5.
13. Ilan Gur-Ze'ev, "Feminist Critical Pedagogy and Critical Theory Today," *Journal of Thought* 40 (2005): 55-72; and Elizabeth Ellsworth, "Educational Films against Critical Pedagogy," *Journal of Education* 169 (1987): 32.
14. Mary Kalantzis, Bill Cope, and Andrew Harvey, "Assessing Multiliteracies and the New Basics," *Assessment in Education: Principles, Policy & Practice* 10 (2003): 16.
15. Other similar tables can be found in Woolfolk, *Educational Psychology*, 342; and Sharan Merriam, Rosemary Caffarella, and Lisa Baumgartner, *Learning in Adulthood: A Comprehensive Guide* (San Francisco: Jossey-Bass, 2006), 295-296.

16. For those of you who are interested in pursuing this topic further, I found appropriate references to pedagogy in several broad areas—the literature of K-12 teacher education and the literature of adult and higher education. Although each of these bodies of literature has a separate audience and applications, I found their agreement on basic educational theory to be remarkably similar. Currently the writings from the K-12 teacher education viewpoint have their basis in pedagogical principles based upon scientific methodology. Speaking broadly, the bulk of these texts propose that Behaviorist and Cognitive strategies are most useful. In contrast, most of the current literature in adult and higher education propose that Situated and Critical instructional strategies are generally more useful. I found the following works to be particularly helpful. John Elias and Sharan Merriam, *Philosophical Foundations of Adult Education* (Malabar, FL: Krieger Publishing, 2005); Merriam, Caffarella, and Baumgartner, *Learning in Adulthood*; Slavin, *Educational Psychology*; and Woolfolk, *Educational Psychology*.

17. Slavin, *Educational Psychology*, 143.

18. Woolfolk, *Educational Psychology*, 320.

19. Slavin, *Educational Psychology*, 199.

20. Peggy Dettmer, "New Blooms in Established Fields: Four Domains of Learning and Doing," *Roeper Review* 28 (2006): 70-78.

21. Seana Moran, Mindy Kornhaber, and Howard Gardner, "Orchestrating Multiple Intelligences," *Educational Leadership* 64 (2006): 22-27.

22. Association of College and Research Libraries, *Information Literacy Competency Standards for Higher Education* (Chicago: Association of College and Research Libraries, 2000). Available online from http://www.ala.org/ala/acrl/acrlstandards/informationliteracy-competency.htm.

23. Slavin, *Educational Psychology*, 185.

24. Beliavsky, "Revisiting Vygotsky and Gardner."

25. James Elmborg, "Critical Information Literacy: Implications for Instructional Practice," *Journal of Academic Librarianship* 32 (2006): 192.

26. Marcia Keyser, "Active Learning and Cooperative Learning: Understanding the Difference and Using Both Styles Effectively," *Research Strategies* 17 (2000): 35.

CHAPTER 2

How Cephalonia Can Conquer the World (Or At the Very Least, Your Students!): A Library Orientation Case Study From Cardiff University

Nigel Morgan and Linda Davies

Authors' abstract: The Cephalonian Method is an innovative means of presenting a library orientation session. It is a simple, effective, flexible, colorful, and fun approach to structuring a lesson. The main features include audience participation, question and answer, humour, PowerPoint, and music; and its objective is to maximise learner engagement. It can be adapted for different levels of learners, any group size, and is suitable for use across all disciplines. We developed the Cephalonian Method at Cardiff University, Wales and it has subsequently been used and adapted by academic libraries throughout the U.K. and in institutions in Australia and Europe. This chapter discusses the origins of the Cephalonian Method, its pedagogical effectiveness, how it works in practice, responses and feedback from learners, and how it is being used and adapted at institutions in a variety of sectors.

Editors' notes: *No, it's not some sort of yoga exercise... the Cephalonian Method was designed by Nigel and Linda when they found that their students were bored with traditional library tours. It all started in a taverna on the small Greek island of Cephalonia. Linda claims she was drinking orange juice at the time...*

Scenario: It's a wet and windy Monday morning, and a large group of soggy Entering Freshmen descend on the library for their orientation session. The uninspiring trudge through the building begins in the foyer; however, by the time the group arrives at the book shelves, students at the rear have abandoned attempts to hear what the librarian is explaining amidst the din of the library environment. A few students wander away, whilst those with the grim determination to stay until the end yawn and count down the minutes until they can escape to the more congenial surroundings of the coffee bar. The librarian himself looks stressed and uninspired as he navigates his diminishing group along the well-trodden route. The prospect of leading six more tours that morning weighs heavily upon him. Oh, how he wishes that he was still on vacation!

Does this scenario sound familiar? Can there be a worse start to a student's relationship with the library? Having delivered library orientation sessions for a combined total of forty years between us, we identified fully with the above. We felt jaded by and bored with the traditional methods, namely the interminable library tour and the lifeless lecture theatre "this is the library" presentation, and couldn't bear to go through with these one more time. We also thought that the students were unimpressed; judging by all those glazed expressions and stifled yawns. Perhaps more significantly, we found that library tours were becoming unmanageable and impractical as we were required to handle larger cohorts of students, necessitating more and more tour slots. It was time to go back to the drawing board and take a fresh look at the situation. What we came up with was a novel and quirky format which was so simple that we couldn't understand why we hadn't thought of it before. Thank goodness for the Cephalonian Method!

The Cephalonian Method has been described as a glorious fusion of music, color and audience participation; it was originally designed for large scale library orientation with groups of medical and biomedical sciences students. This session was often the third of four back-to-back introductory lectures to student life and we wanted to give the students at Cardiff University a light-hearted break from wall-to-wall lectures, whilst at the same time imparting some basic library guidance to help them through their first few weeks at university.

Instructional Goals

Our primary goal was to give students the most favorable initial impression of the library and its services as possible. Moreover, we wanted the experience to be memorable, fun and interactive. We also wanted to convey the illusion that the session was student-driven. Our secondary goal was to promote good attendance at later, more serious, information literacy sessions. We figured that if the initial session were well-received and the students had enjoyed their time with us, then our chances of getting full attendance at the information research-based sessions later in the semester would be maximized. Our tertiary goal was to motivate *ourselves*, to create a session which we enjoyed delivering, one for which we felt genuine enthusiasm. Our philosophy is that it is impossible to enthuse students if we are not enthused ourselves. Finally, we wanted to leave our students with a positive impression, to shatter some of those stereotypical images of librarians, by coming across as lively, humourous and above all, approachable individuals.

Instructional Strategy

The inspiration for our change to library orientation sessions was a vacation company introduction to the Greek island of Cephalonia experienced by Linda:

Dreading the obligatory one-hour poolside lecture in the scorching heat, she was relieved to find herself sitting in a well-shaded taverna, with a long cool glass of orange juice, but was very surprised when, along with several others, she was handed a question card. The two young and enthusiastic company reps turned the traditional session on its head by asking everyone holding a card to stand up and read the question aloud. The questions were designed as prompts to enable them to pass on all the necessary information in an informal and memorable way. Linda's question was "Am I stuck on this island for the whole week?" This was a cue for information about trips to nearby islands and the Greek mainland. "What should I do if I'm bitten by a mosquito?" prefaced an explanation of the location and opening hours of the local drug stores. "I'm really scared of driving on these twisting roads; is there any other means of getting around the island?" prompted information about local cab firms and coach services.

This format was used to convey all the essential information to enable everyone to enjoy their holiday and it struck Linda at the time that it would be possible to adapt this for library orientation. The recent increase in student numbers had already caused us to abandon library tours for all but one or two degree courses with smaller numbers. Instead, for several years, library orientation had been conducted in a trial-by-lecture environment to groups of one hundred plus. What she'd experienced in Cephalonia seemed to be an ideal starting point for a complete overhaul of large and small scale orientation sessions. Questions we considered on her return included:

+   Could we develop a format along these lines to provide an entertaining and informative introduction to the library?

+   Would it work with larger groups?

+   Would it still work with small groups?

+   How could such a session be organized to give a degree of coherence and structure, which hadn't been necessary in Cephalonia?

Match of Goals and Strategy

Our principal goal was to emulate the strategy used in Cephalonia; we recognized that this approach would allow students to participate in the session whilst at the same time providing an unusual and stimulating learning experience. However, to achieve our goals we needed to devise a logical structure whilst not losing either the apparent spontaneity of the original session, or the impression that the students were running the orientation.

Our solution was to use a thematic approach with color coded question cards grouped into categories. The Cephalonian Method required time up front for careful planning and structuring but the time invested was well worth it as we were rewarded with a seamless, stimulating, and stress-free lesson model. We began by identifying the learning outcomes; we considered carefully what we wanted students to learn by the end of our session, and then devised appropriate content to enable these outcomes to be achieved. Indeed, we put much thought into the selection of a valuable core of information to present and carefully considered how best to organise this into logical groupings.

We used a color-coded structure to group content areas together and to ensure a logical sequence within the lesson. Each content group contained a set of questions to be asked by students during the sessions and these were printed on colored cards:

+   Blue—Basic introductory information

+   Yellow—Finding recommended reading

+   Red—Services and facilities

+   Green—Miscellaneous information

The Cephalonian Method is nevertheless suitable for students with color-perception impairments as the color is clearly identified in text on each card. These cards became the catalysts that would drive the session along. Instructions were provided on the back of each card.

We tried to phrase the questions from a student's point of view, to lighten the atmosphere, and maintain interest, e.g. a question that prompts information about computing facilities might be "My mum has e-mailed me a picture of Miguel, my pet iguana—am I able to print it in the library?" A question on study facilities may be phrased as "My tutorial group has to prepare a presentation on the winter vomiting virus, is there anywhere we can work together?" Each question had an equivalent PowerPoint slide of the appropriate color, which we used as a presentational aid. In addition, we used images and music as sensory stimuli; the slides originally featured copyright free clipart but we subsequently opted for a comic strip approach using photographs with speech bubbles, which gave the presentation a loose narrative thread. The photographs featured an imaginary student named Tyrone pictured in various situations including borrowing books, receiving help from a friendly

---

FIGURE 1. Instructions on the Back of the Cards

Instructions

When you hear the colour of your card called by the presenter, please ask the question which you have been assigned.

Please speak loudly and clearly so that everyone will hear.
Please deliver your question with conviction!

Thank you – your assistance is much appreciated.☺

FIGURE 2. My Mum has E-mailed Me a Photo of Miguel, my Pet Iguana. Where Can I Print Him Out?

My Mum has emailed me a photo of Miguel, my pet iguana. Where can I print him out?

IT room in Biomedical Library
IT rooms in Science Library
- Microsoft applications
- Internet, Blackboard, & email

Networked printing payment:
- Laser printing (b&w)
  - 6p per A4 sheet
- Colour printing
  - 20p per sheet

L. Davies & N. Morgan. Information Services, Cardiff University.

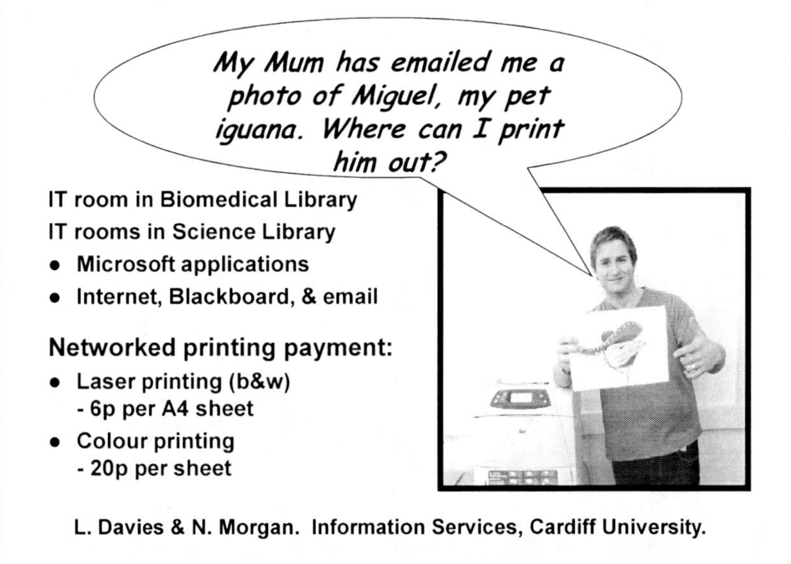

librarian, searching our online catalogue, renewing his books from home during the Christmas holiday season, and proudly displaying his print of Miguel the iguana. Tyrone has certainly proved popular and we have frequently been asked to disclose his phone number!

FIGURE 3. OK. How do I Actually Find the Books on my Reading List?

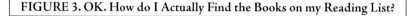

FIGURE 4. What Really Irritates the Library Staff?

Music is also an important feature of the Cephalonian Method; it is a useful tool for creating atmosphere when students arrive, striking a positive and uplifting note at the end of a session, and can be used effectively during activities within extended orientation sessions. The life-enhancing effects of music have been documented in recent years by advocates such as Don Campbell whose celebrated book *The Mozart Effect*[1] provided us with inspiration.

We believe this method has benefits for our students as it enables them to actively participate in the session, and engage with content. It also has benefits for us because no two sessions will ever be identical; within each color grouping we don't know the order in which the questions will be asked, it is a case of randomness within a carefully engineered structure. As a result, there will always be variety, spontaneity, and surprise.

Description of the Instruction Session: What Actually Happened?

We aimed to start most sessions with music, often played as loud as the sound system would allow. If we were in the lecture theatre before the students, we'd set up a CD with several tracks to play as they arrived. However, if we were timetabled in between other lectures and the students were already present, we started the music as soon as possible and left it to play over our preparations. One of us handed out the cards, usually selecting the more talkative and potentially more confident members of the group, whilst the other one started up our PowerPoint presentation and passed around guides to the library and the online catalog. Either way, we used the end of the music to signal that preparations were over and that we were ready to start the session.

We explained that we'd be asking all students with a card to stand up and read the question aloud for the whole group to hear, but added that anyone who didn't want to do this could pass the question on to another member of their group. Generally we found students happy and willing to take part and there was always a rush to stand up when we started by asking for a question on a blue card. Ideally, we wanted the student with the question "So who are you two then?" to stand up first as this raised laughter and provided us with the opportunity to put on a friendly face and introduce ourselves—a great icebreaker. However the beauty of this method is that within the color groupings we were able to take the questions in any order and to adjust the answers depending on the preceding questions.

In response to each question, we selected the equivalent PowerPoint slide and delivered the relevant information content. The questions themselves formed the title of each slide, to ensure that all students followed the presentation, regardless of the volume at which they were delivered. If we thought the student had been too quietly spoken, we repeated the question whilst bringing the slide up. Allowing the students to determine the order of the questions meant that we couldn't simply work through the presentation in a linear fashion, and we have frequently been asked how we were able to display the correct slide seamlessly as the question finished. Our official answer was that we have psychic powers and are able to accurately predict the sequence in advance. The truthful answer is more straightforward, if more mundane. Before the session, we printed out a color handout of the entire presentation which acted as our key. We numbered each slide clearly so that when a question was asked, a quick glance at this told us the position of the relevant slide within the presentation; we then keyed-in the number, hit Return and hey presto! It appeared slick and instantaneous, though of course we had to be extremely careful that we got the number correct!

We each presented two color sections, alternating after each section, to give the students a change of voice and accent (Nigel is a native Welshman, whilst Linda is an exiled Londoner). One of us kicked off with blue and handed over to the other for yellow. The yellow section was in fact only one question, but was the cue for a demonstration of our online catalog. Again, we tried to make this as relevant as possible by demonstrating a search for a book that we knew was on the reading lists that the students had already received, and by searching for a subject that we knew they would be studying. We then tackled the red, and finally the green sets of questions, alternating presenters again.

At some sessions, we threw bright red toy bugs bearing the Information Services logo to the students when they asked the questions; these fluffy novelties could be thrown into the audience without injuring anyone. These were much appreciated and added an additional element of fun. Once we had completed all sections, we invited questions from the floor and were surprised by how many students were keen to stand up and ask something. These additional questions were obviously important to the student, but were often quite peripheral and we took this to mean that we had provided information on all key areas. This was easily tested by asking them a few quick questions to see how much they'd learned, e.g. "How many books can you borrow?" or "How much does it cost to photocopy your friend's lecture notes?" The whole lecture theatre shouted the answers back at us, and we were delighted as we saw this as an indication that we had succeeded in engaging attention and had sustained interest to the end. This was confirmed when we were rewarded with an effusive round of applause. Finally, we sent the students on their way with further rousing musical accompaniment; Linda's preferred choice of "Psycho Killer" being firmly overruled by Nigel, we settled on Talking Heads' "Once in a Lifetime."

Reflection on the Instruction Session: Lessons Learned

So, how successful has the Cephalonian Method been? In short, it's worked like a dream and we certainly do not intend to return to the traditional orientation methods. The friendly informality appeared to suit most people and the element of surprise has helped; at the start, students were intrigued and it was great to see all those quizzical "What's going on now?" expressions. Once the sessions got underway it became obvious that involving the students in this way contributed to breaking down barriers. We were surprised by the degree of interaction within the large groups, and with smaller groups in later years we found that students were encouraged to lose their inhibitions and enter into discussions instead of simply asking questions. In particular, students responded positively to the use of humour and our stars, Tyrone and Miguel the iguana, proved immensely popular.

Indeed, as other United Kingdom institutions adopted the Cephalonian Method, and adapted the content to suit their libraries, we have seen Miguel reincarnated as Sid the ferret, Paulo the polar bear, George the gerbil and several other wonderful zoological manifestations.

We encountered only a few problems. The two most obvious concerns were audibility and spatial orientation (or lack of!) As we had anticipated, the students were unaccustomed to projecting their voices sufficiently in a large lecture theatre to enable all members of the group to hear (after all, we were dealing with medical and biosciences students not drama students!) Repeating the question ourselves and displaying the question at the top of the relevant PowerPoint slide enabled us to overcome this. Secondly, although we have incorporated images of the library into the presentation, we are aware that the sessions do not offer the same level of geographical orientation that students gain during a tour. This has been the most frequent criticism in the feedback we have received and we will address this issue in the future by incorporating 3D interactive library plans, which we hope will help give students a clearer guide to the layout of the library and will also provide visual interest. However, all first-year medical students do visit the Biomedical Sciences Library in small groups with their second-year buddy, usually before our orientation session and therefore can visualize the library to an extent during our presentation.

To monitor our success in achieving our goals and outcomes we handed out questionnaires at the end of every session, and were immensely relieved when the feedback indicated overwhelmingly that the sessions were a success. In 2006, 99 percent of first-year medical students felt that we had succeeded in giving a good introduction to the library service. In addition, 90 percent indicated that this approach was preferable to the library tour. We certainly seem to have struck the right chord with our audience, as the comments were extremely positive:

"Very well presented…loved it. Bravo!"

"It was immense"

"It was a bit strange" (*We took this as a compliment!*)

"It was a creative way of introducing the library. Student participation was a smart idea!"

"Really good idea, made it more fun to watch the presentation."

Whether we struck the right chord with regards to our choice of music is another matter. Choosing appropriate music is always difficult; everyone has their own tastes and preferences. Indeed, we disagree on this more than on any other aspect of the sessions! Our aim is to create an appropriate mood, taking into account factors such as the time of day; a calm, ambient track may be ideal for an early morning orientation but something a little more robust and invigorating is required for a mid-morning session or the dreaded after-lunch slot. We have experimented with classical, punk, new wave, Latin-American, sixties soul, and new age tracks. We have tried various artists, but Paul Weller singing "That's Entertainment" has proved the most popular so far. On one occasion we used J.S. Bach's *Goldberg Variations*; it seemed the perfect choice at the time for small group orientation. However, it was pointed out to us afterwards that this was a favorite of Hannibal Lecter in *Silence of the Lambs*. We decided to drop the track as we had not intended our sessions to have menacing overtones!

When we have asked students what music they would like us to play, suggestions have been extremely diverse and often downright bizarre; for instance, we are not sure whether the national anthem would be a fitting choice or whether Meatloaf's "Bat out of Hell" is a wise selection for a 9:00 a.m. slot on Monday morning, and we're not quite sure what constitutes *thrash metal*! We have decided to rely on our own judgement, accepting the fact that we cannot please everyone. Nevertheless, most students seem to agree that music is a welcome addition to the orientation session.

From our perspective, the Cephalonian Method has been a refreshing change and there are usually lots of opportunities to introduce surprises. For example, librarians in some U.K. universities throw candy to participating students as a reward, and in one particular institution, they invite the students who ask the final two questions to "come on down" for a game show-style play-off with a prize for the winner. Several occasions required initiative and ingenuity when question cards disappeared, with students preferring to hide them rather than pass them on. We have also discovered that some star-struck students will improvise unexpectedly and ask a question of their own devising, instead of the one they have been allocated e.g., "Do you have any Harry Potter books in the library?" We learned to take such incidents in our stride and relished the challenges they presented. In the case of the Harry Potter question, this was a chance to ask the group how they would check for the books and give another quick demonstration. Fortunately, one of our libraries stocks several titles in the famous series, along with analytical and critical texts, as part of a course in Children's Literature. However, the unpredictability that we enjoy is often sufficient cause for other librarians to be wary of adopting the Cephalonian Method. We acknowledge that there are risks; however, for us this is part of the excitement and allure and it gives us a real buzz. We also believe that librarians do not have to be particularly extroverted to run successful orientations in this way (although we concede that the Cephalonian Method will not suit everyone!) Nevertheless, presenters need to be confident as they are required to navigate around a PowerPoint presentation without knowing what is coming next. Some institutions have adopted a more structured approach by numbering the cards in order to provide a linear sequence, however, we think that this robs the session of some of the fun and spontaneity and destroys any illusion of being student-driven.

The Cephalonian Method still has scope for further development; the minimum requirements are colored cards and a PowerPoint presentation, but these can be enhanced by the use of multimedia and lighting effects (of the appropriate color of course!) in order to deliver a truly theatrical spectacle. Some institutions are experimenting by getting students to formulate their own questions whilst others have combined the Cephalonian Method with a traditional tour by planting questions at strategic points en route in the style of a treasure hunt. If you have imagination and the courage to put it into practice, then the Cephalonian Method can help transform your orientation sessions into a uniquely memorable learning experience.

Application to Other Instructional Settings

The Cephalonian Method is, we believe, a versatile and pedagogically sound method of presenting an orientation session. This is not just our view; the Cephalonian Method is popular in U.K. libraries in both the higher education and further education (community college) sectors. It has also been used for purposes other than library orientation. We have been informed by colleagues at other institutions that it has been used successfully to liven up lectures and other factual presentations. The Cephalonian Method was developed for undergraduates, and we have been wary of utilizing it within postgraduate contexts. Therefore, we were surprised to learn that it had been used with and enjoyed by PhD students during information research classes. We were also delighted to discover that the Cephalonian Method has been successfully used to train medical personnel in the use of information resources within the U.K.'s National Health Service. Indeed, we see no reason why its use should stop here; we believe that the Cephalonian Method could also be effectively utilized in the training of new personnel, whether in a library context or in any other environment. Whatever the setting, the Cephalonian Method can be used to get people actively involved, helping to create a more relaxed and enjoyable environment for learning, and hence assisting in the assimilation and retention of information.

We love the Cephalonian Method. It never ceases to amaze us that such a simple idea spotted in a Greek island taverna is proving such a popular and dynamic force; now, no longer confined to its place of origin, the Cephalonian Method has the potential to conquer the globe. Why not bring some Greek sunshine to your own library? We think that you should!

Efharisto!

Notes

1. Don Campbell, *The Mozart Effect: Tapping the Power of Music to Heal the Body, Strengthen the Mind, and Unlock the Creative Spirit* (New York: Avon Books, 1997).

CHAPTER 3

It's Showtime! Engaging Students in Library Instruction

Debbie Crumb and Eric Palo

Authors' abstract: This chapter contains concrete ideas on how to conduct library orientations and workshops that are understandable, meaningful, and enjoyable. We use humor and Universal Design for Learning (UDL) strategies, including active learning, to help engage students in library instruction on information literacy skills. These learning strategies can be applied to most group sizes. Although we have worked with student of all types, most of these approaches have been designed with English-as-a-Second-Language learners in mind. We want to make learning fun!

Editors' notes: Debbie and Eric have created an active presentation format which can be used for library orientation presentations. They apply Universal Design for Learning Strategies–which play on the fact that all students learn in a unique fashion. They also stoop to bribery–by offering students "fabulous, fabulous prizes." Pat Sajak and Vanna White have nothing on these two!

Introduction

OK, everyone, please raise your hand if you want to listen to a lecture about how to use the library. Boring! OK, now raise your hand if you want to play some games to learn about the library AND have a chance at winning some fabulous, fabulous prizes. YES! Gone are the days of talking-head lectures. Librarians need to make library instruction engaging and fun or students will either be drifting off to sleep or text-messaging their friends under the desk-tops.

Over 50 percent of the three hundred plus library orientations and workshop sessions conducted annually by the Renton Technical College (RTC) librarians are done for English as a Second Language (ESL) classes. We have designed several workshops, including our Library Games workshop, specifically for our ESL students with application of Universal Design for Learning (UDL) principles.

Instructional Goals

The instructional goals for the Library Games workshop are to have the students:
+ Learn about the library, how to access its services, and about some of the library-specific terminology that we use.
+ Feel more comfortable being in the library and asking the librarians for help.

Instructional Strategy

Our overriding strategy is to make library sessions accessible, interactive and fun with emphasis on the FUN! We also make great use of UDL (discussed later in the chapter.) The content of a library orientation or workshop may be wonderful but if it is not presented in a manner that students can easily understand, or if they don't see the importance of it or if it's boring, students are not going to be actively engaged in the learning process. They won't get it, nor will they retain it.

Teaching and learning is contextual. Students learn best if they see the value in it for themselves, whether it be learning how to check out or renew a library book, receiving a better grade on their research paper, or being able to better solve life's daily information problems. Most of our library workshops are structured around a class assignment that students have been given or some problem that they are facing in their daily lives.

Make it *fun*! While it's important to take your work seriously, there's no need to take yourself too seriously. Life is too short to sit through boring library lectures. We don't like it; why should our students?

Using humor is not quite the same as making something fun, but not much is found in the literature about having fun in library instruction. However, using humor in instruction is a well-studied technique, even if it is not always well applied. Wanzer, et al.[1] have produced a good overview of the literature on humor in teaching as has Walker[2] in his article on using humor in library instruction. The benefits of using humor are well documented and include reducing tension, fostering group cohesion, gaining and holding student attention, clarifying content, increasing retention of information, and in making it more fun to teach.[3] In his rigidly controlled experiment, Garner[4] demonstrated that the students in a group exposed to a few minutes of humor in a lecture had significantly higher recall and retention of the subject being taught than those getting the same lecture without the added humor.

We all understand humor, but when we try to apply humor we run into problems. Most authors say that telling canned jokes are not all that effective and in our experience at RTC, jokes don't work all that well. Humor is best used when it shows up early in the teaching session[5] and if it appears to come naturally. It could just be something as simple as using a humorous example to demonstrate Boolean searching. But whatever it is, be sure to keep your audience in mind. At RTC we favor self-deprecating humor, using humorous props, and physical humor. These work especially well with students who have limited English proficiency.

The effectiveness of using a Jeopardy-type game, such as those we use at RTC, to make learning fun is also supported by research. Berk[6] used it as one of ten instructional humor strategies tested on both undergraduates and graduate students at UCLA over a three year period. None of the strategies tested was reported to be more effective than the Jeopardy-like reviews in reducing anxiety, improving the student's ability to learn, or in being so effective in improving the student's ability to do his or her best. Maxwell[7] presents persuasive arguments for using game-type learning activities as a way to address multiple learning styles of students in K-12 library instruction.

So the bottom line on humor in library instruction is that, if you make it fun they (the students) will learn (at least a bit more) and you (the instruction librarian) can have fun too!

Another strategy we use in our orientations and workshops is to incorporate Universal Design for Learning (UDL) principles as much as possible. We probably all have benefitted from universal design in architecture and urban planning. A person doesn't need to have a documented disability in order to benefit from curb cuts, automatic door openers, ramps, speakerphones or closed captioned films or TV. UDL helps education institutions and instructors better meet the diverse learning styles and needs of all students—not just those with documented disabilities.

The Center for Applied Special Technology (CAST)[8] is an internationally-recognized, non-profit, charitable organization which was founded in 1984. Through brain research, they developed the UDL principles which use technology to increase access for all students, especially those with disabilities, and to help provide a wider range of options from which students can choose. UDL "encourages the use of flexible methods and resources, emphasizing multi-modal strategies and using research on how the brain learns in order to meet the needs of different types of learners."[9] UDL features multiple methods of presentation, options for participation and means of assessment.

According to Rose and Meyer[10] UDL supports:

+ recognition learning (the what of learning)
+ strategic learning (the how of learning)
+ affective learning (the why of learning)

RTC has been using UDL on campus since 2002 as part of a grant project funded by the U.S. Department of Education.[11]

Match of Goals and Strategy

Some of the different UDL strategies that we use in our various orientations and workshop sessions include:

+ Recognition Learning (presenting information in multiple formats)
  o Having visual aids posted on the classroom walls
  o Providing multiple and real-life examples in demonstrations
  o Using white boards with different colored markers
  o Presenting information in a variety of modalities including lecture, demos, discussion, using PowerPoint presentations with lots of graphics, physically acting out concepts, and providing written handouts with key workshop content
  o Using color screen-shots on handouts when appropriate
  o Using different colored paper to distinguish different handouts from each other
+ Strategic Learning (multiple ways for students to interact)
  o Using lots of interactive hands-on practice, either using low-tech activities or practice on the computers
+ Affective Learning (engaging and motivating students)
  o Using different work groups (allowing individual, partner or team work)
  o Offering a choice of candy treats and fabulous, fabulous prizes
  o Making the sessions informal and fun

In our Library Games workshop we help ease ESL students into learning more about the library by using three types of games which move from a simple and anonymous true/false game to a more difficult, team-centered Jeopardy-like game. This allows the librarians to reinforce the students' success as the students gain confidence.

Description of the Instruction Session: What Actually Happened?

All of the ESL students attend a one-hour, highly-active library orientation prior to enrolling in any workshop sessions. In the follow-up one-hour Library Games workshop, we conduct three different interactive games:

- true/false game (played individually)
- library quiz game (played on teams)
- Jeopardy-like game (played on teams)

Most of the questions' answers can be found on the glossary page of library words and definitions or on the library brochure—both of which are distributed to students at the beginning of the session. The glossary page and other supporting materials are posted online at a Quia[12] Web site where we also have additional games available for instructors to use with their students either before or after our library workshops. Quia is an inexpensive subscription-based online service which allows educational institutions and instructors to easily create surveys and Web sites for their classes. Some Quia options include creating surveys and tabulating the results, creating different web pages for each class or library workshop, maintaining an online calendar, creating quizzes from templates and tracking the results, and creating online learning games from sixteen different templates.

FIGURE 1. A Group of RTC Students Enjoying a Library Session

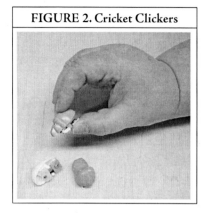

FIGURE 2. Cricket Clickers

The true/false game is a warm-up game; its purpose is to review information that was covered in the previously attended library orientation. Students use low-tech noise makers (inexpensive plastic Cricket Clickers available from SmileMakers[13]) to anonymously ring in with their answers. With the true/false format, students don't need to be able to remember the correct information, they just need to be able to guess at it. With a true/false format, students have at least a 50 percent chance of getting it right (100 percent chance if they hedge their bets and ring in with their clickers for *both* answer options!) While giving the answers, the librarian has an opportunity to reinforce the correct information, sometimes acting out the situation using real-life props (library card, book, video, etc.).

The library quiz game repeats some of the information used in the true/false game but the questions are a fill-in-the-blank variety which means the students needs to know or remember the answer and can't just guess. The class is split into teams and each team has its own distinct-sounding noisemaker (bell, squeaky dog toy, etc.) Teams compete by winning $10 in play Monopoly-like money for each correct answer. The team with the most money at the end of the game wins fabulous, fabulous prizes (fabulous is in the eyes of the beholder; we're talking about packages of post-it notes, highlighter pens, packs of gum, candy bars, calculators, and other cheap prizes easily purchased from the local dollar store.)

FIGURE 3. Teams Compete by Winning $10 in Play Money for Each Correct Answer

The Jeopardy-like game also uses teams and some of the same information from the library quiz game. Questions are in categories of People, Places, Materials, and Actions with the easier questions being worth $5 - $15 and the harder questions being worth $20 - $25. Unlike Jeopardy, students are not expected to respond in the form of a question and are given credit for answers if they are able to act it out or use broken English. There are

FIGURE 4. Fabulous, Fabulous Prizes

FIGURE 5. Props Help Students to Get Involved in Learning

lots of different free blank Jeopardy templates in a PowerPoint format that can be found on the Web by doing a Google search.

There is a wide range of technological props that can be used to engage students in library sessions—from the inexpensive low-tech SmileMakers Critter Clickers or a squeaky dog toy from the local pet or grocery store, to the moderately priced Eggspert from Educational Insights[14] or the Who's First game show buzzer system from Trainer's Warehouse,[15] to the expensive, high-tech audience response systems like Quizdom[16] or TurningPoint.[17]

Often the team competition gets pretty noisy, intense, and even cutthroat as students jockey to make sure they ring in before the other team. The librarian often has to step in and gently and humorously remind the students that the prizes are only worth about 50 cents each and that it's not worth fighting about. It's not like winning a new car or a Hawaiian vacation on the Price is Right!

FIGURE 6. Every Student is a Winner in RTC Library Sessions

At the end of the one-hour session, penny-candy treats are available for all students to choose from so that all feel like winners. It's hard to feel like a disappointed loser with a lollipop stuck in your mouth. Students can also take the Cricket Clickers home to annoy all their family and friends!

In another workshop, Practicing Library Situations, ESL students use written dialogs, lots of real-life props, and not-quite-ready-for-prime-time acting skills to learn how to check out and return library materials, how to renew items both in-person and over the phone, and how to pay bills for long overdue or lost items.

Reflection on the Instruction Session: Lessons Learned

You wouldn't think that giving away little things like penny-candy, cheap fabulous, fabulous prizes or plastic Cricket Clickers would make that big a difference in a student's perception of the library and how user-friendly the library is, but it does. Think about the last time you flew on an airliner and how excited you were when the flight attendants passed out those tiny bags of pretzels (although not excited enough to forgive them for cancelling your connecting flight or losing your luggage.) Or think back to the last library conference you attended and how we all gravitated to the vendor booths with the best freebies!

In various assessments conducted of general college classes attending library orientations and workshop sessions, over 98 percent of the student attendees were satisfied with the sessions and 67 percent of them indicated that they were *more* inclined to use the library as a result of attending the sessions.

In a three-year period (2003–2005), the circulation of our library materials for learning English increased eight times, from 502 to 4,245 checkouts. We lack the statistical data, but we'd be willing to bet one of our fabulous, fabulous prizes that ESL students know more about library procedures than most of the native-English-speaking students on campus. The ESL students have fun learning about the library and, more importantly, make a personal connection with the librarians in a non-threatening environment. After a recent Practicing Library Situations workshop, the ESL instructor sent a short e-mail saying, "Thanks again for an entertaining and helpful class! I'm always amazed at how you can get even the most reticent students involved and laughing."

Because ESL students had fun attending library orientations and workshops, they know the names of the librarians and are often more likely to stop and talk to us as we walk across campus throughout the day. We are looked upon as safe to practice their English with and to ask questions of—and not just questions related to the library.

Using humor to try to lighten and liven up a library session can be like walking a tightrope. What is humorous or fun to one student may not be perceived that way by another. And that is even without the added complexity and danger of accidentally colliding with cultural differences. Again, with ESL students, using physical humor (using a plastic bill-shaped duck call gadget to get the students' attention, dancing like Elaine from the 1990's hit TV comedy Seinfeld when their cell phones' musical ring tones start playing, etc.) instead of verbal humor seems to work best.

Unlike faculty teaching in classes or programs, we librarians work with lots of different students, mostly in one- or two-shot library sessions per quarter. Because of the limited number of sessions and since each session is only one hour in length, we don't have a chance to get to know the students as individuals with their own unique learning strengths and weaknesses. So while we use UDL principles in designing our library orientations and workshops, we do not use specific strategies with specific types of students in mind.

Application to Other Instructional Settings

The Library Games workshop works well with ESL students because there is a lot of hands-on and physical activity with less reliance on verbal acuity. And of course, there is also the opportunity for fabulous, fabulous prizes!

But it would also work well with any student with limited English language skills—whether they were a native English speaker or not. Interactive and fun learning can work with all student groups on campus. With native English-speaking students in academic programs, the game show format could be successful if using harder questions and more technologically advanced clickers like the commercially available audience response systems.

UDL concepts can be readily applied to all classroom and workshop settings. As of April 2007, there were thirty-four instructors from twenty-one programs at RTC who are using UDL strategies in their classrooms. According to a recent survey of 193 students in RTC's UDL project classrooms, "98 percent reported that the UDL strategies being used positively affected their abilities to learn."[18]

Some additional UDL strategies that we have used in other library sessions include:

+ Starting each library session with a trivia question that is pertinent to that particular class and letting the winner choose from a bag of inexpensive fabulous, fabulous prizes

+ Using milk carton, yogurt container, butter box, and cheese packaging props to demonstrate how the library's classification system is like a grocery store where similar or like items are shelved together so that they are easier to find

FIGURE 7. Debbie Crumb	FIGURE 8. Eric Palo

◆   Using plastic word tiles from Learning Playground from the Paper Magic Group[19] to practice alphabetizing skills with ESL students

◆   Playing music files of national anthems from around the world as ESL students are busy working on a workshop assignment to find information about their native countries

◆   Using a deck of playing cards to demonstrate Boolean searching concepts. Deal the deck of cards out to all the students and then call out combinations (red or black, diamonds and face cards, red not hearts, etc.) and have the students hold up the results for all to see. If you use large print cards, it's easy to see which students are getting it and which are still confused by the concepts of Boolean connectors.

American writer Gail Godwin in her novel, *The Odd Woman*, said that "Good teaching is one-fourth preparation and three-fourths pure theatre."[20] Let the show begin!

Notes

1. Melissa Bekelija Wanzer, Ann Bainbridge Frymier, Ann M. Wojtaszczyk, and Tony Smith, "Appropriate and Inappropriate Uses of Humor by Teachers," *Communication Education* 55 (April 2006): 178-96.

2. Billie E. Walker, "Using Humor in Library Instruction," *Reference Services Review* 34 (2006): 117-28.

3. Kristin Trefts and Sarah Blakeslee, "Did You Hear the One About the Boolean Operators? Incorporating Comedy in Library Instruction," *Reference Services Review* 28 (2000): 369-78.

4. R. L. Garner, "Humor in Pedagogy: How Ha-Ha Can Lead to Aha!" *College Teaching* 54 (2006): 177-80.

5. Kwasi Sarkodie-Mensah, "Using Humor for Effective Library Instruction Sessions," *Catholic Library World* 68 (June 1998): 25-9.

6. Ronald A Berk," Student Ratings of 10 Strategies for Using Humor in College Teaching," *Journal on Excellence in College Teaching* 7 (1996): 71-92.

7. D. Jackson Maxwell, "The Library ABC's Game: Sneaking in Learning Through Gaming," *Library Media Connection* 24 (January 2007): 34.

8. CAST: Center for Applied Special Technology, "Universal Design for Learning," CAST: Center for Applied Special Technology. Available online from http://www.cast.org.

9. Cathy Jenner and Cheryl Culwell, *Using Universal Design for Learning in Community & Technical colleges* (Renton, WA: Renton Technical College, 2006).

10. David H. Rose, and Anne Meyer, *Teaching Every Student in the Digital Age: Universal Design for Learning* (Alexandria, VA: Association for Supervision and Curriculum Development, 2002).

11. Renton Technical College, Disability Services, "Universal Design for Learning." Renton Technical College. Available online from http://www.rtc.edu/AboutUs/DSDPGrant/UD/.

12. Quia. Available online from http://www.quia.com.

13. SmileMakers. Available online from http://www.smilemakers.com.

14. Educational Insights. Available online from https://educationalinsights.com.

15. Trainer's Warehouse. Available online from http://www.trainerswarehouse.com.

16. Quizdom. Available online from http://www.qwizdom.com.

17. TurningPoint. Available online from http://www.turningtechnologies.com.
18. *U.S. Department of Education Grant Performance Report (ED 524B) Executive Summary: Universal Design for Learning Project Annual Report 10-106 through 4-15-07(PR/Award P333A050032).* (Renton, WA: Renton Technical College, 2007).
19. Paper Magic Group. Available online from http://www.papermagic.com.
20. Godwin, Gail, *The Odd Woman* (New York: Ballantine Books, 1995), 50.

CHAPTER 4

The Clicky Things Rocked! Combating Plagiarism with Audience Response System Technology

Christine Bombaro

Author's abstract: Charged with presenting the "Seven Deadly Sins of Plagiarism" to every new freshman on campus—twenty-two presentations to groups of approximately thirty students per session—the librarians at Dickinson College developed an interactive presentation on academic integrity following the principles of Robert M. Gagné's "Nine Events of Instruction" and using Audience Response System (ARS) technology. The ARS *Clickers* solved the problem of keeping large groups intellectually involved by entering responses and reacting to the presentation. Students' understanding of plagiarism increased via the presentation as shown by the increase in "yes" responses to "I have committed an act of plagiarism" at the beginning of the presentation and then at the end.

Editors' notes: Presenting information quickly, to a large number of students, can be a thankless task. Christine has found a way to turn this around, however, by using Clicker technology to teach students about the "Seven Deadly Sins of Plagiarism." The thankless has become the thanktified... uh, don't quote us on that...

Introduction

Librarians are often placed in the frustrating position of having to instruct students on certain critical aspects of the research process without ever being given the opportunity to engage in the essential teaching practices that prevent the lesson from being wasted. One-shot sessions usually do not allow enough time for elements such as attention-grabbing, supervised practice, or adequate feedback; nor do they provide the librarian with the ability to forge a trusting relationship that helps to convince the students that what they are learning is relevant, necessary, and valuable.

With this in mind, it was easy for the librarians of Dickinson College to imagine successive classrooms full of bored and annoyed undergraduates when we were asked to participate in first-year orientation by developing a lesson on academic integrity to be delivered to each student by way of a stand-alone session. Dickinson College, a small liberal arts college in Carlisle, Pennsylvania, enrolls approximately twenty-five hundred undergraduate students and admits approximately six hundred first-year students each year. On our campus, previous attempts at imparting the pitfalls of plagiarism to our students through large group lecture and small group discussion had proved unsatisfactory.

As we considered how we might most effectively develop this lesson, we noticed that some of the professors in our science departments were already using audience response systems (ARS) in their classrooms, and we were curious as to whether we could adapt this technology to a session on academic integrity. An audience response system is technology that allows students to respond, by way of small hand-held remote control devices (also known as "clickers"), to questions posted on a screen. ARS technology usually works in tandem with slide show software such as Microsoft PowerPoint. After the students respond to each question, the software generates a chart displaying the students' answers. Although the instructor can track individual responses to each question, by default the results are anonymous and displayed in aggregate. This immediate feedback might give the instructor the chance to adjust the lesson by reinforcing troublesome concepts, to move more quickly through areas in which the students already demonstrate comprehension, or to promote discussion.

Instructional Goals

The goals of this lesson were to prevent the proliferation of plagiarism due to ignorance of citation rules, to point out any poor citation habits in which our students may have been previously engaging, and to encourage positive attitudes about the correct use of other scholars' work. After much discussion and research, we decided to include seven different types of plagiarism in the presentation—a number which handily evoked the title, "The Seven Deadly Sins of Plagiarism: Working Honestly at Dickinson College." From there, we composed the lesson's outcomes:

♦   First-year students will recognize seven specific behaviors – some obvious and some subtle—that constitute plagiarism so that they can avoid these behaviors when performing research. (This outcome would be measured by a short quiz administered at the end of the session.)

♦   First-year students will know the possible consequences of plagiarism both at Dickinson College and in the real world so that they can evaluate the risk factors involved in the decision to commit plagiarism. (This outcome, we recognized, would be difficult to measure definitively, but we were able to compare the answers to questions administered during the lesson with those administered in a quiz afterward, which provided us with some assessment.)

Administratively, this presentation was meant to be a vehicle for communicating consistently one aspect of the college's community standards document, which defines plagiarism as "a form of cheating that refers to several types of unacknowledged borrowing," punishable by course failure and suspension.[1] Prior to the creation of this lesson, the college's associate provost learned by surveying faculty members who had taught first-year seminars that, even though one of the goals of the seminars is for students to understand and practice effective college-level research and writing habits, the faculty members were addressing the issue of academic honesty unevenly. Because Dickinson College imposes strong penalties on those found to have plagiarized, the administration wanted to make it imperative that new students receive clear and consistent information about academic expectations and standards.

Instructional Strategy

In addition to the library director's mandate that the presentation be lively, edgy, and witty, it also had to be a good instructional tool, follow pedagogically sound techniques, and be assessable. For this lesson, which had to be delivered twenty-two times to groups of approximately thirty students per session, resourceful utilization of the ARS allowed us to closely follow Robert M. Gagné's Nine Events of Instruction: (1) Gaining the attention of the learners, (2) Informing learners of the objectives, (3) Stimulating recall of prior learning, (4) Presenting new stimulus, (5) Providing learning guidance, (6) Eliciting performance, (7) Providing feedback, (8) Assessing performance, and (9) Enhancing retention and transfer of skills.[2]

Keeping relatively close to Gagné's Nine Events made it easy to develop a framework for this session, and contributed eventually to its great success. Since we wanted the presentation to be relatively brief at about half an hour, the Nine Events helped us to keep the lesson focused on our outcomes. We made sure that the students knew exactly why they were being required to participate in the program. The clickers were intriguing to the students and piqued their curiosity as soon as we handed them out. With their attention thus gained, we were able, through the course of the instruction to prove to the students that they did not already know everything about writing correctly, while showing them how we could help them. The ARS technology made it possible to quickly accomplish the events of eliciting active performance, providing feedback, and assessing the performance. The ARS method also allowed us to fulfill our goal of delivering the information consistently to many students since it required delivery from a script.

Because it is important to inform the learners early in the lesson what the goals are and what is expected of them,[3] and because the anti-plagiarism session would be completely disconnected from the students' regular classroom experiences, we felt it was especially important to let them know how this lesson would benefit them. Our presentation opened with a statement of goals: (1) to help you succeed in doing college-level research and writing, (2) to introduce guidelines for citing sources properly, (3) to present Dickinson's policy on plagiarism, and (4) to provide sources for help.

Although we hoped that some of our students would have had plagiarism instruction in high school, we were still compelled to base the presentation around an assumption of knowledge,[4] or, in our case, the lack thereof. We chose to assume that none of our incoming students had any formal instruction on the subject of plagiarism, and, further, that some of them may never have written a formal research paper requiring supporting source material. Although this created the additional challenge of keeping the material relevant and interesting to the informed students, we felt that the ARS technology would alleviate this problem by giving them something to do during the lesson, other than passively listen.

Match of Goals and Strategy

After considering several brands of ARS technology, we purchased TurningPoint from Turning Technologies, LLC.[5] At approximately $3000 for the software, hardware, and forty remote control devices (forty being the capacity of the largest classroom in our library), this brand was slightly more expensive than some others; however, the features it offered were best suited to help us achieve our learning outcomes. Our first concern was that, although we wanted the presentation to be somewhat witty and engaging to the eighteen-year-old mind, we did not want the students to dismiss it as a silly waste of their time. TurningPoint remote controls looked less like toys than some of the other brightly-colored competitor products, and we thought that a more subdued-looking device would lend professionalism to the presentation as well as possibly prevent potential misuse of the equipment. Second, the ARS system solved the problem of keeping a large group of students intellectually involved throughout the duration of the presentation, since they would have to enter responses periodically through the last slide. In addition, the TurningPoint system proved relatively easy to use, partly because the software integrates the familiar buttons and features of Microsoft products, and runs from a toolbar embedded in Microsoft PowerPoint, from which the non-interactive portion of each slide is created. More importantly, however, TurningPoint enables the quick and easy collection of data through reports generated in Microsoft Excel, and we wanted above all else to determine at the conclusion of this program whether or not the presentation was helping us achieve the College's goals.

Description of the Instruction Session: What Actually Happened?

In order to give students a simple point of reference to keep in mind throughout the lesson, we first asked them to define plagiarism by choosing among four options: (1) Using unauthorized notes during exams, (2) Collaborating on an assignment when you've been instructed to work independently, (3) Presenting someone else's work as your own, or (4) Copying someone's answers during a test. Ninety-two percent of the respondents answered this question correctly. After explaining to students that all of these activities are unacceptable and represent some form of cheating, we used the correct answer (presenting someone else's work as your own) as the baseline of the lesson and the definition against which the answers to the rest of the questions would be judged.

Before moving on with the instructional portion of the presentation, we asked students to think about their writing prior to coming to

FIGURE 1. TurningPoint Response Card and Receiver (photo used by permission of Turning Technologies, LLC.)]

college and to consider how they used other people's research. This question not only refocused their attention but also obliged them to recall any prior learning on the topic. To accomplish this, we presented a slide stating, "At some point in my academic career, I have committed an act of plagiarism" and asked the students to respond via the ARS keypads with a simple "yes" or "no." We recorded the results and told students that we would revisit this question at the end of the presentation.

Following this introduction, we began to address students' preconceived opinions about plagiarism. Any lesson delivered using Gagné's Nine Events theory requires the instructor to take responsibility for carrying out the learning objectives. However, Gagné also recognized the importance of student attitude in the learning process. Gagné defines attitude as "the establishment of internal states that influence the individual's choices of personal action."[6] In order to help our students shape constructive attitudes about plagiarism, we followed the recall question with two true/false questions pertaining to commonly held beliefs about properly citing source material. The first of these was, "If I didn't plagiarize on purpose, I won't be found responsible." After the results of this false statement were tallied, the librarian offered an account of the plagiarism case against historian Doris Kearns Goodwin, who defended herself claiming that the verbatim copying was the accidental result of her taking notes in longhand.[7] The second attitude question, "Information copied from the internet must be cited," is, of course, true and was reinforced onscreen with a sample from a research paper that correctly cited a chart copied from the Bureau of Transportation Statistics Web site. With these questions, we hoped that

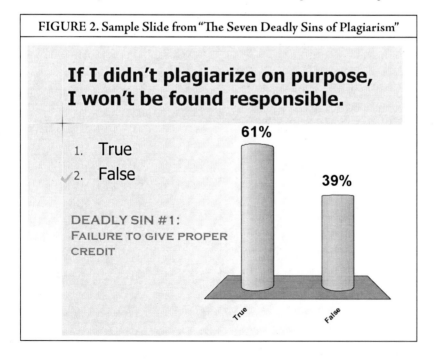

FIGURE 2. Sample Slide from "The Seven Deadly Sins of Plagiarism"

students would begin to understand that any borrowed information must be cited, and that there are no excuses for not doing so.

Knowing that most of our students would not receive controlled follow-up after this session, we had to make sure that there was enough practice embedded within the presentation so that they would be likely to retain the new knowledge they were gaining. We also wanted to include as many opportunities as possible within our time frame of thirty minutes for the students to think about how to properly acknowledge borrowed material, and to discuss some of the less obvious manifestations of plagiarism. We did not want simply to lecture about the dos and don'ts of plagiarism and follow it with a quiz. Rather, after establishing the definition, encouraging recall, and hopefully shaping learning attitudes, we introduced new concepts by asking the students to compare a quotation from a journal article against examples of a student's writing in which the quotation was used, and then by having them vote on whether the example represented plagiarism.

Martin, Klein, and Sullivan define learning examples as "verbal or graphical information that provides additional clarification of rules or information presented to learners."[8] In this presentation we included five examples. The first, which constituted plagiarism, directly quoted the borrowed phrase without quotation marks or citation. The second example, also plagiarism, had quotation marks around the same borrowed phrase but no citation. The third example, plagiarism again, paraphrased the same passage without a citation. In the fourth example, which was not plagiarism, the same phrase was enclosed in quotation marks and a citation was present. The final example was somewhat tricky: we presented students with the correct citation of the article used and then showed them the student's version of the citation, which mistakenly attributed the article to the wrong author. Although this did not technically constitute plagiarism according to our established definition, we wanted the students to understand that carelessness is unacceptable and could be misconstrued by the professor as an attempt to plagiarize by fabricating citations.

Using the ARS voting technology to have students vote on whether the writing samples constituted plagiarism helped us to achieve the most critical objectives of this lesson. First, we were able to present, easily and efficiently, new concepts in the form of different types of plagiarism. The ARS technology naturally elicited performance from the students and then allowed us to provide them with immediate feedback. This, in turn, helped the librarians to guide the learning process by facilitating a brief discussion following each example.

When the instructional portion of the presentation was over, we took the opportunity to warn the students about the possible consequences of plagiarism at Dickinson College, and offered them numerous avenues for help and further information. We countered the "Seven Deadly Sins of Plagiarism" with the "Seven Academic Integrity Commandments." (See table 1.)

Finally, in order to give the students some chance to practice and review what they had just learned, and in order to assess the session, we administered a five-question quiz. Although this is not optimal practice for long-term retention, we thought it was the best way within our allotted time to give students a chance to

| TABLE 1 |
| The Seven Deadly Sins of Plagiarism vs. the Seven Academic Integrity Commandments |

Sin	Commandment
Failure to give proper credit.	Thou shalt not presenteth another's research as thine own.
Copying material from the Internet without citing it.	Giveth proper credit to Internet sites.
Failure to cite even a few words of borrowed language.	Useth quotation marks when borrowing even thy neighbor's brief phrase.
Failure to cite an exact quote.	Includeth footnotes or in-text notes whenever quoting.
Failure to cite paraphrased ideas.	Citeth thou also paraphrased ideas.
Failure to provide an accurate citation.	Verily thou shalt recordeth thoroughly and accurately all sources consulted.
Thinking you can get away with plagiarism.	Do not thinketh thyself immune to being smote with the consequences of plagiarism.

revisit some of the scenarios discussed during the presentation, and to enhance their learning by having them think about plagiarism rules under slightly different conditions. Additionally, the quiz allowed us to compare the students' answers to the quiz questions with their answers registered during the presentation, to see if any changes had taken place. We handed the quiz questions to the students in hard copy, and had them enter their answers via the clickers. The TurningPoint ARS includes a countdown feature, which we used to give the students ninety seconds to read each question and respond. As with the previous examples, we had a brief discussion about each question once everyone had responded. The quiz questions addressed the following scenarios: (1) Borrowing from oneself without attribution (not technically plagiarism by definition, but against college policy), (2) Using a direct quote with quotation marks and citation (not plagiarism), (3) Using a digital photograph from the college archives without attribution (plagiarism), (4) Using a chart copied from an electronic journal article with attribution (not plagiarism), and (5) Paraphrasing without attribution (plagiarism).

Reflection on the Instruction Session: Lessons Learned

Because the TurningPoint ARS so easily collects and reports response data, we were able to conduct two different types of assessment without interruption to the lesson and without keeping the students longer than a few minutes after its conclusion. With the ARS data, we could see how the students answered the questions relating to their knowledge, understanding, and attitudes about plagiarism. Then, in order to determine if the students found the lesson to be memorable and valuable, we asked them to fill out comment cards, on which they were free to comment about any aspect of the lesson, including but not limited to content, format, technology, and the instructor's performance.

The report data demonstrated that, although students could correctly choose definitions of plagiarism from a multiple-choice list, they had difficulty applying those definitions to real-life situations. For example, 75 percent of the respondents correctly agreed with the statement that they must cite a direct quote even if it is only two or three words long, yet only 69 percent correctly identified as plagiarism an example in which a direct quote was used with no quotation marks and no citation, and only 61 percent correctly identified that a direct quote with quotation marks and a citation was properly attributed. Similarly, while 92 percent agreed that copying from the Internet without attribution was plagiarism during the presentation, only 81 percent correctly identified that scenario as plagiarism during the quiz. These are areas of instruction that, looking ahead, we targeted for improvement for the lesson's second manifestation. One area where we did see significant improvement in comprehension after the lesson was in regard to paraphrasing. During the presentation only 49 percent correctly identified unattributed paraphrasing as plagiarism, but during the quiz 70 percent correctly identified a similar scenario as plagiarism.

Perhaps the most significant result of this lesson was the responses to the statement, "At some point in my academic career, I have committed an act of plagiarism," which we asked near the beginning and at the end of the presentation. The first time, 256 out of 496 (51%) respondents answered "yes," and the second time, 332 out of 489 (68%) respondents answered "yes." In every session, the return on "Yes, I have" increased, sometimes dramatically, the second time the question was asked, and in none of the sessions did this trend reverse.

While the quantitative data showed us what our students were learning and where they were still having trouble grasping specific concepts, we were also encouraged by their qualitative feedback. With rare exception, the comments were positive and convinced us that the students found the lesson to be valuable. They overwhelmingly indicated that they not only enjoyed the lesson thanks to the clickers, but that they were better able to recognize problem areas in their own writing, and that the interactivity kept them focused on the lesson. The comments in Table 2 were typical of the hundreds received.

Application to Other Instructional Settings

Delivery of the session via the ARS turned out to be an excellent way to convey information to a large group, particularly as that group had to be subdivided into smaller sections that needed to receive the same information. Standardizing the presentation and incorporating a quiz through the ARS technology alleviated the difficulties associated with the lack of opportunity for follow-up. Even though there would be no formal follow-up, the ease with which the ARS collects data allowed us to make detailed data reports to the college's administration and academic committees, which in turn can help professors in the classroom to recognize and address typical problem areas.

ARS technology also makes it easy to incorporate best teaching practices. As the students mentioned, it naturally produces enthusiastic participation, keeps individuals interested, and promotes frequent feedback from the instructor. Perhaps the greatest benefit of ARS technology is the assessment component. The ARS we used produces detailed response reports in Microsoft Excel, making it simple to analyze data and figure out which parts of the lesson worked well and which need adjustment. Classroom instructors wishing to use the technology to test knowledge and grade assignments can register the clickers to individuals and provide an immediate score. In addition to "The Seven Deadly Sins of Plagiarism," at Dickinson College we are also experimenting with the ARS to deliver a pre-assessment of information literacy skills to selected classes of first-year students.

ARS can be used for long or short presentations, and with large or small groups. Anyone who can write a cogent presentation and make simple PowerPoint slides can use ARS technology. An institution wanting to use an ARS might be limited only by the expense of the equipment.

TABLE 2
Student Comments

About the Clickers	About Paying Attention	About the Material
The clicky things ROCKED!	The interactive clicker made it more interesting. So I paid attention and it was informative.	Not a fun subject, but you made it the most "fun" it could be. Thanks!
I think the clickers were a good idea. It kept me focused on the lecture by actually being a part of the presentation.	The interactive component kept my attention and the program is informative of some subtleties that probably would not have been addressed at my high school.	I think the program was the best you could have done with so serious a topic. I didn't know that a bunch of that was plagiarism.
The clicker made this bearable. It would be very difficult to go through if it was just a lecture.	Good course. The fact that we are active helps us pay attention.	I found the stuff about paraphrasing very interesting and I didn't know that was considered plagiarism. Thanks.
I think the clickers are awesome and make it interesting.	This presentation is effective in that it involves the audience. By having us participate we not only are naturally more interested, but we will remember more of the material.	I thought this was an informative, interactive, and generally painless way to convey needed information. I found it very effective.

Conclusion

Delivering the anti-plagiarism message via ARS technology helped us to deliver a pedagogically sound and interesting lesson that was, at minimum, more effective than other delivery methods such as lecturing formally, administering an online quiz, or relying on students to read and understand the college's academic policies on their own. Although these methods might have sufficed for our purposes, the ARS technology allowed us to keep students directly involved in the delivery of the lesson, which provided an additional sense of importance to the message, facilitated discussion, and encouraged the students to learn from one another.

Formal academic integrity instruction is now a mandatory component of first-year orientation at Dickinson College. "The Seven Deadly Sins of Plagiarism," presented for the first time in the fall of 2006, was subject to considerable revision prior to its second year of performance and will continue to be revised and refreshed in future years.[9] The lesson may not eradicate plagiarism on our campus, and we may never be able to prove that our students will practice plagiarism avoidance as a result of attending this session since only the most egregious cases usually appear before the disciplinary board. However, even if we cannot prove long-term changes in attitude or behavior, we can at least be confident that many of our students began to recognize forms of plagiarism of which they previously had no knowledge, that they have received the message that engaging in this behavior will likely result in unpleasant consequences, and that they have been provided with numerous avenues for help when they need it.

Notes

1. Dickinson College, *Community Standards 2007-2008*. Available online from http://www.dickinson.edu/student/code.html. [Accessed 14 January 2008].

2. Robert M. Gagné, *The Conditions of Learning and Theory of Instruction* (New York: CBS College Publishing, 1985), 246-55.

3. Florence Martin, James Klein, and Howard Sullivan, "Effects of Instructional Events in Computer-Based Instruction." (Education Resources Information Center, 2004, ED 484984): 631.

4. Gagné, *The Conditions of Learning*, 53.

5. Turning Technologies, LLC, "Audience Response Systems," *TurningPoint*. Available online at http://www.turningtechnologies.com/. [Accessed 14 January 2008].

6. Gagné, *The Conditions of Learning*, 219.

7. Doris Kearns Goodwin, "How I Caused That Story: A Historian Explains Why Someone Else's Writing Wound Up in Her Book," *Time* (4 February 2002): 69.

8. Martin, Klein, and Sullivan, "Effects of Instructional Events," 632.

9. A non-interactive version of "The Seven Deadly Sins of Plagiarism" in PowerPoint can be found online at http://lis.dickinson.edu/Library/Faculty%20Services/fyseminars.html.

CHAPTER 5

Daily Doubles, Final Answers, and Library Resources

Julie Maginn

Author's abstract: In this chapter I discuss a variety of interactive and educational games that have been developed particularly for one-shot library instruction sessions at Raritan Valley Community College (RVCC). Students at RVCC seem to react favorably to active learning in general and games in particular. After experimenting with a Jeopardy format, I finally created a game which meets my instructional goal of manageably reviewing the information which has just been presented to students. I examine details regarding how these games succeeded, how they failed, and how they could be adapted to most library instruction sessions.

Editors' notes: Julie created a Library Research Game, to use in a library orientation session, to help students review information they learn during the first part of her session. Julie claims that the Library Research Game is a melding of the finer points of Jeopardy! ("without the pretty blue board") and Family Feud ("without the family and feuding"). You get everything except for the cool little Jeopardy! theme song...

Introduction

On a simplistic level, the primary goal of any library instruction session is for your students to learn about library resources. That may include finding articles, evaluating Web sites, creating proper citations, and perhaps even locating a book. However, after a rather disappointing instruction session, I had a revelation. Possibly, the primary goal of a library instruction session should be to convince the students that the library *exists* and has *stuff*. If the session is longer than an hour, it may even be possible to convince them that this stuff is usually better than the Internet. Standing in front of a room full of students (who seek out distractions including texting friends sitting across from them and applying lip gloss for literally five minutes) is simply not enough when stating or demonstrating information literacy skills or searching techniques.

Instructional Goals

My goals are simple. First, students need to become aware of the existence of library resources.

Throughout my experiences with library instruction, I have learned that students are under the impression that they know everything about finding information. Before most sessions, I ask the class how many of them will still go to the Internet first, regardless of what I'm about to say. There is always an honest handful willing to confess. After asking them to explain why, the most common response is because they are familiar with the Internet. Students are not using library resources because they are not aware that they exist.

My second goal is to have students enjoy the experience. Students need to become involved in the session for learning to occur. Once you have their attention, you can entice them into learning something. Also, entertaining the students distracts them from texting friends, checking e-mail, and surfing the Internet.

So, for the library instruction session under discussion, my goals are to have the students become aware of library resources, to be entertained, and to have the students leave having enjoyed the experience. Krajewski and Piroli reminisce that "memories of favorite teachers exist often because of that teacher's ability to capture students' attention and impart lessons in a fun and seemingly effortless way".[1] Employing games in library instruction sessions allows me to meet my primary instructional goal—to make students aware of library resources.

Instructional Strategy

For the purposes of the following discussion, the concept of game or gaming is not referring to any sort of computer software or simulations; or, for that matter, of fowl and/or hunting of fowl. Rather, my discussion is referring to the traditional concept of games: board games, card games, and most importantly, game shows. Specifically, for this chapter, I am discussing gaming regarding library instruction sessions. Games will be examined as any competition-related activity involving the class, meant to entertain students as they learn key concepts with the instructor being the facilitator, and the students being the active participants.

Why use games at all? I decided to use gaming as a strategy for the purpose of incorporating active learning into my instruction sessions. A quick search of library literature found several articles discussing the use of Jeopardy within library instruction sessions. Doshi[2], Leach and Sugarman[3], Krawjewski and Piroli[4], and Ury and King[5] have all experimented with some type of Jeopardy-related game. Doshi stresses that by including a gaming element in library instruction sessions, he "believe(s) the potential exists to excite this millennial generation about information literacy, and to infuse them with lifelong library skills."[6] Leach and Sugarman explain that Millennial students "find games more interesting than traditional classroom techniques."[7] An added advantage to capturing students' attention is that games engage students in critical thinking. Since 2000-2001, at Raritan Valley Community College there has been a push to teach critical thinking skills in all courses. Active learning within the library instruction setting goes beyond showing where students need to *click*, and forces them to actively think about their research and engage with other students in the class as they attempt to solve the questions posed.

Match of Goals and Strategy

After lecturing with canned examples for several years, I began to notice that the students easily lost interest in the material and were not retaining the information being presented. Deciding to change just the goals or just the strategy would not have solved the problem. Both components needed a re-evaluation. The goal of my previous sessions was for students to be able to conduct independent research after a lecture presentation, demonstration of the resources, and a conclusion with a few hands-on exercises. If I changed the goal to having students become aware of library resources, but continued to only have a session full of lecture, demonstration, and a few exercises, the session would be doomed to fail. Such a broad and abstract overview would not provide the students with the specific skills and knowledge they need. If I left the goal the same—namely, to enable students to conduct independent research—but changed the strategy to presenting the material as a game, it also would have failed. A typical eighty-minute session is insufficient to cover all of the material needed for students to learn how to conduct independent research and still have time for a game. By changing both the goals and the strategy, students were exposed to library resources in an entertaining way, but more importantly, in a way that broke the traditional mold, making the students more likely to view the library, and the librarians, as approachable and fun.

Description of the Instruction Session: What Actually Happened?
My First Attempt at Planning Game-oriented Instruction
As mentioned above, during the previous semester, my classes were failing to catch the students' attention. I realized that the material needed to be covered in a different way with some type of interactive component. After a few discussions with a colleague, I decided to incorporate a game of Jeopardy into the mix. Since two of my goals included entertaining the students and having them enjoy the session, using the strategy of playing a game seemed to fit. To me, the most obvious choice for a game was Jeopardy. At Raritan Valley Community College, library instruction sessions are typically eighty minutes. English I and II classes are required to attend library instruction sessions and have a set curriculum that librarians must administer. Library sessions for all other courses are optional, but highly encouraged. I was assigned to conduct a session for a Speech class. Students in this particular class needed to conduct research in preparation for a persuasive speech, gathering evidence to support their argument. Since the majority of students in Speech classes have already attended one of the required sessions, my focus was to enhance the information the students may have already heard, in addition to covering a few advanced aspects of library research. Briefly, the plan was to lecture for approximately twenty minutes and play the game for approximately thirty minutes, leaving enough time for independent research. Sometimes things go according to the plan; sometimes they do not—just like Wile E. Coyote.

Usually, before any session, I only had to update my lecture. Now I needed a new lecture and had to figure out how best to incorporate a game. I set up the Jeopardy board using one PowerPoint slide. I started with a table of six columns and six rows. I placed the categories in the first row: Catalog Subject Headings, Periodical Locator, True/False, Citation Elements, Academic Search Premier, and Call Numbers. Overlaying the table, I placed one textbox for each answer. On top of that textbox, I placed a second larger textbox for the dollar amount. By setting it up this way, the answer would be revealed by deleting the topmost textbox. I had heard about other programs that would create Jeopardy games, but this primitive way was quick and if I needed to change an answer at the last minute, I could do so easily. For a complete list of category explanations and answers, see Table 1. For the lecture, I knew I had to keep it brief, direct, and simple. I decided to demonstrate

	TABLE 1 Jeopardy Categories	
Category	**Explanation**	**Answer**
Catalog Subject Headings	Use the library catalog to find the proper subject heading for each keyword.	AIDS
		Death penalty
		Adolescents
		Bipolar disorder
		Massage therapy
Periodical Locator	Using the Periodical Locator, determine if the library has access to the following periodicals. (Yes/No)	Sports Illustrated / 1986
		Communication Theory / 2004
		National Geographic / 1930
		New York Times / 1860
		Vital Speeches of the Day / 1934
True/False	Is the following a true statement, or a false statement.	You can check out books with a G number
		The copiers do not accept change
		Cell phone use is permitted in the library
		Circulating books are on the second floor
		Laptops can be checked out of the library
Citation Elements	Determine if the following is a required element of a proper citation. (Yes/No)	Author
		Publication Date
		Article / Place of publication
		Database vendor
		Article / Total # of pages in the journal
Academic Search Premier	Using Academic Search Premier, conduct the search indicated. How many articles are retrieved?	Abstract: Hurricane Katrina
		Subject: atomic bomb
		Keyword & only full-text: bio fuels
		Subject & only academic journals: bird flu
		Subject: e-coli & Keyword: cattle
Call Numbers	Put the following call numbers in the correct order.	D21.F63 / B3.J78 / KF473.L98
		DF846.T56 / DE95.H76 / DA600.R3
		RZ35.P62 / RA35.P61 / R35.P69
		HV67.J23 / HV662.J23 / HV6111.F5
		ML89.S26 / ML89.F26 / ML89.S126

prepared examples illustrating the exact steps the students would have to repeat throughout the game. The plan was to demonstrate how to find subject headings in the library catalog; how to use the library's A-Z periodical title list (the Periodical Locator) to find out if the library had access to a particular article; and how to conduct searches in Academic Search Premier utilizing the abstract and subject term searching features.

My First Attempt at Using Jeopardy

When I made the decision to play the game, I informed the Speech professor of my plans so there would not be any surprises the day of the session. After my usual introductions, I instructed the class of seventeen students to physically move away from their computers and face the front of the room. My objective was to have their complete attention for the lecture part, so that they would be able to answer the Jeopardy questions that would soon follow. I began my prepared searches covering subject headings in our OPAC, finding periodicals in the Periodical Locator, finding articles in Academic Search Premier, and explaining the basics regarding how to create a bibliography. At this point, students had no questions, which is in keeping with student behavior during a traditional lecture presentation. I went through the examples rather hurriedly, stressing their importance and indicating that they would need this information soon. Having students turn their attention from their computers to the front of the room proved effective until the twenty-minute lecture ran to nearly thirty minutes, at which point they began to get restless. I finally covered everything I needed to and introduced the *interactive quiz*. My Jeopardy PowerPoint slide was met with mixed reactions. Some students were excited, some were confused, and some did not seem to care.

The instruction classroom is set up with four rows of computers. I instructed the class that each row was a team and that each team needed to pick a captain and an answer-giver. The captain would be responsible for conducting the searches on the computer and the answer-giver would be responsible for standing up and providing the team's answer. I recorded each captain's name on the board, which had an unexpected positive outcome. In a one-shot library instruction session, rarely do you get to know student names. This, however, provided a nice opportunity to learn some names and make a connection with the students. I then quickly made sure that the class knew the rules of the actual Jeopardy game (some students had never watched the show) and the rules of *my* version.

Before continuing, let me interject a recommendation about rules, based on this first experience. It is crucial that rules are explicitly spelled out prior to the start of the game and followed throughout the entire game. Do not change, add, or detract from the rules that have been set, even if they beg. Debatable rules may include "Do teams lose points for incorrect answers?" and "Is there a maximum bet for daily doubles or can a team only wager the amount they have?" Both of these were debated during the session.

I started the game by arbitrarily picking one of the teams to go first. The first question was rough. Everyone just yelled out the answer, obviously not following the rules. I repeated the rule that only the answer-giver was allowed to respond to the question, and only after standing up and having me call on that team. It took a few questions for that rule to sink in, so the game was somewhat confusing until the students got the hang of it.

The dynamic of the game resulted in various levels of involvement. Due to the time constraints, some teams changed captains after realizing that another team member was able to type faster and able to find the answers more quickly. For obvious reasons, the team captains and answer-givers were very involved, along with a select few of other students who were helping the captains find the answers. There were also those students who sat with their team and watched either their classmates play the game or watch the dust move across the floor.

Those who chose to participate were answering the questions quite well. The questions requiring searching the catalog, Periodical Locator, and Academic Search Premier became more of a race between the captains for the fastest typist. Whereas the Yes/No and True/False questions provided humor when one team answered incorrectly, to see how quickly another team's answer-giver could stand up with the opposite answer. When addressing some of the searching questions, in particular those from Academic Search Premier, teams wanted immediate explanations as to why their answers were wrong. This actually occurred with the first searching question. At that point, I realized I was going to have to go over each searching question. To not do so would only add to the confusion and frustration I saw some of the students experiencing.

Since the game was progressing more quickly than anticipated, I knew this would probably not be a problem and I assured the class that all of their questions would be answered. That's right ... now they had questions—questions! about how the database worked; about why their search was not exactly correct; about subject headings; about library policies; and about why the total number of pages in a journal is not included in a citation. I had been keeping track of the points on the board, which was a feat in-and-of itself. Asking me to perform simple arithmetic in front of witnesses usually results in mistakes, which the class eagerly pointed out. When all of the questions were answered and the game was over, some students were disappointed that there was no Final Jeopardy question. It was somewhat anti-climatic. The winning team received candy as a prize, which I told them alas, they could not eat until they left the library. I then proceeded to demonstrate and explain each searching question. It was satisfying to see those students who were involved, paying attention to see how the correct answer was found. It was disconcerting to see those students who were not involved, packing their things and getting ready to make a beeline for the door. Nevertheless, the majority of students responded favorably: when it was all over, the class applauded.

Reflection on the Instruction Session: Lessons Learned
Reflection on Jeopardy
The first comment I heard from colleagues after the session was over was, "What were you doing in there? We could hear you guys all the way out here!" I made a

mental note to close the door to the instruction room next time. Overall, I thought the session was a success. However, after analyzing the class in more detail, I was able to tease out the successful and unsuccessful aspects of the Jeopardy experiment. The initial facets I felt needed to be addressed included student interaction, the shift in strategy for the students, and how well the questions worked.

First, student interaction ranged from total involvement to total detachment. The majority of the class was involved. I am convinced that it would not have mattered what game was being played; the students would have become highly competitive if I had asked them to play tic-tac-toe. It was amazing to watch how quickly each team demonstrated an overwhelming desire to win. But on the other hand, those students who did not interact at all, failed to achieve the basic goal of the session—to become familiar with library resources. There were also students who became involved in the game, but had no opportunity to directly use the resources themselves; they were merely observers to the captain's actions.

Second, part of the success of the session was a result of the shift in strategy from all lecture to the majority of the session being an interactive game. Ironically, part of the failure of the session was a result of de-emphasizing the lecture component. Some students enjoyed the session because it was completely different from any other session they may have attended in the past. They enjoyed the interaction and the competition. On the other hand, some students were confused and frustrated, perhaps because they could not follow the game.

Lastly, I needed to address the game questions. Some of the questions worked very well, whereas others only confused students, even those who were completely involved in the game. The questions that needed the most work were the database-searching questions. The answer involved a number—a very specific number—which was rather difficult for the students to produce. Unless they repeated the exact steps that I had worked out, their number would be different, even if they successfully carried out the search. The searching questions for the library catalog and the Periodical Locator worked very well since there could be only one answer. And the quick questions, such as the True/False and Citation Elements, were almost too easy. If one team answered wrong, it required no additional thinking for another team to come up with the correct answer.

The Library Research Game

Besides these three facets of conflicting successes and failures, I identified one major success and one major failure. The session was a success since it clearly presented the library in a fun, informal, and approachable way. Hopefully, even the students who decided not to participate in the game would feel a little more comfortable approaching a librarian at the reference desk after having been through the session. The end of the session was a failure, from my perspective, because it did not have that one culminating question that most games lead up to. In order to fix all of the problems described, I developed what I un-creatively call the *Library Research Game*. It is somewhat a Jeopardy-hybrid (without the pretty blue board) and Family Feud (without the family and feuding).

TABLE 2
Library Research Game

Rules and Directions: Each row is a team. Each team should select a team leader and a name for their team. A series of research questions will appear on the screen. The first player in each row is the active player and must conduct the necessary research to find the answer to the question. The first team to have their active player stand up with the correct answer, receives the allotted points. After each question, the entire team stands up, the active player moves to the back of the row, and each player moves up one spot. The team with the most points at the end wins the game.

Questions	Observations
Using the Library Catalog, what is the subject heading for AIDS?	I plan on changing this question. Students have debated that there are numerous acceptable answers, including HIV infections, HIV (Viruses), and the actual answer, AIDS (Disease). Going into the explanation slows down the game, especially as the game's first question.
Using the Library Catalog, what is the subject heading for Al-Qaeda?	Question works well to demonstrate the difference between keywords and subject headings.
Using the Library Catalog, what is the subject heading for wildlife preservation?	Question works well within the RVCC catalog since the students must search through a few records to find the correct answer.
Using Academic Search Premier, what is the subject heading for bird flu?	Students have learned that avian refers to birds with this question. Many have thought they had the wrong answer.
Using Academic Search Premier, what subject term and what company entity can be combined to find articles on e-coli and the Taco Bell incident?	Question works well to demonstrate how students can utilize multiple search options at the same time.
Using Academic Search Premier, conduct a search for the subject term search for identity theft. What is the title of the first academic journal that has full-text access to the article?	This question has been rather difficult for students. I intentionally include searching for identity theft within my lecture, but students seem to have a hard time reading the entire question and that they need to look for the first academic journal with full text.
Using the Periodical Locator, which database(s) provide access to *Communication Theory*?	A basic question that works well.
Using the Periodical Locator, what is the earliest issue of *Vital Speeches of the Day* that the library has access to?	I use this question to show students that the Periodical Locator includes RVCC periodicals, not just those in databases.
Using the Periodical Locator, does the library have access to the following article … ?	This question causes confusion for some since students try searching by article title, instead of periodical title. It reinforces how to find the journal title within a citation.

TABLE 2 Library Research Game	
Final Question **Each team makes a wager.**	**Observations**
Using Academic Search Premier, conduct a search for body image and the media. What are the two subject terms that should be combined for this topic? For 10 extra points: conduct a subject search with those two subject terms. Print out a copy of the first citation retrieved from an academic journal and give it to me with your team's name on it.	Very few teams submit the correct answer. If their subject terms are wrong, the article they submit is wrong as well. The most common error teams make is using two terms for body image and nothing for mass media.

Instead of a Jeopardy board, I made a PowerPoint slide for each question I wanted to ask. Depending on the class, I'll usually end up with about nine questions—three on the library catalog, three on the Periodical Locator, and three using a subject specific database. A possible question may read: "Using Academic Search Premier, what subject term and what company entity can be combined to find articles on *e-coli* and the *Taco Bell* incident?" (For a complete list of questions, please see Table 2.) Each question is worth points related to how difficult the question is. Like the Jeopardy game, each row in the classroom is a team. The first question can only be answered by those students sitting at the first computer in each row—the active players. Their team can help them search for the answer, but they have to conduct it on their own computer and come up with the answer. For the second question, the whole class needs to get up from their seats. The active players sitting at the first computers go to the back of each row, with the other team members moving up one spot—hence the connection to Family Feud. This repeats until all questions are answered.

I started the next session the same way I started the Jeopardy session. I asked students to move away from the computers and face the front of the room. I demonstrated prepared searches in the OPAC, Periodical Locator, and Academic Search Premier, reiterating several times that perhaps they would have to repeat the same searches in a matter of minutes. Whereas most students knew the Jeopardy premise, the students had no idea what was going on with the Library Research Game. I had to repeat the rules and directions several times. I also started having the teams give themselves names in order to get the students to start interacting. I've had Batch of Cookies, Skittles, various professional sport teams, and even the Wikis (a name chosen to irritate me but in a good-natured way).

As with Jeopardy, the first question was rough. Team members did not realize they could help their active player. Active players did not realize the question was on the slide. Team members tried giving the active players the answer—which I did not accept since the active player did not conduct the research to find it. By the second question the rules and directions had been repeated so many times, we were all on the same page. It was gratifying to see team members show the active players how to find the answers to the questions.

This new arrangement solved many of the problems discussed above. With the Library Research Game, each student had no choice but to be involved; each student had the opportunity to conduct searches on their own; each question could be developed further since it did not have to fit in a tiny textbox; each question could become more complex to cover basic searching skills; and students experimented, unknowingly, with team-learning when they *taught* their fellow team members how to locate the answer.

To come up with that *big ending* I initially tried having a Speed Round. That was a complete failure. Each team captain needed to answer a series of ten questions. When the first team was ready to start, I asked the other captains to leave the room so they would not hear the answers. As the first round of questions began, I was talked into letting the rest of the team help their captain with the answers. Does anyone see a problem with this? When the second captain was ready to go, the entire room now knew all the answers to the questions. The lesson learned was to not change the rules during the game. Also, speed rounds inherently require some type of time-keeping—which I failed to do. Upon returning to my office, I quickly deleted my Speed Round document. For future sessions I put together a very hard, but answerable, research question. Each team would place a wager on the question and then work together to find the answer. There was no time limit and it usually took about five minutes for each team to come up with an answer they were satisfied with.

Here are a few suggestions based on my experience using a game for instruction in general. Before starting the game, try some test questions so that the students can get a feel for the game. Questions should not be devised to stump the student. If the questions are too hard, the students will only become frustrated while using

TABLE 3	
Recommended Do's and Don'ts for Using Games	
Do	**Don't**
Have the students move away from the computer.	Tell the students that you have a game planned.
Keep the lecture quick and direct.	Make the rules too complex.
Refer to the game as an interactive quiz initially.	Make up rules along the way.
Make sure the students know the rules.	Change rules during the game.
Conduct some test questions first.	Make the answers debatable.
Start with simple questions.	
Make sure that the questions have only one answer.	
Include some type of "big ending."	
Build in time to review each question.	

the library resources and are likely to return to what they are comfortable with—the Internet. See Table 3 for a complete list of recommended do's and don'ts. It is also important to stress that a wonderfully executed game could still fail. It all depends on the students in the class. Occasionally even a gaming strategy won't perk up an unresponsive class of students. After using the Library Research Game during several instruction sessions, I was dealt a very poker-faced class. Throughout the entire game, I felt as if I were completely confusing the students and pushing them back to Wikipedia and Google. I folded.

On the whole, I prefer game-oriented instruction to lecture-oriented. I have actually yet to repeat a second Jeopardy session since the Library Research Game generally works better. I have had good responses from students in these sessions which convince me that my new gaming strategies are worth continuing, developing, and refining.

Application to Other Instructional Settings

As stated in the introductory chapter of this book, no one theory or strategy works for every outcome, every student, or every situation. Of the two strategies discussed, the Library Research Game is much more adaptable to a variety of assignments and instructional settings than Jeopardy. It is highly advisable that any type of Jeopardy game only be used when students have already been introduced to the basic concepts of the material being covered. Since Jeopardy should progress at a quick pace, the answers should be easy to find. If provided with more than eighty minutes, these games could become even more effective.

Finally, how do you know if your application of the gaming options discussed was a success? After one of my sessions, a student approached me at the Reference Desk and stated that she *remembered me* from when her class visited the library—mission accomplished.

Notes

1. P. R. Krawjewski and V. B Piroli, "Something Old, Something New, Something Borrowed, Something Blue: Active Learning In The Classroom," *Journal of Library Administration* 36 (2002): 178.
2. A. Doshi, "How Gaming Can Improve Information Literacy," *Computers in Libraries* 26 (2005): 14-7.
3. G. J. Leach and T. S. Sugarman, "Play To Win! Using Games In Library Instruction To Enhance Student Learning," *Research Strategies* 20 (2006): 191-203.
4. Krawjewski and Piroli, "Something Old."
5. C. J. Ury and T. L. King, "Reinforcement Of Library Orientation Instruction For Freshman Seminar Students," *Research Strategies* 13 (1995): 153-64.
6. Doshi, "How Gaming Can Improve," 16.
7. Leach and Sugarman, "Play To Win!" 197.

CHAPTER 6

Making Meaning: Using Metaphor as a Tool to Increase Student Understanding

Susan Avery and Jim Hahn

Authors' abstract: We are concerned with maximizing student learning through the use of metaphors, thereby placing learning in the context of everyday experiences. We use metaphors to effectively impart the idea of research as a process. The ethos of metaphor pedagogy utilizes students' framework to build an understanding of database use conceptually and as a transferable skill-set. Students prompted with examples with which they are familiar, helps shape their understanding of research methodology.

Editors' notes: Susan and Jim introduce the use of Cognitive strategies to explain complex concepts. They use a number of metaphors to help their students to understand library concepts. For example: "marking and saving a record is similar to putting things in a shopping cart"; "Facebook is really a database"; and (our personal favorite) "Academic Search Premier is similar to Cheerios." Cheerios actually sound really good about now... go grab a bowl and start reading...

Introduction

The librarians and graduate assistants of the Undergraduate Library at the University of Illinois at Urbana – Champaign provide library instruction to students enrolled in courses that meet the university's Composition 1 requirement. This includes nine different courses that fall under the auspices of the departments of Rhetoric, Speech Communications, and English as a Second Language. Students are placed into the courses based on their college entrance test scores and approximately 20 percent of each class of seven thousand first-year students test out of the course. Two circumstances exist that have a direct impact on the library instruction in these courses. First, there is no university mandate that requires library-led instruction be a part of any of these classes and second, an overwhelming majority of these classes are taught by graduate teaching assistants (TAs). The Coordinator of Instructional Services serves, in many ways, as the evangelist for integrating library instruction into these courses.

Instructional Goals

The library instruction and research components of these classes are intended to fulfill some of the same goals as the writing components: helping first-year students better understand the practices necessary for successful academic coursework. Rather than concentrating on teaching students to search the online catalog or a particular database, the instruction emphasizes essential concepts for understanding research as a process and successfully searching for and using information in a variety of formats from a variety of resources.

The following learning outcomes are the focus of our instructional strategy and, as such, divide our class time into distinct segments related to each of these:

1.   Students will distinguish search engines (such as Google) from online, subscription databases provided by the library in order to select the most appropriate source for their research need.

2.   Students will become familiar with the Undergraduate Library as both a physical and virtual space in order to successfully utilize the spaces and enhance their learning experiences.

3.   Students will create and design effective search strategies in order to better define their topics and more productively engage in the research process.

4.   Students will select and search databases in order to locate relevant resources for their research projects.

5.   Students will evaluate resources in print and online formats, including subscription databases and Web search engines, in order to distinguish academic, scholarly resources and select the most appropriate resources to support their research.

Instructional Strategy

As indicated above, it is extremely important that students do not interpret the instruction that takes place in these classes as only having relevance to this particular course. We emphasize the transferability of the skills and concepts taught, broadening their use beyond the specific course. During the course of our instruction anecdotal evidence indicates that approximately half of our first-year students have never searched an electronic database and many of those that have find it difficult to differentiate a proprietary library subscription database from a free search engine such as Google. This presents us with an additional problem: students who simply do not understand research as a process or the semantics commonly associated with database searching. One strategy we have found that can significantly impact student understanding is the use of metaphor. Metaphors can create understanding and make meaning for students when everyday experiences are used to explain the use of new technologies and processes.

An examination of the literature indicates that employing metaphors in library instruction is certainly not anything new. Nibley notes that the use of metaphors "...will reach out to college students to help them experience some of the excitement librarians feel when we find information we need in a form we can use."[1] Brandt focuses on analogies as mental models that "...provide not only a conceptual understanding of things but also the tools by which we figure out other things."[2] He further goes on to discuss the importance of relevance in those mental models we choose to utilize. Mills likens the metaphor for learning to a journey "so pervasive we don't notice it."[3] This, perhaps, can provide us with some of the best guidance as we utilize metaphors in our instruction: they should be so seamless they weave themselves into the student's thought process.

Match of Goals and Strategy

Our objective is to engage students and help them make connections with what they already do and know. In order for our goals and strategy to meet it is necessary to brainstorm metaphors that will contribute to student understanding. Sometimes it is the case that new metaphors are discovered through student's questions. Other times metaphor invention occurs serendipitously, through the course of explaining a particular database function.

Avery presents the following guidelines for successfully using metaphors in instruction, noting metaphors used in class should:

*   Be understandable to students, allowing them to make the necessary connections
*   Connect to common, real life experiences students share
*   Be relevant to the current context and cultural experiences of the students.[4]

Description of the Instruction Session: What Actually Happened?

The instruction session commences with the library teacher, either a librarian or a Graduate Assistant (GA) employed by the Undergraduate Library (Undergrad) and enrolled at the Graduate School of Library and Information Science at the University of Illinois, prompting these first-year students to recollect their high school research experiences completing reports, papers, or other assignments. Given that the initial college library experience can be quite intimidating for many students, we feel it is important for them to realize they actually have done something like this before. Granted, in many situations the expectations of high school research are quite different from the expectations in a college setting. Nevertheless, this provides a good starting point as we begin our dialog by asking students where they usually start their research. In the vast majority of our classes the top two resources students share are Google and Wikipedia. Each class will have some students who recall using sources such as EBSCO and Infotrac. (They rarely remember the name of the database itself, but rather the name of the provider.) With some prompting on the part of the instructor who share the names of other database providers (Gale, Lexis-Nexis, etc.) we are able to discern that a number of students in the class actually have used a database provided by a library in the course of their high school research. It is interesting to note that many of these students did not realize what the difference was between these resources and free Internet resources such as Google, Yahoo, and MSN.

The hands-on learning then entails students performing a Google search of their topic. We begin with Google to illustrate a major point we want students to appreciate as they come away from the session: This isn't the lottery. A large number of results are not a good thing! Most often their results are in the millions. This contrast is a form of metaphorical thinking; it requires the students to first liken Google searches to the lottery and then sever that likening. Comparing the unmanageably large number of results—many of which lack credibility—of a Google search to winning the lottery (where large numbers are good) emphasizes its shortcomings in terms of the goals of a database search. Further discussion focuses on ways to pare down the results. It is always surprising to us how many of these students, many whom would describe themselves as tech-savvy, are unaware of even simple techniques such as the use of quotation marks when searching for phrases. Before continuing we minimize the Google search so that we may return to it later in the session to juxtapose the Google results with results from a similar search in a library database.

We move on to an introduction of the library as virtual space. Because we are a large research university library with many departmental libraries, our students are walked though the Library Gateway page to the Undergrad's Web site. Students are familiar with Web pages that are solely cosmetic. Consider that a good many Web sites exist merely as a promotional tool.

While the instruction session is always somewhat promotional for the library, we are interested in conveying to our students the fact that the library Web page is *not* cosmetic. One GA has been known to remark, "*This page is a goldmine!*" Here, the gold mine acts as a metaphor for a large amount of valuable information. Resources on the Undergraduate Library's Web page represent a large commitment on the part of the librarians in the Undergraduate Library to select databases and resources that, given their experience at the reference desk, are known to be most relevant and useful for undergraduate research.

The gold mine metaphor employed relates the selectivity of links which we have chosen to place on our Web page. As a librarian will select books for inclusion into the collection she will also choose to select Web page links as a collection to assist in your searching. Students are familiar with the idea of a library being a collection of books. We apply the same selectivity principle in crafting Web pages that serve as a collection of databases, which in turn represent a collection of article abstracts or full-text articles.[5]

Furthering our desire to relate what happens in the library to what happens in our students' lives we strive to contextualize our services. We know students make use of instant messaging services (IM) so our sessions discuss our own Ask-A-Librarian messaging service. In fact, in many of our classes a member of the class will offer a testimonial of sorts on their experiences using the library's instant messaging services. Fortunately all of these testimonials relate positive experiences. We continually emphasize the numerous ways for students to receive additional help after this instruction session. It is surprising to us that many of our students do not realize that librarians have graduate degrees. Here, another metaphor serves us well: seeking professional assistance in the library is not unlike a visit to the doctor's office: to reach the best resolution to your problem you seek the advice of a professional (doctor, nurse, librarian).

Making use of one of those golden Web pages on the Undergrad Web site, we move into a discussion on formulating a topic and choosing keywords for this topic. The extensive use of Web search engines as the primary research tool for first-year students has also resulted in search habits that do not translate well to searching library databases. For example, many students exhibit tendencies to enter complete questions or string unrelated search terms together in the search box. Difficulty understanding that there are multiple ways to describe a topic can be a challenge, as many students tend to lock in on the first keywords they identify. To encourage them to think more critically about the use of appropriate keywords we have made use of a Google mashup: "Guess the Google".[6]

A mashup is one of the features of Web 2.0 combining two disparate Web elements into a new digital tool which may not have a physical world analogue. This resource engages students in the process of guessing what keywords would have produced the arrayed results. We experimented with having students play this game on their desktop PCs but found that students were too immersed in guessing and had to be pulled away from the game. This mashup, as an element of active learning, truly engages students in understanding the importance of varying keywords while searching. We now employ the strategy of playing this game as a class. Intrepid students have been observed locating the game address on their own and playing at their desktop regardless.

At this point in the presentation students are asked the difference between a library database and a search engine such as Google. The metaphor employed to make this point compares library databases to premium pay-per-view cable television programming and search engines to free broadcast television programming. Both will provide results, but quality, on-target results can be more difficult to locate via the free resources. The point is further underscored by appealing to students' desire to get their money's worth. If a portion of your college tuition money is allocated to the library and the library is using the money to pay for your access to these databases, you should make certain that you are receiving the content for which you have paid. This is also an opportune time to discuss how reference books can be somewhat expensive to purchase, but this cost is reflected in the quality of these reference works. The idea of how to make use of a reference work for beginning research is then promulgated.

To illustrate the use of a library database we use the EBSCO database Academic Search Premier (ASP) as our teaching tool. An important practice for students to learn, for citation purposes, is to know the name of the database they are searching. Although we do emphasize the importance of the name of the source that is being searched, after entering the database students are asked to tell the instructor the database name. Invariably they reply EBSCO. Given that the largest, most prominent text on most every database search page will be the name of the provider this is a logical response for our students. We correct this response by explaining EBSCO should be thought of as the brand or company, while Academic Search Premier is the product. The point can be further explicated by asking students what kind of cereal they enjoyed for breakfast: Was the cereal General Mills or Cheerios? Further examination of the drop-down list of all EBSCO databases can further clarify this point as we return to the cereal metaphor. This list of products is similar to a list of cereals produced by General Mills. EBSCO (similar to General Mills) is the company name, while Academic Search Premier (similar to Cheerios) is the product name.

Furthermore, as we are exploring this database, our students are made aware that the library subscribes to numerous databases, and understanding the concepts of searching a database such as ASP, will help them search other databases with confidence. This is similar to transferring your ability to drive a particular make and model of car to driving other vehicles. Although the lights, horn, and other features may be in different places, you know how they will operate and to look for and use them. This helps emphasize that Academic Search Premier is a tool that utilizes specific skills and concepts to locate appropriate resources. Just as a student's driver's permit did not specify they could only drive one particular model of car, likewise they can apply the search skills gained via ASP to other databases. It is clear to us that this metaphor is meaningful to students as they are easily engaged in discussions that recognize what the differences and similarities that exist in various automobiles and, subsequently, library databases.

After we have managed to get some satisfactory results out of our database searching, we talk about marking the records for further use. To mark and save a record is similar to the experience of using the shopping cart in any kind of e-commerce that our students have engaged. Marking the record places the record in a place (in this case a folder) where you can then have the folder's contents e-mailed to you. This is similar to the online shopping experience that utilizes a shopping cart to hold desired items until purchase.

We show that these records can be sent to the student in the citation format of their choosing. We underscore the importance of this function being a time saver for creating your bibliography. Students frequently respond by asking the instructor to model this technique again. Students who may have lost enthusiasm for library database research are suddenly jolted back to attention!

Most students are avid users of the social utility Facebook.[7] We leverage this familiarity to expose Facebook as a database. To explain the closed nature of proprietary databases we ask students to recall that Facebook profiles are not open to viewing by all Web users. One must login to view a profile. Myriad privacy settings remain which further restrict your access to content in Facebook. The referencing of Facebook as a closed database relates the concept of information in proprietary databases. Information in proprietary databases is referred to as encompassing what is called the *deep web* or *invisible web*.

We extrapolate the Facebook metaphor further as one seeks to locate a known article in a proprietary database. Not all databases have the same content just as not all profiles are accessible to all users. Facebook is an exceedingly complex database. A nuanced understanding of Facebook reveals its nature as being a closed database (of databases) undergoing near continual update by its users. Students who have made extensive use of the Facebook platform are urged to make use of this skill set in other database use. When transferring this conceptual framework, they will find a database such as ASP easy to use by comparison.

Students are engaged by instruction which makes use of tools they utilize. Observing student reactions to an introduction of a class wherein Facebook is referenced garners interest and student attention. Building on this initial enthusiasm is a challenge for all teachers. As the instructional session has progressed and we arrive at a point where students may be losing interest, we again infuse Facebook and the unfolding of common database concepts by a static help page.[8] A common critique leveled against the use of Facebook by library staff is the problematic nature of stepping outside of your traditional sphere and into a sphere where you may be trespassing: the student's personal space. A static page such as this allows librarians to use a social utility as a teaching tool while not crossing any social lines and thus avoids violating any personal-boundary-zone-issues.

The final sweeping pièce de résistance of the instruction session: the heretofore minimized Google searches are compared to the Academic Search Premier results. Students are asked to compare the number of results from Google (at best still number in the hundred thousands) with the number of results retrieved in Academic Search Premier. With two or three appropriate keywords they can usually retrieve around fifty quality citations to begin their research. We take advantage of these citation lists to demonstrate the ease with which you can e-mail the results to yourself. This is clearly an added benefit to the class, as students leave the instruction session with something very valuable in hand: a viable start to their research. We like to add to this the qualifying point that Google will not usually point you to content that will be necessary for completing your paper. Google will not provide you access to proprietary databases. We certainly do not disparage Google, (that would be insane) but only seek to help our students form the idea that for success at the university level they will be required to draw on new resources they have not previously employed for their research.

Reflection on the Instruction Session: Lessons Learned

Helping students achieve a light-bulb moment in a library instruction session can present challenges. However, positive responses from both students and teachers indicate that we have been able to achieve many of these moments by utilizing metaphor in our instruction. Nibley reminds us that metaphors must "... appeal to, or be couched in, terms the hearer can understand."[9] This can present challenges to library instructors who belong to different generations than our students and serves to emphasize the importance of keeping pace with current popular culture.

The Undergraduate Library is fortunate to have a number of Graduate Assistants who are closer in age to our undergraduate students and can serve as sounding boards. The environment is one geared toward inventing innovative instruction. For maximizing student learning we are unafraid to attempt that which has never been undertaken in an instruction session.

Application to Other Instructional Settings

Metaphors do not limit themselves to a particular instructional setting. Keeping in mind the subject of a class, the age of our students, and the existing degree of understanding of the topic at hand will dictate what kind and how many metaphors should be employed. Care must be taken not to insult the intelligence level of those in an upper-level class by utilizing metaphors clearly geared toward first-year students.

As reference services and instruction are quite interrelated in a learning environment, the use of metaphors at the reference desk is a great application for enhancing student understanding. Due to the uniqueness of each encounter one must be sure to get a sense of what will be applicable, metaphor-wise, to each given reference encounter.[10] Employed with empathy the use of metaphor in learning will serve to both make meaning for the student and enhance their learning.

Libraries are confusing places. Student learning is improved when we seek to be understood by way of speaking in a manner conducive to learning. Jargon use may make one feel superior but this is never the aim of teaching. Concern for our students dictates we present novel material in the most simple of ways.

Notes

1. Elizabeth Nibley, "The Use of Metaphor in Bibliographic Instruction," *RQ* 30:3 (1991).
2. D. Scott Brandt, "Analogies and the Face of Technology," *Computers in Libraries* 19 (1999): 242.
3. Mills, Jane, "The Concept of the Journey," *Australian Screen Education* 34 (2004): 34.
4. Susan Avery, "Beyond the Mouse Click: Using Metaphor and Analogy in Library Instruction," in *Discover, Connect, Engage: Creative Integration of Information Literacy*, eds. Theresa Valko, Sarah Fabian, and Robert Stevens (Ann Arbor, MI: Pierian Press, 2007), 208.
5. Undergraduate Library, "Find Articles Guide," University of Illinois at Urbana-Champaign. Available online from http://www.library.uiuc.edu/ugl/find/articleguide.html. [Accessed 24 August 2007].
6. Grant Robinson, "Guess-the-Google." Available online from http://grant.robinson.name/projects/guess-the-google. [Accessed 24 August 2007].
7. Facebook. Available online from http://www.facebook.com. [Accessed 24 August 2007).
8. Undergraduate Library, "How Facebook is Like a Library Database," University of Illinois at Urbana-Champaign. Available online from http://www.library.uiuc.edu/ugl/how-doi/facebook.html. [Accessed 24 August 2007].
9. Nibley, "The Use of Metaphor."
10. Richard E. Bopp and Linda C. Smith, *Reference and Information Services: An Introduction* (Englewood Cliffs, NJ: Libraries Unlimited, 2001).

CHAPTER 7

Analogical Storytelling as a Strategy for Teaching Concept Attainment

Anna Montgomery Johnson

Author's abstract: Students come to the library instruction classroom with many misconceptions about online resources. No one likes to listen to a librarian lecture, but Direct Instruction is often the best method for teaching concept attainment. As an alternative to teacher-centered lecture, analogical storytelling is a strategy that harnesses the powerful Cognitive processes of personal narrative to facilitate meaning-making and to personalize the librarian-student interaction.

Editors' notes: Anna used a Cognitive strategy to provide students with information about the library research process. However, she did so by telling students stories from her own research projects. She says, "Anyway, a few years ago, this project my dad works on was featured on the cover of the journal Physics Today, which is a pretty big deal." So we're assuming that Anna's father is "kind of a big deal." (Ten points to you if you catch the reference...)

Introduction

It's not uncommon for college students to think that the library catalog is a search engine and that they can find the full text of peer-reviewed articles with a Google search. The difference between vetted library resources and the wide-open Web is obvious to librarians, but, as T. G. McFadden warns, "the difference is almost entirely opaque" to our students, and the misconception that these are analogous resources carries "pernicious intellectual consequences."[1]

Instructional Goals

Given so much confusion, one of the primary goals of library instruction must be to introduce and explain the library's online resources. Faced with the task of teaching complex concepts, librarians employ many presentation strategies, but most of us agree that lecturing doesn't work. Lectures are boring. Nobody wants to listen to a librarian drone on and on. Lecture forces students to sit still; it's the antithesis of active learning. But what if we had a way to talk to students without lecturing?

In this chapter, I'll discuss storytelling as a strategy for replacing lecture in the library instruction classroom. Storytelling is an instructional strategy that engages students' imaginations, holds their attention, and stimulates the cognitive processes that help them learn. Impressive tools for teaching concept attainment, stories are especially effective when they include analogies to constructs already within students' frames of reference. I will discuss my own use of analogical storytelling in the classroom to clarify three concepts that are often confusing to students: the library catalog, the research process, and the search engine Google Scholar.

Instructional Strategy

Storytelling is certainly one of the oldest instructional strategies. References to storytelling appear as early as 4,000 BCE,[2] and history's earliest teachers, from Socrates to Confucius, are celebrated as tellers of tales. In most cultures, life's earliest lessons are taught in story forms such as religious parables and fairy tales. You don't need to study educational theory to know that narrative is a powerful teaching tool, "one of the fundamental sense-making operations of the mind."[3] Think back to your own early learning experiences: If you're like me, you have no trouble remembering that the third Little Pig built his house of bricks, but it might take you a few seconds to remember that the third U.S. President was Thomas Jefferson.

Why is storytelling so powerfully linked to learning? And why do we rarely remember lectures? Unlike lecture, which is teacher-centered instruction at its extreme, storytelling is an act of performance, designed for and dependent upon the imagination of an audience. Even though the storyteller is the only person talking, "because stories require active listening, people are able to share a depth of experience otherwise not possible through normal dialogue."[4] In an educational setting, this means that students are actively engaged in the story, even while ostensibly enduring the traditional classroom experience of sitting still and listening to a teacher.

Storytelling allows a teacher to do all the things we hope to accomplish when addressing a classroom: it emotionally engages students, allows them to grasp new concepts, and promotes active listening. Craig Eilert Abrahamson examines storytelling in terms of cognitive processing: "The teller and the listener come together on a cognitive and emotional level that allows the listener to relate to the teller from his or her own personal framework and thus grasp the teller's perception of the content at the same time. This represents a remarkable, and yet very common, interpersonal experience."[5]

Master storyteller Amy Spaulding believes that storytelling "is an organic art and, as more and more of life becomes technologized, it grows in importance as an antidote to impersonality."[6] I'd add that, as more and more of library instruction becomes all about the Internet, it's increasingly important that librarians bring personality to the classroom.

Telling stories is always an effective way to personalize a presentation, but not all stories are educational. For the purposes of this discussion, I'm using the term *storytelling* to refer to a presentation style that relies on personal narrative as a delivery method for instructional content. My stories are about library resources, not fairy tale characters; they begin not with "once upon a time..." but with "last term..." When I tell stories about my own experiences using library resources, students are able to understand new concepts by imagining themselves in the story's situations.

Educational strategies featuring the use of story appear in the literature of many different learning theories. Storytelling is perhaps most often analyzed from a Constructivist framework wherein students tell their life stories to each other.[7]

Autobiographical narrative assignments are especially prevalent in English as a Second Language (ESL) classes for adult learners.[8] In discussing the meaning-making power of autobiography, theorist Jerome Bruner proposes that the cognitive processes involved in telling our life stories can actually shape our memories of lived events.[9]

Storytelling is also discussed in the literature of business communication, where persuasive delivery is equally important. Storytelling is serious business. Corporate leaders recognize stories as powerful delivery methods for sales pitches and motivational communications.[10] By presenting just the facts, speakers risk alienating their audiences and suffering "Death by PowerPoint."[11] Executive coach Robert Dickman teaches CEOs to see storytelling as a sales tool because "a story is a fact wrapped in an emotion that compels an action which transforms our world."[12]

Witness the hugely successful *Chicken Soup for the Soul* series, created by motivational speakers who told stories "with such universal themes as a mother's love, obstacles overcome, misunderstandings resolved …and the boundless wisdom of children."[13] A favorite source of material for many public speakers, the *Chicken Soup* stories are carefully constructed to elicit a specific emotional response from the listener, such as crying or laughing out loud. Story has the power to make listeners feel what the teller intended them to feel: personal narrative, properly employed, can have equally persuasive power as a teaching tool.

The most successful stories used for instructional purposes often incorporate analogies. Analogical learning occurs whenever the student can recognize consistent similarities between concepts.[14] Analogy "provides a concrete link to the new concept, notion, or process that is being introduced so that the learner can adapt or assimilate to held mental models."[15] Instructional stories are therefore doubly effective when they are relevant to students' previous experiences.[16]

Match of Goals and Strategy

Analogical storytelling is a powerful strategy when concept attainment is critical to student success. In the library instruction classroom, story can replace lecture as a delivery method for teaching new information. Embedding instructional information in personal narrative lets the librarian engage and relate to students and—more importantly—stimulates the cognitive processes that will help students remember. As Abrahamson observes: "There is a true need for didactic instruction in education, integrated with inspiration, satisfaction, and fascination, for people often remember information the longest that has had an emotional impact on them."[17]

Storytelling is sneaky teaching; it's slipping lessons into a story like Mom used to sneak eggs into your milkshake. Students don't really notice that they're learning while they listen, and they pay attention because nobody ever really outgrows story time.

Description of the Instruction Session: What Actually Happened?
The Online Catalog
Librarians take a lot of professional pride in the fact that we were early Internet adopters, moving our card catalogs online way back before there was a World Wide

Web. For a while, this made library catalogs the very latest in online databases. But for today's "digital native"[18] college students, who grew up with Google, the library catalog looks like just another search engine. It doesn't matter that all similarities between library catalogs and search engines end as soon as you click Search. Students have a hard time understanding the concept of the library catalog; part of the problem is that they don't know what's in there.

The old card catalog, with its hundreds of drawers of thousands of cards, gave users a visual, visceral sense of the size of the library's collection. This sense of scope was lost when the library catalog moved online. As McFadden explains it, "the Internet is a typical 'black box.' Very complicated things happen inside of it, but nothing about the box itself reveals what is going on."[19] Lacking visual clues to its contents, and superficially looking a lot like a search engine, the library catalog becomes a confusing concept. Students have no idea of the size of the database they're querying and no idea that they're not searching every word of every page of every book.

I use size analogies to teach the concept of library catalogs. I begin by asking if my students remember the card catalog. Many of them (for now at least) do, so we reminisce about the scope of the old system: how much room the card drawers used to take up in the library, the length of the drawers, the number of cards in each drawer. I ask students to visualize the size of the cards themselves. Was the entire book printed on that little card? Of course not, there wasn't room. This discussion provides students with a realistic sense of scope when they encounter the new concept of the online library catalog. Armed with the mental image of the extinct card catalog, they now understand that the familiar library catalog has simply evolved to an online environment; we still use the library catalog to find out about a book, not to access the book itself. It's not like Googling a Web page; the catalog isn't searching every word on every page. And they won't be able read the whole book on the computer ... at least not yet.

The community college where I work belongs to a regional consortium of over thirty academic libraries with reciprocal borrowing privileges.[20] When students search our library catalog, they may click a button to repeat the same search in the consortial union catalog with its millions of additional titles. Students rarely realize the research potential of this resource, so I again use size as a starting point to teach an unfamiliar concept. Since the two catalogs function in very much the same way, I tell a story to emphasize the enormous difference in scale between our local catalog and the union catalog:

"We share a humongous library catalog with almost every other college library in the Pacific Northwest. It's called the Summit catalog, and it's really, really, really big. Our library has about fifty thousand books. Summit has eight million books. That number is just huge. It's so huge it's hard to visualize. Let's try to figure out how big that is.

"We can see how big our library collection is. We want to know how much bigger Summit is, so let's try to figure out how many times bigger than fifty thousand is eight million ... okay, fifty thousand goes into one hundred thousand ... twice.

One hundred thousand goes into a million ... ten times. So, two times ten is ... twenty. And then one million goes into eight million ... eight times. And twenty times eight is ... one hundred and sixty. So, wow, the Summit catalog is a hundred and sixty times bigger than our library catalog.

"Wow. One hundred and sixty times. How much bigger is that? There are about eleven weeks in each quarter of school ... five days in a week times eleven weeks is fifty-five ... fifty-five times the three terms of the school year is one hundred and sixty-five. Give or take a couple of holidays, call it one hundred and sixty. So, if Summit is one hundred and sixty times bigger than our library catalog, that's the same difference as one day of school compared to the entire school year. Wow!"

The Research Process

Of course, when I introduce the concept of the research process, I want students to learn that they should search for reliable information in many different resources. In the process of researching and writing a paper, there are many ways to get from beginning to end, but careful research involves investigating several types of resources. In trying to arrive at an analogy to explain this process, I shied away from models that were too linear; it doesn't really matter where students begin their research, as long as they ... cover their *bases*! So now I tell an analogical story about baseball: When you're at bat (assigned a paper), you want to hit a home run and get back to home plate (finish the paper), but first you have to hit the ball (choose a topic) and run the bases (explore reference sources, the library catalog, and the library's article databases). I also talk about Web sites, which are, of course, in the outfield.

Google Scholar

Like many academic librarians, I spend much of my time teaching students how to access articles electronically. Typically, students have topics in mind when they begin the research process, which means they are searching for any relevant articles across many (often thousands of) journals. But some students approach research assignments by trying to locate a specific article based on the remembered bits and pieces of something they've read.

To give one recent real-life example, a student wanted to find "a piece from the New Yorker a few years ago about Muslim girls in France who weren't allowed to wear the veil at school."[21] This student remembered a great deal, including the crucial detail of the periodical title, but his database keyword searches weren't turning up any results. Knowing what the article is about won't get you very far if you're thinking *veil* but the database thinks *HIJAB (Islamic clothing)*.

The specificity and complexity of controlled subject terms, the very features that make subscription databases so powerful, can render an article invisible to a searcher who only knows what (he thinks) that article is about. Ambiguous "aboutness" is where search engines shine; good thing there's Google Scholar.[22]

By putting those magical Google algorithms to work in scholarly Web spaces, Google Scholar is a librarian's best friend for those "I know I read an article about" questions. Because it is such a useful tool for identifying citations, I teach students to use Google Scholar when they know some, but not all, of the publication details for an article. In the library instruction classroom, I tell the following story:

"My dad is a physicist at a national laboratory. He works at a particle accelerator. That's a device that speeds up subatomic particles to pretty much the speed of light, sends the beam of particles around a really long track, and then lets the particles bang into each other, so the physicists can study what happens. Now this stuff is way over my head ... literally; the machines they use are made out of magnets as tall as houses!

"Anyway, a few years ago, this project my dad works on was featured on the cover of the journal *Physics Today*, which is a pretty big deal. When they took the picture for the cover, they wanted somebody to stand next to the enormous equipment, for scale, so my dad ended up being on the cover of *Physics Today*, as this tiny little person down in one corner. We teased Dad a lot about being a model ... a scale model.

"So now Dad's birthday is coming up, and I had this idea to make him one of those photo mugs with his *Physics Today* cover on it. I need to get a copy of that cover photo, but I can't remember which issue it was.

"Let's see what I have to work with ... I know the name of my dad's project, and I know that the journal is called *Physics Today*. That's not very much information, but I think maybe Google Scholar can help."

At this point in the story, I walk over to my podium computer and *Schoogle* (perform a Google Scholar search of) this information, which very quickly identifies the *Physics Today* issue featuring my dad's project.[23] A Web Search link takes me to the official *Physics Today* Web site, where I browse the archives of past issues and click on the cover photo, and there's my dad, in all his (scale) model glory.

While we're looking at the Google Scholar results list, I start a discussion about the differences between a Google Scholar search and a "regular Google" search. When they follow Google Scholar links, students are understandably frustrated; Google Scholar may look like a search engine, but it functions like a citation index. Because links in a Google results list lead to Web pages, students expect the links in their results list to take them directly to the full text of articles. Instead, they are taken to a citation and an offer to buy the article from British Library Direct for thirteen pounds.[24]

Full Text Library Databases

The thought of college students whipping out their credit cards to happily pay for articles, woefully ignorant of the wonders of their library's free interlibrary loan service ... it's enough to make any academic librarian apoplectic. Talk about a teachable moment; it's time for some analogical storytelling.

"Now I know that there's a link where you can buy the article online, but you do NOT have to do that! You can get a copy of this article from the library, and it won't cost you anything at all, except your time. Let me tell you how this works.

"Have you ever been flipping through the TV channels and come across a channel that's showing movie previews? And while the preview is playing, they'll flash on the screen a phone number to call, or a remote button to press to buy the movie? Now you could certainly do that. You could pay $9.99 or whatever it is and watch the movie right then, right there on your TV.

"But you know that'd be kind of silly because you could rent it for cheaper, or you could even borrow that movie from your library and watch it for *free* if you would be willing to wait a little while.

Those are your same choices when you find an article with a Google Scholar search. What you're seeing is the citation, which is like the preview for the article. You can pay for the article with your credit card if you really, really want it right away. But that's pretty silly because you can – guess what! – get it from your library, for free."

Reflection on the Instruction Session: Lessons Learned

Time is at a premium in a one-shot library instruction session. Why, then, do I choose to tell stories, which take longer to deliver than traditional lectures? Because, as any standup comedian will tell you, it's all about the delivery. For a story to succeed, the storyteller must be a strong enough performer to keep the audience actively engaged in the story. This is something to think about before you attempt storytelling in the library instruction classroom. If you're a reluctant public speaker, or if you get nervous when you teach, the added pressure to perform might make you want to stay away from storytelling. But I hope not. It's a lot of fun to tell a story, and it's a wonderful feeling to realize that all of your students are actually paying attention. They may roll their eyes, but at least that means they're listening.

Application to Other Instructional Settings

While the stories I've described here were told in a classroom setting, analogical storytelling can also be a useful strategy in one-on-one reference encounters. Drawing analogies between library resources and items within a student's known experience helps the student learn the new concepts, but it also helps to humanize the librarian-student interaction. If you're trying to teach someone how controlled vocabularies work (without, of course, using the words *controlled vocabulary*), it's much more fun to open up the local Yellow Pages and have them flip all the way from *Windshield* to *Auto-glass* than to make the poor soul try to navigate those Big Red Books of Library of Congress Subject Headings.

Notes

1. T.G. McFadden, "Understanding the Internet: Model, Metaphor, and Analogy," *Library Trends* 50 (2001): 87-109.
2. Craig Eilert Abrahamson, "Storytelling as a Pedagogical Tool in Higher Education," *Education* 118 (1998): 440-51.
3. Janice McDrury and Maxine Alterio, *Learning Through Storytelling in Higher Education: Using Reflection and Experience to Improve Learning* (Sterling, VA: Kogan Page, 2002).
4. Terrence L. Gargiulo, "Power of Stories," *Journal for Quality & Participation* 29 (2006): 4-8.

5. Abrahamson, "Storytelling as a Pedagogical Tool," 441.

6. Amy E. Spaulding, *The Wisdom of Storytelling in an Information Age: A Collection of Talks* (Lanham, MD: Scarecrow Press, 2004).

7. McDrury and Alterio, *Learning Through Storytelling.*

8. Marsha Rossiter, "Narrative and Stories in Adult Teaching and Learning." (Education Resources Information Center, 2002, ED 473147).

9. Jerome Bruner, "Life as Narrative," *Social Research* 71 (2004): 691-710.

10. Assaf Keden, "It's All in the Delivery," *Communication World* 22 (2005): 14-7.

11. Marshall Goldsmith, "Storytelling and the Art of Persuasion," *Business Week Online*, 14 August 2007, http://www.businessweek.com/careers/content/aug2007/ ca20070814_ 386968.htm.

12. Ibid.

13. Andrew Ferguson, Deborah Edler Brown, and Andrea Sachs, "A River of Chicken Soup," *Time Canada*, (8 June 1998), 25.

14. Keith J. Holyoak and Paul Thagard, "The Analogical Mind," *American Psychologist* 52 (1997): 35-44.

15. Daniel Callison, "Analogy," *School Library Media Specialist* 16 (1999): 35-8.

16. Abrahamson, "Storytelling as a Pedagogical Tool," 446.

17. Ibid., 449.

18. Mark Prensky, "Digital Natives, Digital Immigrants." Available online from http://www. marcprensky.com. [Accessed 27 August 2007].

19. McFadden, "Understanding the Internet," 89.

20. Learn more about the *Orbis Cascade Alliance* at http://www.orbiscascade.org.

21. Jane Kramer, "Taking the Veil: How France's Public Schools Became the Battleground in a Culture War," *The New Yorker* (22 November 2004): 59–71.

22. Learn more about *Google Scholar* at http://scholar.google.com/intl/en/scholar/ about. html.

23. The cover image is online at http://ptonline.aip.org/dbt/ dbt.jsp?KEY=PHTOAD& Volume=56&Issue=10. *Physics Today* 56 (Oct. 2003).

24. Libraries can configure *Google Scholar* settings to display local journal holdings, but my library has not yet implemented a link resolver. Learn more about Google's "Library Links" program at http://scholar.google.com/ intl/en/scholar/libraries.html.

CHAPTER 8

Keep Them Engaged: Cooperative Learning with the Jigsaw Method

Linda Reeves, Judy McMillan, and Renata Gibson

Authors' abstract: Northwest Vista College librarians use a modified version of the Jigsaw method, a popular cooperative learning strategy, to immediately engage students with the research strategies they need to know. Student groups explore a particular kind of information resource and then teach the rest of the class not only how to use the resource but also what kind of information it provides. The theory behind the Jigsaw and our Half-Jigsaw is that students learn better when they immediately apply what they have learned by teaching it to others.

Editors' notes: Linda's, Judy's, and Renata's goal was to present a puzzling topic in as effective a manner as possible. They used a Cognitive strategy called Jigsaw, in which, the students themselves became the presenters of the information to be covered in the session. Student groups explore pieces of a topic and put them together in a presentation—like an educational Jigsaw Puzzle. (This has nothing to do with that scary old dude Jigsaw in the Saw movies ~Ryan)

Introduction

As opposed to behaviorism with its focus on observable change, cognitive theory holds that learning involves mental changes that may not be observable. While the focus in behavioral theory is on the presentation of material by the teacher, the focus in cognitive theory is on the processing of material by the student. In lessons based on cognitive theory, students play an active role in their own learning. Cognitive theorists believe that students must interact with material and make their own connections in order to learn. Students engage novel material through discovering for themselves the information they need to acquire to solve a problem. Rather than simply having information transmitted to them by the teacher, students must engage in critical thinking about the new material.

Librarians and Learning Theories

It is important for today's instructional librarians to be knowledgeable about learning theories and various effective instructional strategies. Librarians are increasingly stepping away from the podium—or the multimedia teaching station—and trying more student-centered approaches. Karl Bridges and Leigh Estabrook, in *Expectations of Librarians in the 21st Century*, explain why librarians need to embrace active and collaborative learning:

As instruction moves ever more to the front and center of academic librarianship, librarians, too, must embrace [more collaborative models of teaching] in order to become more relevant and better classroom instructors and to be understood within our campus cultures as instructional professionals in our own right.[1]

Northwest Vista College

The authors are reference and instruction librarians at Northwest Vista College, a fast-growing community college in San Antonio, Texas, with an enrollment just over ten thousand students as of Fall 2007. Most of our students (63 percent) are older than eighteen, the traditional age for first-year college students.[2] Fifty-nine percent of our students attend college part-time, and 44 percent intend to transfer to a four-year college. The library has one teaching classroom with a multimedia station and twenty-four student computers. Our library classroom stays very busy. In September of 2006 librarians taught 104 sessions. We have worked hard to market our library instruction program and to make it valuable to students—and to the faculty who assess their research projects. The number of library instruction sessions has grown from 109 in the year 2001 to 380 in 2006. We anticipate the number for 2007 to be higher still. We have noticed an increase not only in the number of library instruction sessions but also in the number of positive comments from faculty since we began using strategies embraced by the faculty of Northwest Vista College: active and cooperative learning.

Instructional Goals

For some time we had been looking for a way to make class more interesting and engaging for the students. We had noticed that when we used lecture and demonstration to teach students about library resources, we lost our audience rather quickly. In addition, faculty members shared with us that their students did not seem to remember what they learned about library research and fell back into their old ways of relying exclusively on free Internet resources. Therefore, we knew we needed a lesson plan that would keep students interested and involved.

Tenets of cooperative learning

We decided that a cooperative learning lesson might be what we needed to keep students engaged, develop their critical thinking skills, and make their overall experience more enjoyable. In addition, many studies suggest that cooperative learning provides for greater levels of retention. Cooperative learning can be defined as "the instructional use of small groups so that students work together to maximize their own and each other's learning."[3] The terms *collaborative learning* and *cooperative learning* are sometimes used interchangeably, but many agree that *collaborative learning* is an umbrella term that encompasses the more structured approach, cooperative learning.

Instructional Strategy
Background on Jigsaw

One of the most effective cooperative learning techniques is the Jigsaw method. The Jigsaw method was pioneered by Elliot Aronson for use in elementary schools as an alternative to the traditional lecture method. At its core is the idea that students must cooperate with each other and depend on each other to learn the material. The instructor does not lecture to the students, but introduces the lesson and allows the students to learn both individually and by working together. In the traditional Jigsaw method the students are divided into teams and then further divided within the team, with each student being made responsible for a portion of the material. The goal is to have the students teach each other in these small groups. Aronson explains the Jigsaw classroom in this way:

> A Jigsaw classroom is not a loose, "anything goes" situation. It is highly structured. Interdependence is required. It is the element of "required" interdependence among students that makes this a unique learning method, and it is this interdependence that encourages students to take an active part in their learning. In becoming a teacher of sorts, each student becomes a valuable resource for the others...Within this cooperative paradigm, the teacher learns to be a facilitating resource person, and shares in the learning and teaching process with the students instead of being the sole resource. Rather than lecturing to the students, the teacher facilitates their mutual learning, in that all students are required to be active participants and to be responsible for what they learn.[4]

The Jigsaw method and other cooperative learning techniques motivate students to become involved in their own learning. Barkely, Cross, and Major maintain that the "*Jigsaw is helpful in motivating students* to accept responsibility for learning something well enough to teach it to their peers."[5] An additional explanation for the success of the Jigsaw method is that *students may learn material more thoroughly when they teach it to their fellow students.*[6]

Proponents and related literature

Eliot Aronson's book *The Jigsaw Classroom*, published in 1978, is the first mention in the literature of the ground-breaking Jigsaw method.[7] In the book, Aronson explains that he and his colleagues developed this technique as a way for recently desegregated Texas schools to allow all students to achieve their highest potential. Aronson and his colleagues contrast the Jigsaw method with the traditional competition-centered, lecture-intensive classroom and stress that learning by competing is not always the best way. Instead they propose a combination of both competitive and cooperative learning environments and proceed to show how well students responded academically and socially with the inclusion of the Jigsaw method into their weekly lessons.

In 1997, a newer version of *The Jigsaw Classroom* was published under the same title.[8] It incorporates recent research and reflection on the Jigsaw method. In addition to Aronson's books, other books on collaborative learning that we found useful are *Leading the Cooperative School* by David Johnson and Roger Johnson, *Collaborative Learning Techniques: A Handbook for College Faculty* by Elizabeth Barkley et. al, and *The Nuts and Bolts of Cooperative Learning* by David Johnson et.al.[9] Especially pertinent to library instructors is an article written by Michael Lorenzen entitled "Active Learning and Library Instruction," in which the author outlines what active learning is and how to apply active learning techniques, including Jigsaw, in the college library classroom.[10] Frances Anderson's article "The Jigsaw Approach: Students Motivating Students" summarizes Jigsaw history and focuses on how peer instruction can be a strong motivational tool that fosters healthy social interaction.[11]

Goals of the Half-Jigsaw Lesson Plan

The following lesson, which employs a modified version of the Jigsaw teaching strategy that we have dubbed the *Half-Jigsaw*, illustrates many of the components of cognitive learning theory. The major goal of the lesson is to let students discover that not all information resources are the same and that in fact resources differ in currency, audience, scope, and disciplinary focus. Other goals include students learning how to construct an appropriate search strategy and quickly evaluating search results. By the end of the lesson students should be able to select appropriate resources for different purposes, construct successful search strategies, and quickly evaluate the potential usefulness of the titles they have retrieved.

The Half-Jigsaw Strategy

Due to time constraints and other concerns, we made modifications to the original Jigsaw method, resulting in our Half-Jigsaw. Our institution does not have an ongoing information literacy course. Currently our only instructional model is a one-shot, seventy-five-minute class in the library teaching lab. We have found that doing both the Jigsaw lesson and an individual assessment does not allow time to include group processing, which is one of the components of the traditional Jigsaw but which takes additional time.

Time constraints also led us to experiment with grouping students only once instead of twice. Rather than dividing students into groups and then subdividing students again within these groups, we divide students only once. Instead of students teaching each other in small groups, student groups teach the rest of the class. By the end of the class the different pieces of information are combined together when the groups present their findings to the class, as in a jigsaw puzzle.

We found that having students teach the entire class also solved the problem of students possibly teaching each other incorrect information. In Aronson's original method, the students depend solely on each other and report only to their own small teams. In our Half-Jigsaw, each individual team reports their findings to the entire class. They are assigned a particular information resource to explore, given some basic access directions, and instructed to explore what kind of information is available on their research topic (see Sample Jigsaw Piece). Having the student teams report to the entire class allows the other students to learn about the various resources set forth in the lesson, and allows the instructor the opportunity to assess, and if needed, correct or add to what the teams are reporting.

As a way to stress that they are responsible for their own learning, students are told that they will have to complete a short exercise on the information presented by the groups. We allow students about ten minutes to use their computers to complete this final exercise. Then the librarian collects and reviews the exercises after class. Reading these exercises gives us feedback on how much students learned. We then return the exercises to the course instructor.

In Aronson's Jigsaw method the students are the sole instructors, and there is not as much control over how the students are teaching each other and what they are learning from each other. By modifying Aronson's method, we are able to allow the students to teach and learn from each other, while at the same time monitoring the accuracy of their content.

Match of Goals and Strategy

The overall goal of our Half-Jigsaw lesson is to help students become independent researchers. To this end, students need to be aware of various library resources and know how to use them to access information. Therefore, one of our goals is to allow students to discover that not all information resources are the same and that in fact resources often differ in currency, audience, scope, and disciplinary focus. In addition, we want students to learn how to construct an effective search strategy and quickly evaluate search results. By the end of the lesson, therefore, students should be able to select appropriate resources for different purposes, construct successful search strategies, and quickly evaluate the potential usefulness of the titles they have retrieved.

Because we want students to be able to do research independently, we want to get them involved in the learning activities as soon as possible and to take ownership of their learning. The Jigsaw Method is ideally suited to getting all students involved in the learning task.

Since the Jigsaw method keeps students involved, it is more engaging than traditional library instruction. And because the Jigsaw method involves teaching new material to others, it is likely to result in deeper learning and longer retention than approaches in which students remain in a passive role. Although it seems that students are more receptive to library instruction from peers than from a librarian, we underline the importance of paying attention to all presentations by announcing in advance that there will be an individual exercise at the end of the lesson. The individual assessment lets students know that they will be accountable for the materials covered in class. (See Library Research Exercise.)

Description of the Instruction Session: What Actually Happened?

We have used several different topics for the Jigsaw. The most successful has been Hurricane Katrina. Hurricane Katrina remains a relevant topic, as more information comes to light about the causes and effects both in terms of climate and society.

We typically give a very brief introduction to the library home page, pointing out links for the catalog, the databases, and the citation manager, in addition to the hours and phone numbers of the library. We call this five-minute orientation the Five-Point Tour because we draw students' attention to five different parts of the library home page. During this short orientation we often walk students through the process of signing up for a free account for NoodleTools—bibliographic management software—and the library's electronic book collection.

After this introduction, the librarian becomes a *guide on the side*, and it is up to the students to explore the resource their group has been assigned and become familiar enough with it to teach it to the rest of the class.

To begin the Jigsaw portion of the lesson, we divide the class into groups of three or four students. The number of groups depends on the number of components to the lesson, and, realistically, the size of the class. In a class of twenty-four students, for example, we typically have six groups of four students each. One group is assigned reference books, another group is given circulating books, a third group is assigned the electronic book collection, and the remaining groups are asked to examine one of the following databases: Opposing Viewpoints Resource Center, Science Resource Center, and Business Resource Center (Gale Group Databases). With smaller classes, instructors can assign fewer students to a group, and/or have fewer groups. The Half-Jigsaw lesson plan is very flexible. The instructor can decide the number of groups, the number of students in each group, and what components of the lesson will be taught by student groups.

Once assigned to their group, students are tasked first with discovering how to search their assigned resource so that they can instruct the rest of the class on how to use it. Second, they need to decide what kinds of information their resource has on the topic of Hurricane Katrina. We ask the students to find and summarize three articles or books to show the class what kinds of information their resource provides. In their presentations, students demonstrate how to use the resource, as well as address questions such as the following: What aspect of hurricanes does this resource discuss? How could this resource contribute to our understanding of Hurricane Katrina? What perspective on the hurricane does this resource offer?

Groups have about fifteen minutes to explore their resource and to prepare their presentation and to assign a speaking part to everyone in the group. Next, groups come to the teaching station and have about five minutes to teach the rest of the class about their resource and the kinds of information available from that resource. Finally, students have ten minutes to complete an individual exercise in which they must choose for themselves where to find certain kinds of information, e.g., background information about hurricanes, scientific theories about the causes of Hurricane Katrina, the connections between Hurricane Katrina and poverty, or the impact of Hurricane Katrina on U.S. businesses.

The Hurricane Katrina Half-Jigsaw lesson plan continues to be very successful as an interactive way to introduce students to the variety of resources available through their college library. It has been used with classes in English, speech, and government. Students enjoy the lesson because it involves an interesting, real-world topic, and because they are actively engaged and working together collaboratively. Students tend to pay more attention to a fellow student explaining how to use a resource than they would to a librarian. Knowing that they will have an individual exercise at the end of class also keeps students attentive. The individual assessment provides the librarian and the course instructor with feedback about students' understanding of how to select and use information resources. In our experience, the exercise reveals that by the end of the library session students are able to select and search appropriate library resources to find the information they need.

Reflection on the Instruction Session: Lessons Learned

Our first experience with the Jigsaw method was with the traditional Jigsaw model. We had learned about this approach in faculty development workshops and were interested in trying it in our library sessions. We actually only used the traditional Jigsaw method once before making our adaptations. Our weekend college professors wanted the librarians to try the traditional Jigsaw method with their weekend college class. Because there were forty-seven students enrolled in this multidisciplinary class, we arranged for two librarians to facilitate the session. The librarians gave a very short overview of the library Web site, databases, and catalog. The professors had already divided the students into ten teams and further divided students within each team and assigned each a resource to research. Because of the size of the class, two groups covered each assigned resource. The groups spent about fifteen minutes working with their assigned resource. Then, they went back to their original groups to teach the assigned resource. The problem with a large group such as this was that the librarians could not observe how and what students were teaching. Also, because of the class size, groups moved out of the library teaching lab, which has twenty-four student computers, in order to use the computers in the library. This was not an ideal arrangement; in fact, some of the students were frustrated and left the library. A short individual assessment was given at the end of the class. All of the students did well, with most of them missing only one question. The instructor said that the students were surprised that they did this well on the test because they had felt overwhelmed by the task and feared they would not retain as much as they did.

This experience encouraged us to modify the Jigsaw method. With the Half-Jigsaw, students teach their assigned resource to the class. At that point the librarian can correct any mistakes or misconceptions. The full Jigsaw may work better with a smaller group or under different circumstances.

Application to Other Instructional Settings

The Jigsaw has been used successfully in educational settings from elementary through college level and with a variety of disciplines. Michael Lorenzen mentioned the Jigsaw method as an example of a useful active learning strategy for library instructors. We discovered that, with some adaptations to accommodate the constraints of a one-shot library session, our Half-Jigsaw can be an extremely engaging and effective way to introduce students to the variety of available library resources. Another way to implement the Half-Jigsaw is to divide a topic into separate components, and assign each group one aspect of the topic, e.g. of a particular country. The Jigsaw and Half-Jigsaw can be used with any topic or discipline. It is especially useful when students must master a large body of information that would be onerous to present through lecture or individual reading. We have used the Half-Jigsaw with courses in English, history, government, sociology, speech, world civilization, Hispanic cultures, and even the Student Leadership Institute, an organization of students preparing to discuss various social problems with elected officials in Washington. Interestingly, we initially tended to reserve the Half-Jigsaw for classes in which the students had already had some experience with the Jigsaw or with library research. However, we have also used the Half-Jigsaw successfully with students in the Student Development Seminar, a course designed for first-time-in-college students. It has been our experience that after course instructors have experienced library instruction through the Half-Jigsaw method, they specifically request this method for future library sessions.

Notes

1. Karl Bridges, *Expectations of Librarians in the 21ˢᵗ Century* (Westport: Greenwood Press, 2003), 214.

2. Northwest Vista College, Institutional Research, Planning & Effectiveness, "Institutional Student Data. Fall 2006," Northwest Vista College. Available online from http://www.accd.edu/nvc/employees/lrpe/dw/nvc_studentfacts.htm. [Accessed 12 September 2007].

3. David W. Johnson, Roger T. Johnson, and Edythe J. Holubec, *The Nuts and Bolts of Cooperative Learning* (Ednia: Interaction Book Company, 1994), 1-3.

4. Elliot Aronson and Shelley Patnoe, *The Jigsaw Classroom: Building Cooperation in the Classroom* (New York: Longman, 1997), 11.

5. Elizabeth F. Barkley, *Collaborative Learning Techniques: A Handbook for College Faculty* (San Francisco, CA: Jossey-Bass, 2005), 156.

6. Barbara J. Millis and Philip G. Cottell, Jr., *Cooperative Learning for Higher Education Faculty* (Phoenix: Oryx Press, 1998), 10.

7. Elliot Aronson, Nancy Blaney, Cookie Stephan, Jev Sikes, and Matthew Snapp. *The Jigsaw Classroom.* Beverly Hills: Sage Publications, Inc., 1978.

8. Aronson and Patnoe. *The Jigsaw Classroom.*

9. David W. Johnson and Roger T. Johnson, *Leading the Cooperative School.* Edina: Interaction Book Company, 1994; Barkley, *Collaborative Learning Techniques*; Johnson, Johnson, and Holubec, *The Nuts and Bolts of Cooperative Learning.*

10. Michael Lorenzen, "Active Learning and Library Instruction." Available online from http://www.libraryinstruction.com/active.html. [Accessed on 12 December 2007

11. Frances Anderson and Jesse Palmer, "The Jigsaw Approach: Students Motivating Students". *Education* 109 (1988): 59.

Teaching Resources
Sample Jigsaw Piece

This is a sample *jigsaw piece*: A group of three or four students would receive this handout and work together to explore what kind of information this database provides on the assigned topic. The box at the bottom of the page, **Features to Explore & Teach Others About**, identifies some elements to address in their presentation to the class.

Sample Jigsaw Piece
Library Research Tool:
Online Database – Science Resource Center

Science Resource Center
+ Contains thousands of topic overviews, experiments, biographies, pictures and illustrations
+ The latest scientific developments are covered in articles from over 200 magazines and academic journals and links to quality web sites.

To Access:
o From the NVC library web page, click on Online Databases. Click on Alphabetical Listing and click on the letter S. -OR- Under Databases by Subject, click on the Sciences link.

To Search:
o Click on *Science Resource Center* to start searching the database.
o Click on one of the subjects in the list –OR-
o Do a keyword search on **Hurricane Katrina** and global warming. You might also search these topics separately.

Features to Explore & Teach Others About:
+ How do you access this database?
+ Search term used
+ Printing/e-mailing
+ Pull up and skim through 3 relevant articles on Hurricane Katrina and global warming.
+ Summarize the main topics covered in the articles.
+ What aspect of the hurricane does each article discuss?
+ What perspective on the hurricane do articles in this database offer?

Hint: For search tips, try the Help section of Science Resource Center.

Individual Assessment

This is the individual assessment that students use their computers to complete after all groups have presented their assigned resources. The individual assessment addresses the "individual responsibility" element of the Jigsaw lesson. We call the assessment an exercise.

Name: _____

Class: _____

Class Instructor: _____

Date: _____

Library Research Exercise

Find the following information:

1. A general overview and background information about hurricanes.

_____

Title   Call Number

2. A book about hurricanes or climate change.

_____

Title   Call Number

3. An article on a scientific theory about a possible cause of Hurricane Katrina

Title of Article: _____

Name of Database: _____

4. An article about the connections between Hurricane Katrina and poverty.

Title of Article: _____

Name of Database: _____

5. An article about the impact of Hurricane Katrina on U.S. businesses.

Title of Article: _____

Name of Database: _____

CHAPTER 9

True and Terrifying Stories: Using Peer-Led Discussion Groups to Evaluate Information Texts

Karla M. Schmit

Author's abstract: University students in an adolescent literacy course are given the assignment to evaluate an information book. The students use the evaluation skills that they gain in choosing an exemplary information book to be used in a final class project that asks them to create an integrated unit that pairs a fiction and nonfiction title as the seminal pieces. As an expert in information literacy, book evaluation, adolescent fiction and nonfiction literature I can provide a library instruction session in which the students learn about criteria that can be used in evaluating information books to be used with middle school students. The use of small-group interaction, cooperation, and discussion as a library instruction strategy is used to guide and help the students to understand, as well as internalize, the criteria for evaluation. Students are given the opportunity to negotiate and socially construct their understanding of the criteria for evaluating an information text.

Editors' notes: Karla takes a potentially terrifying assignment—critiquing a nonfiction adolescent book—and squeezes the screams out of it. She supports dialogue by facilitating its occurrence in small groups of peers and by the use of a powerful graphic organizer to direct the discussion.

Introduction and Instructional Goals

University students in a course on adolescent literature and literacy were given the assignment to evaluate an information book (a work of nonfiction) to be used with middle school students. The book to be evaluated was *An American Plague: The True and Terrifying Story of the Yellow Fever of* 1793 by Jim Murphy.[1] The instructional goal was to provide practice in information book evaluation and to help students prepare for an end-of-semester final project that involved creating an integrated unit for adolescents using a fiction and a nonfiction title as the core selections. The overall goal was that when the university students become classroom teachers they will know how to use evaluation criteria effectively in determining exemplary information texts to use with their future students. They will also be able to guide their future students to evaluate information texts for accuracy in text and illustrations, freedom from stereotypes, promotion of analytical thinking, logical organization, and writing style appropriate for the age the book is intended.

As a librarian knowledgeable in information literacy, book evaluation, adolescent fiction and nonfiction, I taught the students in a library instruction session about criteria that can be used to evaluate information books. There are many ways that this type of library instruction can be structured, but I have found that using small, interactive, peer-led discussion groups is one of the most effective. Through small-group discussion and hands-on work with information books, students begin to internalize the criteria for the information literacy skill of evaluating information texts and other materials.

The instructional goal of using small-group discussion and interaction is to allow all of the students to be actively involved in their own learning. Students are situated in the opportunity to experience the evaluation of an actual information book while constructing their knowledge of information books—structure, criteria for evaluation, and use in adolescent classroom settings. In this strategy, students are not relegated to the role of passive listeners and note takers of the criteria for evaluating information books. Instead, they are active participants in developing the information literacy skills of analyzing, synthesizing, and evaluating information books for adolescents, using techniques such as discussion, higher-level questioning, and close reading of the text.[2]

Instructional Strategy

In a small, peer-led group discussion, students bring together the information text, plus their own life experiences and perspectives within the context of the shared interactive event. The students' responses to the text and each other are constructed by experiences and mediated through language within a social context. The group participants guide each other towards deeper or alternative interpretations of the information text changing themselves and their view of the world in the process.[3] Johnson and Freedman[4] describe a pedagogy which brings a questioning stance to discussions and creates a space where students discuss texts, ideas, and discourses that are important to them. In this kind of environment a questioning stance is prized because it provides for students' personal voices, individual growth in the learning process and, in this case, the development of the skill of evaluating information texts for adolescents to be used within other contexts.

In a discussion group, each participant has his or her own rights and obligations for participation.[5] These rights and obligations can be realized in the turns that participants take in the discussion. Students position themselves and each other based on complex, interpersonal dynamics and by their interpretations of the purpose of the small-group activity. Students come to peer-led discussions with assumptions from previous experiences for what will happen, how and when they are to talk, as well as existing social relationships and positions.

Eeds and Petersen[6] claim that for some students a peer-led discussion group will be a new, social practice. This is particularly true in a library-instruction session. Hopefully, the use of peer-led discussion groups can keep it from being a terrifying experience. A student's own interpretation of an information text may not have been valued in previous experiences. There will be students who have experienced discussion situations in which there is one accepted interpretation of the text as mandated by the teacher. In that type of discussion, fewer student voices are heard and the teacher directs all of the action.

However, through peer-led discussion groups, students are able to voice their own understandings, persuade others, and begin to internalize concepts as defined by Vygotsky.[7] The cohesiveness of a group is often a determining factor for whether a group will be cooperative and friendly with each other during a small-group discussion.[8] Cooperation among the group members will make the goals of the group more attainable. The students in the adolescent literacy and literature course were all members of the same peer group: females in their junior year of college with approximately the same goals for becoming teachers. The information book evaluation lesson took place about mid-way through the semester and the students seemed to have developed a community of learners that were used to working together cooperatively. The students could work together towards internalizing their understandings through discussion. They were able to raise problems that they saw as important in the text while making personal connections to their own lives.[9] Through this active learning process, students were consciously engaged in dialogue and reflection.

Match of Goals and Strategy

I felt that the strategy of using small, peer-led discussion groups met the immediate instructional goal of providing the students with practice in using evaluation criteria to analyze an information text. Using this strategy creates a safe environment for the students and provides them with feedback from their peers. It isn't as scary a proposition to do an assignment like this on one's own if there has been a chance to try out the how-to of evaluation. The students are given a chance to critically think about and analyze the importance of evaluation criteria in using materials with their future students. As a librarian and an educator, I believe that the freedom to think about and construct meaning is essential for students to learn how to critically evaluate the world in which they live.

Description of the Instruction Session: What Actually Happened?

The library instruction session took place in the classroom where the students met each week for class. The session was an hour and fifteen minutes long. Because of the short amount of time for the library instruction and discussion activity it was decided that evaluation criteria developed by Donna E. Norton[10] from recommendations made by the National Science Teachers Association[11] and the American Association for the Advancement of Science as identified by Kathleen S. Johnston[12] would be used. The criteria include the following:

1. All facts should be accurate.
2. Stereotypes should be eliminated.
3. Illustrations should clarify the text.
4. Analytical thinking should be encouraged.
5. The organization should aid understanding.
6. The style should stimulate interest.

The criteria are in a condensed form that highlights the most important evaluation points and could easily be covered through group discussion in the allotted time period.

Students came to class having read the information text *An American Plague: The True and Terrifying Story of the Yellow Fever of 1793* by Jim Murphy. They had been instructed in previous sessions that information books for adolescents are nonfiction, or true books, on almost any subject. Often information books can be written in a style and format that is inviting to students in a way that textbooks can never emulate. There are a variety of types of information books; and the quality of information books can range from exemplary to extremely poor. It is important that high-quality information books be used in the school curriculum.

In the previous class, the students had read and discussed a fiction book that could be used as a companion book for the nonfiction piece that was being evaluated. The students were gaining practical and progressive classroom experience for the integrated units that they would be creating for their final class projects. They were getting firsthand experience in how to find and pair fiction and nonfiction titles to create meaningful learning experiences for their future students.

There were thirty-two students in the class and they were seated at round tables with four students at each table. I typically prefer that peer-led discussion groups consist of three or four students in each group. This seems to be a size that allows all students to get a chance to talk within the group and since the students were already in groups at tables it didn't take precious extra time to form the groups. I asked the students to clear the eight tables of everything except the information text and writing utensils.

Each student received a graphic organizer that outlined the evaluation criteria to each student. The graphic organizer was a visual reminder of what the group was looking for in the text and it could be saved as a resource guide for evaluating future information texts that they used. The organizer included questions to help the students to critically think about each of the criteria that they were evaluating in relationship to the book. I also gave each table an extra organizer to write on and complete as a group.

I briefly discussed the evaluation criteria and mentioned that there were other evaluation guides available that were more detailed. I asked the students to complete the organizer by having each group member take a turn in writing for each of the criteria. The students were asked to discuss the criteria and write on the organizer what was discovered and decided within the group regarding the quality of the book. Students were asked to cite page numbers from the text as the documentation for the conclusions that they arrived at as a group. The students were told that they had thirty minutes to discuss the information text and to complete the graphic organizer. The completed organizer was evidence of the work completed in class and class activity points were awarded for completion of the project. The introduction of the activity took about fifteen minutes.

The students took a few minutes to decide who was going to begin writing first. The students began to discuss the information book in their groups. I was in the room to offer assistance if any group needed it but I allowed the groups autonomy to get the process started without interference.

Eventually as the groups settled into the interactive activity and discussion, I moved from group to group to observe. I noticed that the students were paging through the text as they talked to find evidence for their assertions in regard to the criteria. Some of the groups engaged me in their discussion by asking specific questions about some of the criteria. I noticed in the discussions it seemed that a number of the groups brought up the fiction title that they had read and discussed the previous week and were comparing the differences in the structure of the fiction and nonfiction titles. Some of the students mentioned that they felt they should have read the titles in reverse. They felt that by reading the nonfiction title first it would have given them accurate background information and some prior knowledge for reading the historical fiction text. The students were making suggestions for the next time the course was taught.

Many of the students were from the Philadelphia area where the yellow fever of 1793 happened and found that the historical topic was highly interesting to them. A number of groups brought up the fact that the true story of the yellow fever from 1793 and the ways in which the people of the time and government officials reacted were relevant to today's concerns about catastrophic and contagious diseases that affect the world. The students were making connections to their own world through the discussions they were conducting during the interactive group evaluation of the text. They were comparing and contrasting what happened in the past with what is happening in the world now.

They were also getting a firsthand opportunity to learn about the importance of primary sources, such as illustrations, letters, newspapers and government ledgers. The students were actively searching the text and talking about the evaluation criteria as they made determinations about the information book's usefulness as a classroom tool in middle-grade education.

The small groups share their information with the larger group at the end of the work period. As the librarian, I moderated this sharing time among the groups. It is interesting to note that many more students are willing to share their ideas and thoughts in the larger group because they have had a chance to do so in a smaller group and they have built a level of trust and confidence as a result of sharing within that smaller group.

Following are several samples of documentation from the college students which illustrate the kinds of information that they were able to glean using the evaluation criteria as a group. In regard to the accuracy of the facts in the book, one group wrote, "He thoroughly documented his research and makes this clear through his arrangement of sources by topic. He has a large variety of sources. The index takes you back to pages in the text where the terms and concepts are defined and/or explained." Another group wrote, "The author discusses all sides of the racial issues. He told the story from the point of view of an outsider. It was clear that the author stuck to the facts rather than to his own opinion and he was not biased."

The evaluation criterion is also discussed as similar to criteria that may be used to evaluate a Web site or information in a newspaper or magazine. The importance of knowing how to critically evaluate information across texts and various media was considered during the discussion with the whole group.

Reflection on the Instruction Session: Lessons Learned

Based on student engagement, I felt that this library instruction session was extremely successful. The students were actively involved in the learning process and through the discussion they were able to better internalize a broad set of criteria used in evaluating information texts. The students were allowed to create meaning and understandings that were greater than the specific activity. They were able to discuss with their peers ways in which an information text can be used and were able to discover new ideas in the process.

The library session created opportunities for further, more personal, librarian assistance when the students were working on their final, integrated-unit projects. Many students commented that it was helpful to come to someone for other resources whom they knew from the previous library session. I also had a greater understanding of what kinds of materials and resources would be the most helpful to the students because of the time I had spent interacting with them in their classroom setting.

Application to Other Instructional Settings

The strategy of using small-group, peer-led discussion groups could be used in a variety of other library, information literacy, and instruction areas, such as citing sources, paraphrasing and plagiarism to name a few. Of course the amount of time available for the library instruction and the size of the class would play into decisions about using small-group discussion as a strategy. Certainly library sessions that take place over more than one class period would be optimal for incorporating small-group discussion.

Notes

1. Jim Murphy, *American Plague: The True and Terrifying Story of the Yellow Fever of 1793* (New York: Clarion, 2003).
2. Michael Lorenzen, "Active Learning and Library Instruction," *Illinois Libraries* 83 (Spring 2001): 19-24.
3. Paulo Freire and Donaldo Macedo, *Literacy: Reading the Word and the World* (Westport, CT: Bergin and Garvey, 1978).
4. Holly Johnson and Lauren Freedman, *Developing Critical Awareness at the Middle Level: Using Texts as Tools for Critique and Pleasure* (Newark, DE: International Reading Association, 2005).
5. JoBeth Allen, Karla J. Moller, and Dorsey Stroup, "Is This Some Kind of Soap Opera? A Tale of Two Readers Across Four Literature Discussion Contexts," *Reading & Writing Quarterly* 19 (2003): 225-51.
6. Maryann Eeds and Ralph Petersen, "Teacher as Curator: Learning to Talk about Literature," *The Reading Teacher* 45 (1991): 118-26.
7. Lev S. Vygotsky, *Mind in Society* (Cambridge, MA: Harvard University Press, 1978).
8. David Jaques and Gilly Salmon, *Learning in Groups: A Handbook for Face-to-Face and*

Online Environments (London: Routledge Taylor & Francis Group, 2007).

9. Alex Kozulin, Boris Gindis, Vladimir S. Ageyev, and Suzanne M. Miller, *Vygotsky's Educational Theory in Cultural Context* (Cambridge, UK: Cambridge University Press, 2003).

10. Donna E. Norton, *Through the Eyes of a Child: An Introduction to Children's Literature* (Engle Cliffs, NJ: Merrill Prentice-Hall, 2003).

11. National Science Teachers Association, "Criteria for Selection—Outstanding Science Trade Books for Children," *Science and Children* 29 (March 1992): 20-7.

12. Kathleen S. Johnston, "Choosing Books," in *Vital Connections: Children, Science, and Books*, ed. Wendy Saul and Sybille A. Jagusch (Washington, D.C.: Library of Congress, 1991): 97-103.

Teaching Resources
Graphic Organizer—Information Book Evaluation Group members:

Group Work Activity Points—10 points

Evaluation criteria are from Donna E. Norton, *Through the Eyes of a Child: An Introduction to Children's Literature*, 6th ed. (Engle Cliffs, NJ: Merrill Prentice-Hall, 2003).

Evaluation Criteria
1. All facts should be accurate.
2. Stereotypes should be eliminated.
3. Illustrations should clarify the text.
4. Analytical thinking should be encouraged.
5. The organization should aid understanding.
6. The style should stimulate interest.

Note: The factual data in information books may be made credible by citing research, quoting authorities, quoting original sources, and providing detailed descriptions of the setting, circumstances or situations. Photographs can add to a piece's authenticity.

Use the following questions to help determine the suitability of the information book that you are evaluating. Provide evidence from the text including the page numbers from the text that support your claims.

a)   Accuracy.
Does the author have the scientific qualifications or did the author document thorough research conducted on the particular subject? Are facts and theory clearly distinguished? Are significant facts omitted? Is the information as up-to-date as possible?

b)   Stereotypes.
Does the book violate basic principles against racism and sexism? Are the illustrations accurate?

c)   Analytical Thinking.
Do students have an opportunity to become involved in solving problems logically?

d)   Organization.
Is the organization logical? Does the information book have the following book parts: Table of Contents? Index? Glossary? Bibliography of Further Readings? Additional Internet Sites That Provide More Information? Other?

e)   Style.
Is the writing style lively and not too difficult for students of a certain age to understand?

CHAPTER 10

Constructing Narrative to Situate Learning in Library Instruction: Counseling an Imaginary Undergraduate

Susan M. Frey

Author's abstract: In this chapter I describe a lesson plan that I use to teach information literacy to undergraduates. I work with students to create a fictitious undergraduate student who is looking for information. The class then works together to brainstorm research strategies to help the fictitious character. I relate the successes and frustrations of my experiences teaching this lesson and I relate my classroom activity to constructivist models of experiential learning.

Editors' notes: Susan uses dialogue, in this case, with the whole class, to have students create an imaginary peer who needs to do a research project similar to their own. The research skills she eventually discusses with the students flow completely from their own experiences. Imaginary peer... kind of Donnie Darko-esque... without the giant rabbit suit...

Introduction

As I glance down at my notes to make sure I've covered all the databases I'd planned to demonstrate, I can hear a faint swooshing of notebooks being closed and book bags being stuffed and I know that the students, sensing the end of the demonstration, are preparing to bolt. I look up from my notes and ask, "So does anyone have any questions about searching the Newspaper Source database?" The students, treating my question as rhetorical, ignore me as they continue packing up. But I had planned for questions and informal discussion after my overview. This was to have been when I would dialogue with the students and really connect with them. So I repeat the question with a large, friendly smile, and move away from the display screen at the front of the classroom to walk towards them.

Now I do have their attention, but not quite the reaction I'd hoped for. My stepping down from the podium to get closer to them is, for these undergraduates, an invasion into their territory. In crossing the invisible teacher/student boundary I have just jeopardized their security and complacency. "Ya mean she really wants us to talk with her?" aptly describes their wide-eyed expressions. I continue smiling, (It's what you're supposed to do when you encounter skittish people) and say, "Okay. Well what we're all going to do for the rest of the lesson is practice some searches! Does anybody have a topic for their paper that they'd like us all to try out?"

The packing abruptly stops as they realize that the lesson hasn't ended, and that I'm not going to let them off the hook. But having spent the last twenty minutes watching me wave my arms about in maniacal enthusiasm, these students are not itching to have me call on them. Instead, they desperately employ clever ways of being invisible. One method is immobility. Another is to avoid eye contact. They have become the hunted. I walk about the classroom, looking for a cooperative face, and as I do I realize that my brilliant plan—to start my lessons with a few demonstrations followed by some hands-on practice—needs retooling. Instead of introducing these students to research methods and getting them excited about the databases, I am lulling most of them into a soft, comfy silence. I am failing to engage them.

Instructional Goals

As a reference and instruction librarian at Indiana State University (ISU), it's my job to teach information literacy to our students. ISU is categorized as a research institution by the **Carnegie Commission on Higher Education,** and offers extensive baccalaureate programs and select master and doctoral degrees. The university accepts many transfer students from two-year colleges, and a large segment of our student population is the first generation in their family to attend college. The library instruction program at ISU primarily consists of librarians teaching guest lectures at the request of the course instructors. This means that in most instances I have the opportunity to teach only one instruction session for any given class. As my scenario of the typical instruction session shows, I was having difficulty in making meaningful connections with many of these novice researchers in the limited amount of time I had with them.

The traditional demonstration/lecture format was preventing me from helping students learn that performing research is an action-oriented experience requiring independence of mind and sound critical thinking skills. I began to realize that by remaining passive while watching my demonstrations, students did not understand the process of online research because they were watching me do the research instead of doing it themselves. The more interactive, hands-on portion of my lesson wasn't as effective as I hoped for either because the students were not relating the classroom activity to their real-life experiences.

Realizing the ineffectiveness of my traditional approach of a demonstration followed by hands-on practice, I decided to design a lesson that would simulate the experience of the researcher. Knowing that people learn best by doing, my new lesson would incorporate no demonstrations or lectures. I would offer students the opportunity to experience a process of discovery, with its accompanying frustrations and triumphs, by searching the databases themselves. I would create an environment in which students could begin to own their lesson while still being a supportive and positive facilitator. It was time, I felt, to take the training wheels off of their bicycles.

Instructional Strategy

In thinking about how to address this problem, my goal was to plan a lesson that would effectively teach students the rudiments of information-needs assessment and database selection. To do this I wanted to get them thinking as professional researchers. Although research can be a collaborative process, it requires independence and tenacity. Experienced researchers know how to define their information needs and how to redefine these needs over time. They know how to consult experts and colleagues for advice. Most importantly, even if they have impatient personalities, the more successful among them understand that research requires time and hard work. In my opinion what researchers are looking for is the data that will fit their information needs. They concentrate more on their needs than on whatever information tools they are using at the moment. I believe that effective researchers are process driven, not tool driven. How then could I get my students to think as researchers do?

Many teaching practices presume that knowledge can be taught when it is taken out of the context of true experience and distilled into the classroom environment. Educational researcher and mathematician Alan Schoenfeld believes that the way schools teach math, concentrating on mathematical formulae, is divorced from the ways mathematicians operate in the real world. He asserts that mathematical education does not truly teach students to think mathematically. For Schoenfeld, concentrating only on mathematical formulae to teach mathematical thinking is simplistic and is like focusing solely on grammar to teach how to construct prose.[1] Researchers like Schoenfeld argue that knowledge is not gained by memorizing rules or protocols, but instead knowledge is the product of activities that are rooted in real-world experience. When learning is experiential, it is embedded in a culture of practice. A good example of this is the internship, in which a student learns the ropes by working alongside professionals. An internship has the potential to not only provide a student with skill sets, but also an introduction into the culture of that profession or group. When this enculturation occurs learning is situated because it is anchored in experience.

Proponents of experiential teaching methods, such as John Seely Brown and his colleagues, argue that all learning and thinking is situated in experience.[2] These authors believe that traditional classroom activity, such as lectures and teacher demonstrations, take place within the culture of schools, not the culture of practitioners in the real world. Separated from authentic cultural content, students have difficulty relating their classroom lessons to real-world situations. Thus my students, who passively watched me construct online searches projected on a screen in a dimly lit classroom, were having difficulty relating my database demonstrations to what they had to do in the library on a Saturday afternoon. The culture that I was failing to immerse them in is that of the researcher.

If learning is to be situated, it must be embedded in an authentic activity. Unfortunately, unless the teacher has the power to take students out into the field, the authenticity of the activity must be simulated in the classroom. This appears to be oxymoronic. How can one simulate authenticity? One method is to construct a thinking exercise that will help students conceptualize a real-world environment. So instead of an actual internship or apprenticeship, a teacher can help to create a *cognitive apprenticeship*.[3] My approach to creating a cognitive apprenticeship to situate learning is based on Lampert's practice of teaching multiplication through collaborative storytelling in the classroom.[4] Whereas Lampert does this by asking students to use everyday objects, like coinage, to perform calculations, my method is to have the class create a fictitious student in need of research assistance.

Description of the Instruction Session: What Actually Happened?

I begin the lesson by telling students that I would like to do more than just a demonstration of the university's online resources, and I ask them if they would agree to work with me to do something different. I propose the creation of a fictitious undergraduate that we can counsel. I say, "Let's create an imaginary student and pretend to help this person out with his research. That way, we can focus more on research and forget about ourselves."

I realize that asking for consent is a gamble since students can decline to engage in this lesson. But because my aim is to help empower these students from the get-go, I feel that this strategy sends a powerful message. I want the students to see me more as a facilitator than an instructor; and I want them to feel that they have the power to co-create the lesson with me. To my relief, all classes to which I have offered this lesson have accepted. Perhaps this is because they see me as an authority figure that should not be contradicted? Maybe my offer has the faint promise of novelty? For whatever reason, initial student response to my offer is consent mixed with patches of curiosity and slight suspicion.

Once the students accept my offer, I move from the podium at the front of class and sit down in the student seats with them. I do this deliberately to show them that we are going to be working together as a team. By posing questions and soliciting responses I begin by helping the students give the fictitious character a gender, name, age, and major. We briefly describe the character's taste in clothes and music, and elements of the character's personality, circumstances, and lifestyle (i.e., impatient, confident, passive, has kids, has two jobs, witty, just broke a leg, etc.). Most of my questions are specific. "Let's make this person real", I suggest, "Do you guys want her to drive a crappy car?" One question that usually enlivens the group is, "So is this the kinda person you wanna strangle, or are they okay to be with?" I commit the description to memory, but in some instances students have volunteered to take notes on who we decide the character shall be.

After we've spent about five minutes fleshing out the character, I ask the class to come up with at least two research problems the character has to deal with for the current semester. The research topic can come from any class the character is taking. If the students are at a loss for research ideas, I suggest we use their own research projects. Some of the best ideas have come from the most unexpected sources. A particularly interesting paper topic on the influence of baseball on American culture was offered by a doleful student who quietly said, "I've got this really dumb thing for English I've gotta write." This comment sent the class into bubbles of laughter. "Great!" I said, "Dumb thing for English? Excellent! Since Bob [that class's character] is impatient and overworked, let's give him a dumb assignment! What is it?"

Once the two research topics are identified I suggest the topic that has the most research potential and invite the students to come up with research strategies. I act as a facilitator, using discursive techniques to help the class stay on-task, such as playing devil's advocate, restating students' comments to encourage further examination, and modeling self-reflection and collegial debate. "Okay," I say, "Now Bob has gotta write this paper on baseball and he's come to us for help. What do we tell him?" If the class response is, "I don't know" then I say, "Okay but let's pretend that we've *got to* help him, even though we don't know how. Where can we start?"

With the baseball assignment, the first suggestion was to use the Google search engine. This is not the resource I would have suggested as the first choice. But I did not discourage the class from following this route. "Okay, let's use Google. Someone needs to go to Google and give it a try." Unbeknown to the students, I become queasy the first time I make this suggestion in the lesson because I do not intend to touch any of the classroom computers and I secretly worry that no one else will. But if I were to sit down behind a monitor I fear the lesson would degrade into a demonstration. I do not care if they use the student computers or the instructor computer connected to the projector at the front of the room. For me, the important issue is that I am not searching the databases for them. Fortunately someone always offers to work on the computer, and the class investigating baseball Web sites was no exception.

The class did find some useful baseball sites and I gently steered them towards Web site evaluation by asking them about the authority of the sites, and how the information could be used in a paper. Google is often the first resource students think of and since I, a professional researcher, use Google I cannot in good conscience forbid them this resource. But at this point in the lesson students may be in danger of getting lost in endless pecking down blind alleys. Although I wish for this lesson to be a process of discovery, in practical terms I have from sixty to ninety minutes with them. So if a student doesn't suggest a library resource I might say, "Listen guys, this library spends beaucoup bucks on some really great databases. Many of them are full-text, so you can get the journal articles right off the computer. What do you think about that?" Most students are perceptive enough to understand that I see that the class is losing momentum and I'm throwing them a line.

When I refer to specific resources, I try to frame my suggestion in the context of real-world experience. "Look", I say, "If Bob had come to me at the reference desk with this paper topic I would suggest one of the ProQuest databases because they are multidisciplinary. Why don't one of you give it a try?" Once in a library database, the class can go in one of several directions. If there are students who are familiar with online searching they will usually take the lead in coming up with search strategies that we can test out together. If the class is particularly inexperienced then we talk it out as one brave soul staffs the keyboard and types in what we devise. During the process I question them. "Wow, two thousand articles!" I say, "That's an awful lot. How can we help Bob limit his results?" I try to make the fictitious character real, so that they focus more on what the character's needs are than on the library resources. The effects of this strategy are often gratifying, as in the case of one student who remarked that our character would be too impatient to construct the search we were developing; and her comment led to a brief class discussion on the actual versus the imagined time burden of online searching.

I judge the lesson to be the most successful when students begin teaching each other. In one class a young woman taught everyone how to nest search terms in parentheses. Impressed by her knowledge and by the quality of the results she produced, a classmate asked her, "How did you know that?" She responded that a librarian had taught her how to do it at the reference desk. When the second student looked over to me and asked, "Do you know how to do that?" I responded that I did. "Oh then can I come and ask you this stuff downstairs [at the reference desk]?" Of course I encouraged her to do so! Although moments like this are rare, they are intensely rewarding. It's my belief that a fellow student promoting the reference desk carries great weight, because peer assessment and advice can mean a lot to these students as they often ask each other for advice on how to complete their assignments. What better way for the reference desk to be promoted than by another student who is demonstrating the efficacy of well constructed search technique!

In this lesson I also look for opportunities to help the students learn of the potential tedium and frustrations of research. When students vent that the process is going too slowly I tell them that it can go slowly for me, for their professors, and for other students, but I make sure to not be sarcastic or preachy about it. Many students have told me that this one observation has helped them feel more secure about database searching. They had made the false assumption that they were doing something wrong if they could not find their answers in a few minutes. As experienced researchers know, research takes time.

The casual camaraderie that I encourage in class can swiftly deteriorate into non-productive socializing. So I do sometimes have to steer the class back on-task by making comments like, "Yeah, this is why I spent two hours searching last night when I could have finished my research in twenty minutes. I was gabbing with other people! Let's get back to Bob and why he's so pissed at not finding the articles he needs. Why isn't this database working for him? Is it because he's so impatient? Is this the right database for the topic?"

About five minutes before the end of class I do ask the students if they have any observations, and I encourage them to seek me out for help in future. As would be expected, some students are more engaged in the process than others, but all students have told me that they enjoy the class. One student told me that she felt freer in class to bring up her research needs and concerns because she ascribed them to the fictitious character and made him the dummy. Another student said that it was fun to talk it out in class because he usually falls asleep during demonstrations. Yet another told me that he was happy to see the class hit a few brick walls in the research process, because this helped him to realize that one doesn't always find answers within the first few attempts at searching.

Reflection on the Instruction session: Lessons Learned

It's my belief that for many of these students learning became situated. As they progressed in this lesson, they behaved less like students and more like consultants who were responsible for helping the fictitious character. Like researchers, they defined information needs, discussed strategy with their peers, assertively looked for resources, and readjusted strategy. Once having collaborated with me to construct searches for the fictitious character, some of them view research as a dynamic process that involves inquiry and investigation. By the manner in which they consult me for advice after class, I believe that they see me more as someone who can help them think through their own research agendas, rather than a person who will hand them the answers.

Since my time with these students is confined to a one-shot guest lecture, I do worry that I am depriving them of important information. I find this lesson fun to teach because students are engaged in the research process. I also feel a greater connection with them because we are co-creating the lesson together. But I am sometimes disconcerted when they leave the classroom and I realize that I have not used precious class time to go over my laundry list of important library databases. I am also frustrated by time constraints. Doing anything by consensus takes time and I realize that this lesson would work better if it could be expanded to at least two hours (with a short break at the mid-point) so that the students and I could really dig into the databases and discuss the complexities of research strategy.

I find that this lesson works best with juniors, seniors, and graduate students because they have had time to acclimate themselves to college life. When I have used this lesson with incoming freshman, I find that the process is too drastic a change from their prior classroom experience. Course instructors usually ask me to teach early in the semester. But this is the time when freshman are still trying to negotiate the physical, educational, and social terrain of their new world. So I believe that with freshman, it will be better for me to use this lesson later on in the semester when they are more secure about their environment.

One stumbling block I have encountered is class size. For this lesson to work effectively, a small group of six to nine students is advisable. When I tried to run the lesson with a class of twenty-five students, many of them broke off into sub-groups and began to socialize. Because of this it was more difficult to keep the class on-task. A good way around this problem would be to have a large class break up into smaller groups, each with its own facilitator. As yet, I have not tried this but I see potential in asking the course instructors to work with me as co-facilitators in this respect.

Because this lesson requires the librarian to cede so much control of lesson content to students, this is not the lesson to use when instructional goals include exposure to specific resources. Since I cannot promise a course instructor what information resources will be covered in this lesson, I use the traditional demonstration/lecture format when the instructor asks me to include specific information tools in my presentation. However, for course instructors who are more interested in a general introduction to basic research processes, this lesson plan works well because it focuses more on the research process than on the research tools. For course instructors who have observed this lesson, some see promise in my methods. Others are concerned that I miss the opportunity to teach the mechanics of searching specific databases.

Although student response to this teaching technique has been positive, it is anecdotal. As yet, I have not used any assessment instrument to prove that students are learning more about research strategy. Currently we are not using any pre- or post-testing in our library instruction at ISU, however, because students are obviously engaged in the process I plan to continue using the lesson.

Application to Other Instructional Settings

Currently the ISU library does not offer a course of study in information literacy. But we are working towards the possibility of offering a one- or two-credit course in the subject. Ideally, I believe this lesson would work best by being incorporated into a student workshop or credit course on information literacy. In this way the lesson could be blended with other class activities and formats. Alternately, this lesson could be embedded in any college course, such as an English or history course that requires a research paper. Regardless of its application, creating imaginary students who need research help is a powerful teaching tool which situates learning in a real-world context.

Notes

1. Alan H. Schoenfeld, "Learning to Think Mathematically: Problem Solving, Metacognition, and Sense-Making in Mathematics," in *Handbook of Research on Mathematics Teaching and Learning*, ed. Douglas Grouws (New York: MacMillan, 1992), 334-70.
2. John Seely Brown, Allan Collins, and Paul Duguild, "Situated Cognition and the Culture of Learning," *Educational Researcher* 18 (1989): 32-42.
3. Ibid.
4. Magdalene Lampert, "Knowing, Doing, and Teaching Multiplication," *Cognition and Instruction* 3 (1986): 305-42.

CHAPTER 11

Using a Personality Test to Teach Boolean Logic

Kathleen Lowe

Author's abstract: Using Boolean logic to construct a search strategy is widely held to be a legitimate performance indicator of an information literate undergraduate. In this chapter I describe how to use an online Personality Test to teach the concepts of Boolean logic. An added benefit is that by making the instruction personal, engaging, and inclusive freshman students hopefully make the connection that the librarian is approachable and accessible both in and out of the classroom.

Editors' notes: Kathleen uses dialogue to discuss Boolean logic after the students have participated in a common experience – taking a Personality Test. This lively encounter provides a mutual basis for students to discuss an apparently unrelated library topic. We bet the ENFPs have a great time with this activity.

Introduction

Learning to teach is an evolutionary process. I look back at my first years of teaching and think, "What an amoeba! What was I thinking?" At the start of my career I would stand in front of the bright–eyed and bushy-tailed class confidently demonstrating database searches making certain to point out quirky characteristics of individual databases (that pesky ProQuest, that obtuse ABC-CLIO interface). I basically checked off a list of tips and hints for efficient catalog and databases searching.

Instructional Goals

Now, when preparing for a class I ask myself the questions set out in the introduction to this book. What do I want my students to learn? How can I structure my teaching toward those goals? How do I construct an environment in which students can learn?

I generally look for ways to:
- Engage students through different teaching methods
- Incorporate the assignment into the library class presentation when possible
- Engineer group work and problems that foster critical thinking.

I finally learned to stop talking all the time. Now my instructional goal is to engage students in discussion about themselves, about the assignment, and to encourage them to think about the big issues. What made me change? The students really did not respond as well to my lecturing them as you would expect a bright-eyed and bushy-tailed group of students to respond. Instead of eagerly nibbling nuggets of my knowledge, the class looked tired and bored out of their noggins.

Another epiphany occurred while I was sans professor with a freshman English class. Yes, early on in my career I naively said I would work with the class while the professor was out to a conference. This was his first year teaching; this was my first year teaching: and we had a failure to communicate. He thought I would have something prepared for the class and I thought he would have something prepared for the class. I naively asked the class what the assignment was for them to do in the Library. The students were savvy to this; of course they had no idea what they were supposed to do in the Library. Instead of just letting them get up and go as they urged me to do, I whipped them into groups, gave them assignments and the rest is history.

Years older and much the wiser, I now structure instruction in very different ways. Structuring group work around the assignment is my favorite plan of action. For the particular strategy I am sharing with you, my overall goal is to engage students in a conversation so that together we can use information about them to come to an understanding about how to best formulate a database search. Interesting information the students discover about their personality types become the basis for this conversation on Boolean logic.

Instructional Strategy

My overall instructional strategy for freshman English composition classes incorporates active learning techniques, collaborative learning, and constructivist methods that design opportunities for engaging students. Depending upon the assignment, I like to promote critical thinking skills by introducing sources that present opposing viewpoints. Ken Bain's *What the Best College Teachers Do*[1] poses some questions I find helpful to ask myself when preparing for a particular class.

1.   What information will my students need to understand in order to answer the important questions of the course and challenge their assumptions?

2.   How will students best obtain that information?

3.   What big questions will my presentation and assistance help students answer? How will I encourage students' interest in these questions?

4.   How will I create a neutral critical learning environment in which I embed the skills and information I wish to teach and challenge students to rethink their assumptions and examine their mental models of reality?

5.   How will I create a safe environment in which students can try, fail, receive feedback, and try again?

More specifically, for freshmen just learning to search a database, my instructional strategy combines cognitive and social learning theories. I use examples that build on a student's personal store of knowledge. Placing students in small groups as much as possible supports social constructivism. I refrain from lecturing too long. I see myself as a guide, someone who can point out the constellations; it's up to the students to connect the resources and see the big picture. I provide the topic and some sources; the students do the research. Group members are free to form opinions and discuss their results based on the evidence I give them and what they discover in print material, database searches, and Google searches if applicable. I look for a topic that bumps students into the big questions in life. Bain explains that the very best teachers "search for ways to build these conflicts into the class."[2] Preparing for a class includes mapping out my sources of information so that the topic includes resources that propose several ways of approaching the issue or historical problem. Learning is a conversation.

Description of the Instruction Session: What Actually Happened?

The purpose of this section is to provide the nuts and bolts of an active learning strategy I've successfully used in an instructional setting. All freshmen at our university are required to take a two course sequence English 101 and English 102. English 101 students generally have one fifty-minute introduction to the library facilities and services. Building on the introduction to the Library and to databases in English 101, English 102 classes often schedule two or more class periods in the library. The English 102 students are assigned a paper requiring scholarly analysis and sources appropriate for undergraduate research.

A typical introductory English 101 session touches on Boolean logic. Using Boolean logic to construct a search strategy in library databases is widely held to be a legitimate performance indicator of an information literate undergraduate. How to teach Boolean logic successfully and why it's applicable to an undergraduate more familiar with Googling is another thing.

A successful lesson plan requires careful preparation, often hours of groundwork and constant revision to ensure learning occurs. The lesson plan must build on a foundation established by previously learned capabilities. I would agree with Gagne that "instructing means arranging the conditions of learning that are external to the learner. These conditions need to be constructed in a stage-by-stage fashion; taking due account at each state of the just previously acquired capabilities of the learners, the requirements for retention of these capacities, and the specific stimulus situation needed for the next stage of learning."[3]

The steps in the English 101 Boolean logic lesson plan are constructed to take students stage-by-stage from what they know best themselves to something they are unfamiliar with—using Boolean logic to search a library database. The library objectives of English 101 are simple—get to know the library as a place and introduce the librarian as a teacher and resource.

I begin by asking students to take an online personal inventory quiz. Students have a keen interest in finding out who they are and what career may best suit them. Most of us have taken some kind of personal inventory test, many of which are far from reliable. For example, *Cosmopolitan* magazine offers tests that promise to reveal how hot a lover you are on a scale from one to ten; such tests are designed around what they predict test-takers want to hear. *Cosmo* offers all varieties of this kind of test, engineered to ensure women rate as sex goddesses—even librarians who prefer the company of other librarians who like to go to conferences and collect oodles of bookmarks and free tote bags.

Monster.com offers a large online library of quizzes: the Resume Readiness Quiz, the Interview Image Quiz, or the Office Romance Quiz. I have students take

the Discover Your Perfect Career Quiz.[4] Discover Your Perfect Career is a four question test designed to identify your basic personality preference types. The questions
are all about you. Essentially it's a very short test based on the Myers-Briggs Type
Indicator (MBTI). I tell students up front that the test does not provide definitive
or fixed results, so they should not take it too seriously. But I add that their answers
should reflect the way they really are—not as they wish they could be or what their
boyfriend, girlfriend, or parent wishes they were.

Students will need five to ten minutes to complete the test. When time is up I
ask the class to look up from their computers. I begin a conversation with the class
to draw their thoughts about their results. What happens is a fundamental shift in
who controls the flow of information. The students are now telling me who they
are, what they want to be, was the test accurate, and did the test really discover the
perfect career for them. The lines of communication are open and flowing fast. This
is a hallmark of constructivist learning: learning is enhanced by social interaction.

It is essential to the process of active learning that group interaction occurs. A
conversation begins; the class and I are energized, engaged and ready to connect with
one another. I believe this is the best exercise to initiate the conversation; welcome
to this class and tell me a little about whom you are and your future.

The test reveals two things. First, it reveals one instrument's assessment of your
personality characteristics. For example, I am an ESFJ: Extrovert, Sensor, Feeler,
Judger. Second, based on your result, the Discover Your Type software links your
four personality traits to careers that best suit someone of your type. For example,
an ESFJ is best suited to be a real estate agent, a personal fitness trainer or a massage
therapist. I always get laughs when I mention how much I hate people's *toes* and
would therefore never be a massage therapist. At every opportunity, I am asking
students to share their results and reactions. It can get a little noisy.

Throughout the sharing of types and careers I quip and ask quick questions
about what would happen for example if you worked at Google and your team
was composed of all feelers? Is there a psychology major in here? If you are the
corporate psychologist, why is it important to have a diversity of personality types
on a team? Again, what happens if you get a whole group of feelers? How do you
think decisions would be made? How do you think a group of feelers would handle
conflict? There is no right or wrong answer, only a chance for any student to chime
in. I avoid absolutes and accept all answers and often will simply echo the students'
comments.

The Boolean logic lesson comes in once they have settled down a bit. I've asked
them to jot down their four types. Using a document projector I will display on the
screen a sheet of paper with the following statement:

Extrovert AND Feeler
Extrovert OR Feeler

I then ask by a show of hands how many people are both an Extrovert *and* a
Feeler. Perhaps four out of twenty-five will raise their hands. I then ask by a show

of hands how many are an Extrovert *or* a Feeler. Now about ten out of twenty-five will raise their hands. I ask the class if this is what they would have predicted: that *and* reduces a set of results and *or* increases your results. Most are not aware of how Boolean logic works. The show of hands and projection of the results bear out the nature of Boolean logic: seeing is believing. I reinforce this part of the lesson with additional sets designed to give students at least one chance to raise their hands and participate. I write beside or under each combination the total number of hands raised for the *and* question and the *or* question. For example:

Extrovert AND Feeler   4

Extrovert OR Feeler   10

Next piece of paper on the document projector

Introvert AND Judger   3

Introvert OR Judger   9

Next piece of paper…

How many people are just like me?

Extrovert AND Sensor AND Feeler AND Judger 1

How many share at least one of those types?

Extrovert OR Sensor OR Feeler OR Judger   16

You can see what happens right away. Light bulbs go off. Students begin to catch on to the concept of *and* and *or*. It's possible to lecture all day about Boolean logic (and I have) and construct great examples in databases to illustrate Boolean logic (and I have) but I believe in the power of *showing*, versus merely *telling*. By raising their hands and curiously looking around to see who is an Introvert or Extrovert, etc. and drawing the class's attention to writing down the results I get the light bulb and the *Aha* moments precious to every teacher's heart.

The next stage is to apply a little Boolean logic in a library database. I typically use Academic Search Premier in the advanced search mode to demonstrate. At our library we chose to default to the advanced search. Again, the students each have a computer and I ask that they follow along with me. I use predetermined examples adapted to current topics of interest to undergraduates. Some examples I've used include:

Facebook AND College students   **Facebook OR College students**

Binge Drinking AND College students   **Binge Drinking OR College students**

Dating violence AND College students   **Dating Violence OR College students**

At this point most students can follow the logic:

1. Put one concept into each search box.

2. Determine your results based on your choice of Boolean logic.

The final stage is to construct connections between Google and Library databases. Most undergraduates have used Google; however, few students are aware of the relationship between Google and Boolean logic. Associating a library database's use of Boolean logic with Google's similar searching mechanisms can work to our profession's advantage. Librarians must learn to sequence their teaching; in Bain's words, they must ask, "How can I provide a sequence of experiences that will encourage students to refine their reasoning abilities?"[5]

The sequence of personality test results connected to Boolean logic connected to library databases connected to Google is based on another hallmark of constructivist learning: students construct knowledge based on existing structures they understand. Ken Bain puts it this way when he describes what the best college teachers do: "Students must use their existing mental models to interpret what they encounter, they [best teachers] think about what they do as stimulating construction, not transmitting knowledge."[6]

You can find several ways to demonstrate Google's connection with Boolean logic. Google has an Advanced Search Help screen I've used to demonstrate how Google uses Boolean logic. The Google Basic Search Help tips clearly indicate Google defaults to *and* to refine a search. Students are often amazed to know they have cracked one of the reasons why Google seems to be *intelligent*.

Reflection on the Instruction Session: Lessons Learned

Without a doubt the group exercises and conversational learning are fun, lively and thought provoking for students, professors and me. This type of learning engages students in the process. The drawback is that it takes time to do it all. Finding connections between what students already know and the discussion topic is a challenge; I'm constantly scanning for new ideas. I've been told that I make it seem easy but the truth is that I carefully choreograph and orchestrate the process.

The missteps are few but once in a while I get a student who dominates a group. I've used body language and visual cues to draw out other members of the group. I've only encountered one time when it was destructive to the process. The professor was well aware of the problem and we worked together to see that the other group members were not bullied or harassed for their opinions.

Application to Other Instructional Settings

Actively connecting students to a new topic can be used in any learning situation where conversational learning is important. In other classes, rather than using a group exercise like the Personality Test to start the conversation, I have used rhetorical questions which grab student's interest in a similar fashion. For example in an English 102 class, researching topics related to the criminal justice system, I begin by asking if all people in jail are criminals? I follow that conversation by asking if Martin Luther King is a criminal? This question enacts the knowledge that they already possess about Dr. King's tremendously positive reputation as a leader during the twentieth century. We use that information to discuss problems inherent in the criminal justice system—which leads us to potential research topics. Teaching conversationally is hard work, but I find that it is ultimately rewarding.

Notes

1. Ken Bain, *What the Best College Teachers Do* (Cambridge, MA: Harvard University Press, 2004), 51-60.
2. Ibid, 54.
3. Robert M. Gagne, *The Conditions of Learning* (New York: Holt, Rinehart and Winston, 1970), 28.
4. Paul D. Tieger and Barbara Barron-Tieger, "Discover Your Perfect Career Quiz." Available online from http://resources.monster.com/tools/quizzes/perfectcareer/. [Accessed 3 January 2008).
5. Bain, *What the Best College Teachers Do*, 51.
6. Ibid, 27.

CHAPTER 12

Plagiarism Instruction Online: Beyond the Citation

Lyda Ellis

Author's abstract: In this chapter I discuss a plagiarism instruction program that is part of a one-credit online research course offered at the University of Northern Colorado. The plagiarism program requires that students conduct peer interviews to learn about the plagiarism habits of their fellow undergraduates. Students participate in hands-on activities addressing the issues of cyber-plagiarism and paraphrasing. Through continuous open dialogue students gain a more complete understanding of the complexities and implications of plagiarism.

Editors' notes: Lyda uses dialogue, in an online class, to help students understand plagiarism. First she has her students interview a peer regarding his or her habits of plagiarism. Then, an open, online discussion follows which helps students, as a group, to come to some conclusions about cutting-and-pasting. She says that she makes "it very clear that what is said in discussion stays in discussion—it's sort of like Vegas!" Hmm... We wonder what the odds for success are for trying that with our students? (I'm giving 2:1 ~Ryan.)

Introduction

The first step to avoiding plagiarism is having an open discussion about the issue. Many college educators assume that college students are aware of what plagiarism entails and how to avoid it once they arrive on campus. Many students, therefore, hear their professors say "Don't plagiarize," but are rarely given a review about how to avoid plagiarism. This chapter describes four sessions of a one-credit, online, research course offered at the University of Northern Colorado titled Introduction to Undergraduate Research (LIB 150).

Instructional Goals

The first goal of the plagiarism instruction program described here is to allow my undergraduate students to openly discuss plagiarism. I want my students to discuss all aspects of plagiarism freely without fear of retribution from a professor. Once my students are comfortable discussing the issue and they understand different aspects—such as cyber-plagiarism[1]—the goals become more specific.

The second goal of the program is to assist students in understanding the power of search engines such as Google. The desire to copy/paste text into one's own paper is strong, especially if a student procrastinates on an assignment. Understanding the ease with which teachers can catch cyber-plagiarism is necessary, especially at the college level when students often feel strapped for time along with a pressure to earn high grades.

The third goal is to ensure that students understand how to properly paraphrase. Paraphrasing is a skill that students struggle with continuously. Learning to create a citation properly is the easy part—what and when to cite is the difficult part. My goal is for each student to leave class with the skills to properly paraphrase scholarly articles and to recognize proper paraphrasing in the work of others.

Instructional Strategy

My plagiarism instruction program has four parts so there is more than one strategy involved. The main strategy is open dialogue. There must be an open discussion about plagiarism among the students. To facilitate discussion I assign a peer interview where the students interview two of their peers outside of the class about their plagiarism habits. The students bring the results of their interviews to a larger class discussion and the students talk with each other about the issues that came up during the interviews.

The other strategy used in this program is hands-on learning. The program is part of a larger research course where hands-on learning is essential. The plagiarism program consists of assignments that require the students to seek out cyber-plagiarism, practice paraphrasing, and evaluate a paper from an Internet paper mill site. These hands-on activities follow the initial discussion of plagiarism and then each piece of the program is followed by more group discussion that further helps the students grasp the concepts of plagiarism. Essentially there is an open dialogue among the students throughout the entire twelve-week research course.

In 2002 Brandt asked "Can it be possible that students today don't really understand what plagiarism is?"[2] Well, it is not only possible, it is the reality. Many of our undergraduates do not understand plagiarism. An open dialogue about the issue and hands-on activities to teach the skills of avoiding plagiarism, such as proper paraphrasing, are essential for students' understanding of the concept.

In 1988 Kroll stated that "What is conspicuously missing in most discussions…is any consideration of how students conceptualize the issue of plagiarism."[3] The peer interview addresses this issue by giving the students a chance to figure out how they understand plagiarism. This gives the instructor insight about what the students lack in their comprehension of plagiarism and at what level instruction is needed.

In 2006 Jackson presented results of her research about online plagiarism instruction. According to Jackson, the results of her study "make it clear that students need more instruction and practice with proper paraphrasing."[4] Undergraduates have trouble synthesizing an original passage and writing it in their own words.[5] The paraphrasing unit of this plagiarism instruction program gives students an understanding of how to paraphrase properly and then requires the students to apply what they know to technical articles in their field of study.

During the summer of 2007, I conducted a brief online survey of academic librarians about plagiarism instruction offered at their libraries.[6] Based on the responses, 84 percent of the participants' libraries offer plagiarism instruction to undergraduates. Among the participants, 54 percent offer plagiarism instruction in both a typical fifty-minute library session and through online tutorials. The survey shows that 63 percent said that their libraries also include instruction in proper paraphrasing to their undergraduates. I am often asked if I feel it is a librarian's place to teach students how to avoid plagiarism, so I asked the same question in the survey; 69 percent of participants answered "Yes". I agree wholeheartedly with one respondent's statement that "If we're supposed to help them understand information retrieval in a comprehensive way, then using info legally & responsibly is part of that." Similarly, one respondent said that "It is part of teaching students to become information literate."

When using the strategy of open dialogue, especially when you are dealing with plagiarism, the number one rule is trust. Students must trust that you will not penalize them for their answers or comments in the plagiarism discussion. The students are asked to talk about personal plagiarism and they will not answer honestly if they think you will penalize them or if they feel you will look down on them because they have plagiarized in the past. I make it very clear that what is said in discussion stays in discussion—it's sort of like Vegas! Another important rule is that there should be very little teacher involvement in the discussions. I don't get too involved in the class discussions except to ask for clarification or to build on a student's comment. As an observer you will learn a lot about your students' plagiarism habits and beliefs; the students learn a lot about different perceptions of plagiarism through the discussion, which is the goal.

Match of Goals and Strategy

The main goal is to have undergraduates openly discussing plagiarism. The use of a peer interview is perfect because the students are taking this discussion out of the classroom and into the dorm room. Not only is there a plagiarism discussion in class, but for a brief time on campus there could be fifty or more students discussing the issue. This allows students to become comfortable talking about plagiarism and begin understanding everything that is involved in attempting to avoid it.

Because I am teaching students a skill, hands-on learning is crucial. Identifying cyber-plagiarism by using a search engine to find plagiarized text is the best way I know to show students how easy it is to find. I can show students example after example of improper paraphrasing, but until they sit down and attempt to paraphrase a section of text they will have no idea what they are doing. Hands-on learning is the key.

Description of the Instruction Session: What Actually Happened?

Before I delve into what happened, let me give you some background about the plagiarism instruction program. In the LIB 150 class students are taught how to use library resources, how to evaluate sources, how to use bibliographic software, how to compile an annotated bibliography, and how to cite sources based on the Modern Language Association (MLA) Style. The four-part plagiarism program offers in-depth discussion and practice on how to avoid plagiarism. In Part I, Peers &

Plagiarism, students interview two of their peers about their plagiarism habits—past and present. This portion of the program begins an open dialogue about plagiarism, not between student and professor but among students on campus. The result is a very honest discussion since a professor is not directly involved.

Part II, Plagiarism & Google, takes the students to Google and addresses the issue of cyber-plagiarism that is so rampant on college campuses. In preparation for Part II, I collected a series of paragraphs from freely available online sources to create a document for the students to work with. Students search on Google for specific paragraphs using their own keywords as well as full sentences. Because the sentences were chosen from Internet sources, students learn how easily cyber-plagiarism can be detected.

Part III, Proper Paraphrasing, is a hands-on activity designed to get students involved in understanding and practicing proper paraphrasing. This is done in multiple steps. Students read about proper paraphrasing and do some exercises on their own. Next they work in groups to properly paraphrase a passage from a technical journal in their field of study. They edit this passage on the course wiki so they can easily collaborate. This gets students into a new environment and working together to solve the problem. Students are also using the research skills learned in LIB 150 to prepare the paraphrased section.

In Part IV, Evaluation, students evaluate a paper that I purchased from an online paper mill. This is a good lesson in not relying on paper mills, but it is also a culmination of the entire research course. The purchased paper is evaluated for good use of sources, solid research, proper citation, and proper paraphrasing.

As soon as Peers & Plagiarism begins there is an open, ongoing discussion of plagiarism through an online discussion forum. All answers to the interviews are discussed, opening up numerous avenues to pursue in discussing plagiarism. Each semester is different. Students come from different backgrounds; some know a little and some know a lot. Peers & Plagiarism lets the instructor know how much each student brings to the table and assignments can be adjusted accordingly. Debate about the power of Google and about proper paraphrasing are also part of the ongoing discussion.

So, what happened? I implemented the program in two online sections of LIB 150; first during the fall 2006 semester and again in the spring 2007 semester. In the fall of 2006 parts I-III were implemented. I was a little nervous when I first assigned Peers & Plagiarism. I was afraid the students might hate interviewing people and I was also afraid that they would just make up the answers. What I found was that the students really liked the interview portion and came to the discussion with honest answers. Many of the peers interviewed had plagiarized papers and other assignments in high school but, according to my students, they were not going to do that in college because there is more at stake. When responses began to pour into the online discussion forum, one student commented that "It's interesting the number of people who in our interviews said they didn't plagiarize. I wonder how many of them truly understand the extent of plagiarism!"[7] And this is the ultimate question: who truly understands the extent of plagiarism?

What I like best about the Peers & Plagiarism assignment is that it allows me to really gauge where my students are in their own understanding of plagiarism. Many comments appeared in the discussion that surprised me, such as "I think a lot of the misconception of how much plagiarism encompasses is due to the fact that oftentimes students in middle school and high school are not taught what plagiarism is."[7] Another student noted that "If you didn't take AP, you didn't get taught research."[8] These comments are surprising, and at first I was inclined not to believe the students. Surely they were taught about plagiarism in high school whether they took an Advanced Placement (AP) course or not. But, I had to remember my number one rule—trust! I had to trust that if the students were taught about plagiarism they may not have been involved in in-depth discussions. I also kept in mind the possibility that teachers did in fact take the time to discuss plagiarism but my students did not pay attention or fully grasp the concept and implications.

During the fall 2006 semester some students did seem hesitant to answer the interview questions about themselves, even asking for the ability to post anonymously. I pondered the anonymous posts for awhile, and in the first semester I decided against allowing anonymous posting. My biggest fear was that students would be rude to each other knowing I could not track them. Since the first discussion moved slowly I allowed anonymous posts for all plagiarism discussions after the initial discussion following Peers and Plagiarism. I had to know that the students were working on the assignments and participating, but to really get the conversations going, anonymous posts proved helpful. The discussions did get heated sometimes, but no student was ever blatantly rude to another.

Many undergraduate students understand the power of search engines such as Google but they were still surprised at the ability for Google to find a specific sentence out of all of the Web sites Google searches. More students in the fall 2006 semester were surprised that Google was so exact at finding their passages. I believe this is because more freshmen take the course in the fall semester. During the spring 2007 semester I had more upperclassmen and even some adult students returning to college. It did not surprise me that upperclassmen knew Google's ability because they have been exposed to cyber-plagiarism more fully than some freshmen. For those students who were not surprised by the outcomes of the assignment, I made it a bit more challenging. I asked them to pick out their own keywords from the passage and type those into Google to see what the search engine would find. This then became a lesson in choosing proper keywords. If the students chose good keywords the appropriate Web site appeared. It did surprise the upperclassmen that Google could find one particular Web site from a keyword search with just two terms.

Part III, Proper Paraphrasing, became the most difficult portion of the entire LIB 150 course during both semesters. Students struggled with putting ideas into their own words. They also struggled with understanding why they still had to cite the source! To begin Part III students were sent to a plagiarism site developed by the University of South Florida, "The Fraud of Plagiarism."[9] The "Examples and Tips" section of this tutorial discusses copying, sentence rearranging, and proper paraphrasing. Currently this is my favorite plagiarism Web site and the students seem to like it too. During the fall 2006 semester the students worked in groups of three or four to paraphrase a passage from a history text and each group paraphrased the same passage.

During the spring 2007 semester I changed the assignment and had the students work on paraphrasing a passage from a technical journal. Students were grouped by discipline and given a passage from a scholarly journal article in that area. Having the students paraphrase a more difficult passage required them to do some research about the topic covered in the article. Once they made sense of the technical jargon they were able to paraphrase the passage. Since each group paraphrased a different passage, we were able to look at different examples of proper, or improper, paraphrasing. This gave the students more practice and the discussion centered on what each group could have done to improve their paraphrased passage. This was one discussion where I was more involved; students tend to get defensive when others critique their work so I acted as the mediator. Also, to ensure proper behavior in the discussion forum anonymous posts were not permitted.

Finally we come to Part IV where the students evaluate a paper bought from a paper mill site. This was not part of the course in the fall 2006 semester; it was added for the fall 2007 semester. First the students evaluated the purchased paper by analyzing the types of sources used in the paper (popular or scholarly), and the use of proper citation and proper paraphrasing. This requires students to locate some of the sources used in the paper, which allows them to use their research skills acquired in LIB 150. The second step is to have the students choose keywords for the paper and type those into a search engine. All online paper mills are searchable by a search engine; just because a student buys a paper does not mean it cannot be found through Google. This is a valuable lesson for college students. Again, this also gives students practice in choosing good keywords for searching. One thing to remember when implementing this assignment is never link to a paper mill site from another Web site. When you do this it increases the Web site's ranking in search engines like Google and makes the site appear closer to the top of the search results on a given topic. Also, I suggest that instructors buy one paper and reuse it each semester to avoid giving financial support to these sites.

There have been unexpected outcomes of the plagiarism program. I am quite surprised at how honest the students are when they are discussing this issue. A few students admitted they had plagiarized papers, even in college. Their honesty angered some students but allowed us to have a more open discussion about the issue. Many students are surprised at the complexity of plagiarism and appreciative of the discussions in class. I also find that discussions about plagiarism seem to be a rare thing on campus. One student said "maybe I'm just dense, but I think it should be talked about more in college by professors right away. An example would be like a freshman English writing class should discuss the topic more in depth than just saying 'don't do it.' Instead, I have gone through my whole college career only talking about plagiarism more specifically in this class."[10]

Reflection on the Instruction Session: Lessons Learned

I have only been working with this program for two semesters. I consider it in perpetual *beta*! Each semester the students will know a little more or a little less about the issues surrounding plagiarism. The program is successful because the students feel they know nothing about how to avoid plagiarism and feel overwhelmed when their professors tell them not to do it, but do not tell them how to avoid it. If this program is filling a void for them, it is a success.

It was a struggle getting the students interested in the program during the first semester. After all, there seem to be a lot of assignments about plagiarism in this class if you consider that most students have had little plagiarism instruction beyond the citation. During the first semester I did not require the continued discussion throughout the entire semester. This stifled discussion of the topic and the remaining assignments seemed somewhat disconnected. In the second semester continued discussion was mandatory, so the students were discussing plagiarism, cyber-plagiarism, and paraphrasing as the semester progressed. My other mistake was in assuming that undergraduates would not know the full power of Google. Most of my upperclassmen were not surprised and I had to make adjustments to the Google & Plagiarism assignment during the spring semester.

One thing I learned was not to require a certain number of posts in the online discussion; students usually post the required number and never look again. Now I tell my students that their discussion grade is based on quality, not quantity. The students must be fully involved in the discussion to say something meaningful, which requires that they frequently check the discussion board. And, as I mentioned earlier, I participate very little in these discussions. Students enjoy the open discussion without much involvement from me. Once the students became comfortable with each other the discussions really took off!

Online instruction is tricky, especially the paraphrasing unit. Group work online can be difficult, but not impossible. Another lesson learned is that students taking online courses must know at the beginning of the semester that there will be group work. Many students take online classes to avoid groups and will withdraw from the course if group work is required.

This program is important for our student's academic success and therefore requires continued revamping. We cannot teach research without talking about plagiarism and without teaching students how to avoid it. We must go beyond the citation. During the 2007 Association of College and Research Libraries (ACRL) Conference I was asked if I really thought it was my responsibility to teach students how to properly paraphrase. My answer—"*if they don't know how to do it and they are attempting to do research and write a paper, it is 100 percent my responsibility.*"

Application to Other Instructional Settings

Keep in mind that the plagiarism instruction program is part of a larger research course taught online. The nature of online learning gives the students at least one week to complete each assignment. Using the entire program in a typical library instruction session, in which faculty members bring their students to the library for a general introduction, is not feasible. However, I have brought the Google & Plagiarism assignment into a short library instruction session and that has proven successful. It gives the students a quick activity to demonstrate cyber-plagiarism. I use this when teaching students how to use subscription databases and why they should use library databases instead of the Internet.

The best part about this program is that it can be implemented in both an on-line and face-to-face setting, so if you are teaching a research course in a traditional classroom all of the assignments will work. In a face-to-face class students may be more hesitant to be honest about their own plagiarism habits but they will probably have no trouble discussing the habits of their interviewees. The hands-on portion of the program is probably easier in a face-to-face setting because students can see what others are doing. I expect that the paraphrasing is a bit easier in a traditional setting because you are with the students if they are struggling with paraphrasing. A face-to-face setting is also more conducive to group work, which I find useful when teaching paraphrasing skills. In this setting students become peer-teachers and help other students. Elements of peer-teaching may be found in an online discussion board but it is not as effective as in the face-to-face environment.

If you are one of the lucky librarians who works closely with faculty before their students come to the library then each section of this program may be useful. If a faculty member will include the peer interview in his/her syllabus then you are able to have a good discussion about plagiarism with the students once they come to the library. If the faculty member will include the paraphrasing assignment in his/her syllabus then you will have a good lesson on paraphrasing once the students get into the library. Working with faculty members on plagiarism instruction is one of the many ways librarians can make an impact. It is hard to get into an established syllabus, but if you can find a faculty member willing to let you then you should jump at the opportunity!

Notes

1. Cyber-plagiarism is plagiarism done via the Internet. It is sometimes referred to as copy/paste plagiarism because students copy from a Web site and paste the text into their paper.
2. Scott Brandt, "Copyright's (Not So) Little Cousin, Plagiarism," *Computers in Libraries* 22 (May 2002): 39-41.
3. Barry Kroll, "How College Freshman View Plagiarism," *Written Communication* 5 (April 1988): 203-21.
4. Pamela Jackson, "Plagiarism Instruction Online: Assessing Undergraduate Students' Ability to Avoid Plagiarism," *College & Research Libraries* 67 (Summer 2006): 418-28.
5. Ibid.
6. Lyda Ellis, "Plagiarism," University of Northern Colorado. Available online from http://www.surveymonkey.com/s.aspx?sm=PT2_2fSzT0K1Dh4qZeGRQ4RQ_3d_3d. [Accessed 20 October 2007].
7. Response given in a Blackboard Discussion Forum on September 22, 2006.
8. Responses given in a Blackboard Discussion Forum on November 12, 2006.
9. This tutorial can be accessed at http://www.cte.usf.edu/plagiarism/plag.html.
10. Response given in a Blackboard Discussion Forum on November 12, 2006.

CHAPTER 13

Web 2.0: Using a Wiki to Extend Learning beyond the Classroom Walls

Carl DiNardo

Author's abstract: This chapter discusses the use of Web 2.0 applications to enhance the learning environment of library, research or information instruction, especially in the single-class setting. While an instructional wiki serves as the main example, the techniques for successful integration are applicable to other Web 2.0 tools as well. A wiki provides the students with the opportunity to continue to discuss the information received in class, after the class is over. The wiki format also allows me to continue to interact with the students.

Editors' notes: Carl extends student discussion outside the classroom session with the use of a wiki—an easily editable Web site to which a whole group of students can add comments. With the advent of Web 2.0 sites, such as Facebook, students expect to be able to add their observations to the Web. (When I read about wikis I get wacky because my version of the Web never got past Web 0.9, much less to Web 2.0! ~Doug.)

Introduction

As a library and information instructor, a large part of my classroom environment is inherently technology-based. Some of this technology is fairly standard, such as a computer-generated slide show or a demonstration of a technique projected to the front of the classroom. But there are many other ways in which technology has entered, altered, and expanded the classroom environment. Some instructors have added relatively new technology to their classrooms: online applications that are known collectively as *Web 2.0*.[1]

Academic librarians are typically faced with the *one-shot class* as opposed to teaching a lengthier *course*. We often do not have much time to convey a mountain of information. I have had as little as twenty minutes to address a classroom full of students on topics as specialized as the resources and techniques for researching Early American Literature. Though I spend a relatively short span of time with students in a teaching capacity, they can benefit from the opportunity to have their learning environment extended beyond the classroom walls. Web 2.0 tools, particularly wikis, have helped me do this.

The Web 2.0 moniker has precipitated a debate concerning the nature of the Internet, the technology driving it, and the social body using it. While entering this debate is outside of the scope of this chapter, it is important to understand what is meant by Web 2.0. Web 2.0 does not really refer to a new World Wide Web in the technological sense, though advancements in technology are an important component. The term more accurately describes a shift in how users interact with the Web and other Web users. What O'Reilly calls "Web 1.0" was a more static, less interactive World Wide Web.[2] Users could read text, view pictures, and follow hyperlinks, but short of uploading their own coded Web page could not interact very much with that environment.

From a user's perspective what sets Web 2.0 apart is a level of interaction that developed out of the framework of Web 1.0. Within the Web 2.0 paradigm, users are able to quickly and easily structure a personalized version of the Web without the fuss of learning much about computer languages and codes. Table 1 lists some common types of tools and their general characteristics, but it is important to recognize that there is a great deal of variety both within and outside of these types and that new ideas and iterations are constantly being developed.

Table 1 Web 2.0 Resources	
Resource Type	**General Characteristics**
Blog	One voice speaking to many listeners. Comments can be made by listeners. Discussion may be difficult.
Wiki	Quickly editable Web-style pages for collaborative construction. Contributors may be a large or small group, and may access the site for editing from any connection.
RSS/RSS Readers	Allow a user to keep track of updates on multiple selected Websites without visiting each one individually.
Social Networking	Participants are able to find others based on common interests, hobbies, etc. Messages may be posted by the user and commented on by others. Music, video, picture and other types of files can be linked to and shared.
Podcasts	Method of digital file syndication usually associated with audio and video files. Designed for easy listening/viewing on portable devices. Often associated with RSS.
Mashups	Allow the combining of information from two or more Web sites to form a separate body of information.
Video Sharing	Allow the easy uploading, viewing and exchanging of digital video.
Image Sharing	Allow the easy uploading, viewing and exchanging of digital images.
Virtual Worlds	Participants navigate through and interact with a virtual 3-D world and with each other.

To date, the Web 2.0 resource that has worked the best for me has been the wiki. Simply put, a wiki is a Web page that can be set up for online editing by one or more participants. Editing is meant to be fast and easy; I sometimes will do this on-the-fly in class. The term wiki is an abbreviation of *wikiwiki*, the Hawaiian word for *quick*. The name is a reference to the speed with which a wiki can be edited, as compared to coding html from scratch. There are wikis with different bells and whistles available from the various hosting companies; however the ability to be quickly and easily edited by multiple contributors is the hallmark of a wiki. I have used other tools, and have started combining tools (one of the merits of many Web 2.0 tools is their ability to work well together), but wikis have worked out for me as a type of home base.

Instructional Goals

My reasons for using a wiki derive from instructional goals that are well served from its use.

1. I want my students to be receptive to learning.
2. I want to accommodate various learning styles.
3. I want to promote the sharing and discussion of ideas.
4. I want to provide an avenue for communication/feedback outside of the classroom.

Kim, Grabowski, and Sharma identify several elements of a good learning environment including: "teachers' teaching strategy, supporting tools, learning climate, characteristics of learner-centered classroom, peers, and technology support."[3] I have found that these elements can work harmoniously or compete with each other. When these elements begin to clash, it seems that I start to fall short of my expectations. When they are working well together, however, I find that my teaching life is good, and while I may not be able to walk on water, my goals are more easily met.

Wikis have helped me to meet these goals by offering an appealing technology that can be used creatively yet can still remain authentic from the student perspective. That is to say the technology is genuinely used for learning, not just for the sake of using it. Also, while I consider all of these goals important, it is the last that truly lends itself to using a wiki and can extend learning beyond the classroom.

Instructional Strategy

More specific strategies, such as the following, which stem from my goals are aptly supported by the use of wikis.

1. Use technology that will offer appeal without being distracting or merely for show.
2. Provide an online handout. It will be informative without spoon-feeding information.
3. Incorporate an interactive activity that will require a level of student involvement.
4. Use an online forum for discussion and communication outside of the classroom.

I found that experimenting with wikis helped me to shape my objectives, such as in the use of a forum. I knew I wanted a way to extend communication outside of the classroom, and as I experimented with this feature of some wikis, I structured an objective around that. When designing my objectives I endeavor to make my strategy seamless, as I do not want my use of these tools to create a distracting learning environment.[4]

The idea that there are several ways in which people think and learn in the classroom suggests that offering alternative methods for receiving or processing information is important for connecting with more students.[5] In an effort to better reach my students I try to integrate strategies that will address more than a single style of learning. Lecturing, discussion, handouts, and student participation all can serve a different purpose. A strategy that increases the ways in which students can learn is at least worthy of investigation, and my use of wikis to meet my instructional objectives has been successful.

There are growing bodies of literature that connect libraries and the use of Web 2.0 applications. Similarly, the higher-education literature has also begun to explore suitability for course use.[6] Little has surfaced, however, concerning the potential of these applications to aid in the one-shot library instruction session. Looking into the course-oriented literature that explores Web 2.0 offered guidance for setting up a sound instructional strategy.

An interesting and inspiring quality of wikis is their collaborative potential. The hurdle for the one-shot instruction session is that this type of joint-effort takes time. I wanted to develop a strategy that incorporated some collaboration, but with the understanding that this would take place outside of class. This would not only extend the learning environment outside of the classroom, but also act as a way to share valuable sources as they were discovered.

Using a wiki to extend the learning environment outside of the one-shot class is considered web-based learning.[7] Even though the majority of the class occurs within the traditional classroom there is a part that includes online participation. Again, it is this potential to go beyond the classroom that makes wikis most exciting and valuable.

Match of Goals and Strategy

Exploring the uses and relative strengths and weaknesses of various wikis available has enabled me to try to match up the tool with my objectives as a means of meeting my goals. Sometimes I find that more than one goal can be achieved with a single new strategy. An example would be setting up a forum within the wiki to facilitate communication and discussion. This helps with two of my goals: promoting the sharing and discussion of ideas and providing an avenue for feedback. I definitely made mistakes (more on these less-than-glorious moments later), but I learned from them and moved ahead.

As is the case with most technology, careful and considered preparation is critical for these tools and techniques to be useful.[8] Without planning, you can actually induce the opposite effect of what you are trying to achieve by creating confusion and frustration. At best, you will end up with a distracting environment. At worst, learning can grind to a halt.

Another important factor has been communication with teaching faculty before and after the class. Discussion and demonstration of this strategy with a faculty member ahead of time has helped in several ways. Since I want to use wikis for assessment, it is important to have the course instructors' support. After all, I may not ever see these students in a classroom again. While some of them might be inclined to provide feedback on their own, many will not. When I am in touch with an instructor early enough I can tailor a wiki to a class assignment or desired outcome for the collaborating instructor. The instructor can also guide and encourage students to provide feedback following the completion of an assignment.

Description of the Instruction Session: What Actually Happened?

My first use of a wiki in a class, while decidedly not my ultimate vision of student interaction, proved to be an encouraging start. In this case I simply created a wiki as an online version of what would have otherwise been a paper handout for a general research class for a freshmen-level English course. I set up an account, and then began placing links to appropriate databases and, via the library's online catalog, to print sources that would be useful for the assignment. I wanted to see if there would be positive or negative reaction to this format, so I conducted the class as I normally would have, using the wiki page I had created to guide the discussion of sources. From my perspective this had the added benefit of quick one-stop access to those sources I had linked to as I taught the class. I encouraged the students to write down the wiki's Web address and to use it as they worked on their papers. About a week later the faculty member teaching the course thanked me specifically for setting up the wiki, as her students had apparently made good use of it. Success on both fronts!

With that encouragement I met with another member of the English faculty who wanted me to do a research session for her writing classes. During our meeting I proposed a more ambitious wiki strategy that would include more active participation. After discussing some of the details, she agreed to allow me to try my strategy.

Since all of the students in the class had a common general theme for their research (nutrition), I decided that the wiki might again start its life as sort of pathfinder, but this time it would be dynamic; the students could contribute to it. Similar to the previous class—but to a lesser degree—I added links to just a few appropriate reference tools, as well as several governmental and organizational Web sites that might benefit a number of students.

My aim was not to hand out all of the information to the students (I was teaching research, after all), but to stimulate interest in the tool so that it could become more than what I had started. If I could generate this interest based on real student-benefit, I believed that I would meet all four of my goals.

I operated in the classroom as usual, and I handed out a sparse page which included highlights for discussion, space for notes, and a brief description and the address of the wiki. I guided the end of the research discussion toward the evaluation of online materials. As we began, I projected the wiki at the front of the class and encouraged the students to follow along at their terminals. We discussed some hallmarks of good and not-so-good Web sites and I used the links on the wiki to highlight certain points that were made.

Before I wrapped up the session, I explained that this site was theirs to use, and that they should add to it, and that I felt I could learn from them, too. I likened the adding of a resource to telling a friend "I found some great info over here. You should check it out." The payoff would be that we could benefit from each other, rather than just one person telling another about one source. I also felt it important to point out that the students should not worry about making mistakes, as any changes could easily be reversed. The software keeps a record of changes made which can be referenced if something goes wrong.

I demonstrated how to add content to the site, as well as where to go for help. The professor of the course wanted me to allow time for database-searching practice as I walked around the room taking questions and generally helping out. Some students decided that they would use the time to search the Internet for sources, and when the students found valuable information, I encouraged them to add it to the site. As they did, the wiki began to grow and take on a new character based on the resources the students were discovering.

I also showed them the forum component. An online forum is an excellent platform for discussion and questions. The students really liked knowing that I was making myself as available to them as possible if they had questions outside of class. I also wanted them to know that I was open to their thoughts about how the class went and what they thought of my teaching.

In addition to making myself more widely available, I was able to post follow-up discussion topics. For example, I used this feature to follow through on an insightful student question concerning requirements for involvement in editorial oversight in Wikipedia. Of greatest benefit to me, however, was the ability to get feedback from the students not only concerning the wiki itself, but also on my teaching. I always encourage candid responses from my students, and a forum is a fairly non-threatening environment for this. This is a point at which having support from the course instructor has paid off. I had not considered it prior to my first attempts at using the forum for direct feedback on my teaching, but the times that I have asked teaching faculty to encourage their students to provide feedback have generally evoked more student response.

Responses ranged from the predictable and uninformative "I thought it was a good class" to somewhat more telling comments indicating a lack of understanding of topics. Excluding the sparse paper handout in a different class elicited two responses from students who felt that something to take with them would have been helpful.

An item of some importance is that the sessions that this seems to work best with are longer than many of the one-shot classes librarians often get to teach. I was given nearly two hours with these students. Because of that I was able to show them the wiki and a bit of how it worked. In subsequent instruction sessions I have walked students through the registration process which is usually simple and straightforward. As I had made these wikis open to public viewing, registration was not required to view or even edit them, but it was required for participation in a forum discussion. I was fortunate to have lengthier classes. In a shorter class this is a much more difficult thing to squeeze in as we try to sprint through the basics of research towards a non-existent finish-line.

Reflection on the Instruction Session: Lessons Learned

There were, of course, some glitches. Learning from the students helped me to begin to debug the process. With the wiki experiment, I found that there was a great deal of potential if I could tweak a few things. The first wiki I chose was quite powerful and had quite a few unique features. Unfortunately, implementing these features made for a very complicated wiki. The forum component, in particular, was a bit unwieldy and discouraged student use. I soon set up shop on a different wiki hosting site. This wiki didn't have as many features, but it did have a straightforward forum which allowed for easy use. Once this easier forum was set up students began participating outside of the class more than other classes had.

It also became apparent that if I wanted this strategy to work in the one-shot environment, there would be a great deal of time spent in set up, maintenance, and follow-through. Time spent in preparation helped me keep problems to a minimum, and I was more prepared to handle those problems that might still crop up. Again, it is important for the tool to be a good fit for the strategy.

Before I turned to wikis, I tried using a blog. The first time I tried to get a blog to fit my instructional situation, I ended with a room full of annoyed students; and simply annoying students has never been one of my goals. Due to the typical blog structure, there is a main voice delivering information (which was me), with provisions for readers (the students) to post comments. Additionally, blogs are typically structured in a reverse chronological order, not according to a topical classification scheme.[9] Ideas were shared, but mainly by my voice. The students could respond to main posts, so there was some feedback. However, the way in which these responses are structured within a blog did not allow for easy discussion.

Because of this structure I have had little success using a blog as an avenue for feedback, and the response I did get was more than offset by the difficulties in achieving other goals. The blog did not help me to achieve most of my goals, and was a poor choice for what I was trying to accomplish. Looking back this should have been obvious to me during the planning stages. I was certain that I could make this tool fit in my classroom environment, but I was wrong. I may have had a good idea, but I certainly did not choose the right tool for my particular situation. This stumble sent me searching for other tools, ultimately leading me to the wiki format.

An incredibly interesting and unexpected outcome of using wikis has to do with non-traditional students. The first time I successfully tried this approach, I brought up the wiki after discussing Wikipedia and some peculiarities of evaluating internet sources. When I switched from saying "Wikipedia," which everyone clearly understood, to "a wiki" I had far more confused faces than I had anticipated—I hadn't anticipated any. Most of these confused faces were from the non-traditional students in the class. I found that many of these students were feeling technologically deficient compared to their younger classmates. But despite their insecurities they were, on the whole, very willing to at least try using the wiki. These students were very thankful to learn about some of the online applications they had heard of. They also appreciated learning about other tools that were important but unfamiliar, such as the library's online databases.

Not all students were enthusiastic. A few cited a lack of time as reason for not participating, indicating that this was just one more thing for them to have to deal with. Others indicated that they had visited the wiki to shop for information but had not contributed. These responses were not surprising, but they do imply a need for student-perceived benefit if the strategy is to succeed.

One thing that soon became apparent with the wikis was that quick and simple is relative. There are many wikis available, and looking around a bit online helped me find those with features that were appealing. With the more difficult of the available wikis however, students can become frustrated and have little or no interest in participation. Some of these wikis even frustrated me because they were indeed complicated and difficult to operate. This isn't typical, but I found I should watch out for it and promptly adopted a simpler-is-better philosophy.

This teaching strategy is not always going to be appropriate or applicable to every classroom situation. Instructors who have very little time in the classroom may find it difficult or even counterproductive to try to extend learning outside of the classroom with a wiki, though setting one up simply as an aid to student research has worked quite well for me in these instances. Having the support of the course instructor is also important. A short-notice instruction session will not allow enough time for a good set-up, though having a dedicated instructional wiki already in the queue can certainly make this less of a problem.

Application to Other Instructional Settings

While personal experience limits me somewhat to a discussion of wikis and other Web 2.0 applications in a single-class setting, there seems to be even more potential for the course setting. A study by Rayburn and Rayburn found a difference between the critical thinking of undergraduates in longer (sixteen weeks) and shorter (eight weeks) courses.[10] Though the total amount of time spent in the classroom was equal between the groups, student performance on final exams was significantly better in the lengthier course for those questions requiring critical thinking.[11] If you are fortunate enough to be teaching your students through a course (as opposed to a one-shot class), the temporal constraints lessen. A blog, for example, might simply be used to keep students updated on your course. This application of a blog would likely not improve the environment for a single class, but could be an excellent bulletin board, especially in the absence of course management software.

A major consideration in teaching a course on information is the way information is packaged. Web 2.0 has had a major impact in this area. Users are able to narrowly define not only where they receive information from, but also what that information is. To an extent, that seems to be the point.

This degree of information-personalization has created an interesting dynamic. On one hand we can better manage the glut of information that bombards us daily.

On the other hand, we need to try to stay guarded so that the information we receive is not simply what we want to know, but also what we need to know. If you are showing these tools to students in an information-management style course, be sure to discuss this issue. After all, you can just as easily add a news source to your RSS reader that is typically contrary to your views as add one you usually agree with. When you take that step, the information is more complete and will offer a perspective that is much closer to balanced.

Are wikis absolutely necessary for your teaching? No. Are they appropriate for every situation? Probably not. They are simply versatile tools that instructional librarians can use to extend the learning environment beyond the classroom and encourage collaboration. Selecting tools and implementing strategies that reflect your classroom goals creates solid scaffolding for success. Communication and follow-up with faculty and students helps ensure that your strategies will continue to evolve and improve.

Notes

1. Tim O'Reilly, "What Is Web 2.0: Design Patterns and Business Models for the Next Generation of Software." Available from http://www.oreilly.com/pub/a/oreilly/tim/news/2005/09/30/what-is-web-20.html. [Accessed 4 December 2007].

2. Ibid.

3. Kyoungna Kim, Barbara L. Grabowski, and Priya Sharma, "Designing a Classroom as a Learner-centered Learning Environment Prompting Students' Reflective Thinking in K-12" (paper, Association for Educational Communications and Technology Conference, Chicago, IL, October 19-23, 2004).

4. Wiley B Lewis and Duane G. Jansen, "Characteristics of Hypermedia Presentations" (paper, American Vocational Association Conference, Vocational Instructional Materials Section, Las Vegas, NV, December 12, 1997), 8.

5. Thomas Armstrong, *Multiple Intelligences in the Classroom* (Alexandria, Virginia: Association for Supervision and Curriculum Development, 2000); Bette LaSere Erickson, Calvin B. Peters, and Diane Weltner Strommer. *Teaching First Year College Students* (San Francisco: Jossey-Bass, 2006).

6. Mary Bold, "Use of Wikis in Graduate Course Work," *Journal of Interactive Learning Research* 17 (January 1, 2006); Stuart Glogoff, "The LTC Wiki - Experiences with Integrating a Wiki in Instruction." *Using Wiki in Education*, ed. S. Mader. Available online from http://www.wikiineducation.com. [Accessed 4 December 2007].

7. Harold F. O'Neil and Ray S Perez, eds. *Web-based Learning: Theory, Research, and Practice* (Mahwah, NJ: Lawrence Erlbaum Associates, 2006), 5.

8. Ulla K. Bunz, "'Theoretically, That's How You Do It...': Using Narratives When Computers Let You Down in the Technology Classroom" (paper, Southern States Communication Association Convention, Lexington, KY, April 5-8, 2001); Glogoff, "The LTC Wiki."

9. Robert Godwin-Jones, "Emerging Technologies: Blogs and Wikis: Environments for On-line Collaboration," *Language, Learning & Technology* 7 (May, 2003).

10. L. Gayle Rayburn and L. Michael Rayburn, "Impact of Course Length and Homework Assignments on Student Performance," *Journal of Education for Business* 74 (January, 1999).

11. Ibid.

CHAPTER 14

An "Amazing Race" through the Library: Reality Television Meets Problem-Based Learning

Dawn Eckenrode

Author's abstract: In this chapter I discuss using a problem-based approach for teaching library instruction. Based in constructivist theory, this student-centered strategy for learning presents them with situations in which they are asked to solve problems through reliance on prior knowledge, experimentation, and trial and error. The lesson plan I have designed is modeled on the reality television game show, The Amazing Race. The students learn by doing and working collaboratively in groups to solve problems and co-construct knowledge through dialogue and experience.

Editors' notes: Dawn uses a TV reality show activity to absorb students in a simulated experience of finding information in the Reference area. Dawn says, "When class began, I was definitely outside the comfort zone of my usual teaching methods… To top it off, the class was being videotaped." The "Amazing Race through the Library" could make some serious cash on late night TV… any producers want to buy the tapes?

Introduction

When a professor requests a teaching librarian to present to her class, the communication of her goals and expectations for the session is crucial to the lesson planning process. While many professors come to the library with clear-cut skills they would like their students to learn—such as how to find empirical studies in the database PsycINFO—there are also faculty members who take more abstract or unconventional approaches to the planning and goal-setting process. While these interactions are often more challenging, they also open the field for more creative lesson planning.

A talented theater professor, who approached me about planning a library session for his Freshman Seminar course, decided to take the unconventional route. Freshman Seminar courses at our institution are designed to expose students to various services available on campus and to build a sense of community among the classmates. This professor's course design was highly creative, with each class focusing on a different campus service and a different reality television game show theme. For example, a visit to the Career Development Office was modeled on an episode of The Apprentice—a television show that depicts a group of businessmen and women competing for a job running one of Donald Trump's companies. Following the reality television game show format, each unscripted class was videotaped and edited into short episodes, portraying the dramatic and humorous situations of our students while they competed in a variety of tasks designed to orient them to campus life. The professor's vision for the library's session was unconventional to say the least:

1. He wanted the class to be based on the reality television show The Amazing Race.
2. He wanted the students to be running around the library.
3. He welcomed chaos.

These are definitely not the typical stipulations received when negotiating a library session and some outside-the-box thinking was required in order to establish the logistics for the class and to create well-defined learning outcomes.

Instructional Goals

Since the professor had given me free rein to decide what the students should learn about library services, I used my knowledge of the Association of College and Research Library's (ACRL) Information Literacy Standards[1] and my first-hand experience with freshman learning behaviors in the library to establish the goals for the class. First, I wanted the assignment/game to be a confidence-building exercise. Students are often overwhelmed by the physical presence of the library, the variety of resources available, and the respective locations of those resources.[2] According to a study conducted at the University of Georgia by Van Scoyoc, freshmen students' perceptions of library staff are a major part of their overall anxiety in relation to using the library.[3] So not only did I want the library to be perceived as a helpful, friendly, and inviting place — I wanted librarians to be perceived as helpful, friendly people. To that end, I wanted the students to leave class with an understanding of the following concepts: (1) that the library has a variety of research tools available; (2) that the library provides access to information in a variety of formats (not just books); (3) that materials are organized differently in various locations; and (4) that librarians are available to assist them in their research.

Once I had solidified the goals for the session, I wrote its learning outcome based on a model for writing meaningful learning outcomes taught by Deborah Gilchrist, an outcomes-based assessment expert and Dean of Library/Media Services at Pierce College in Lakewood, Washington. This model states that good learning outcomes should be measurable; clear to the student, faculty, and librarian; integrated, developmental, and transferable; match the level of the course; and use the ACRL Standards as a basis, not an end.[4] My outcome read: "At the end of this process you should feel confident using several research tools in order to effectively locate multiple types of information sources in a variety of formats." I was sure to provide both a copy and an explanation of this learning outcome to the students when I introduced the class session. I feel this is an important part of any class I teach, and it is especially imperative when learning takes place in the form of a game. It is my experience that when education is fun, students can often be skeptical that they are actually learning. In order to make the learning process more meaningful to the students, I have found that it is integral to explain, right at the beginning of class, what the students should be able to do at the end of the lesson. Students appreciate knowing the method behind the madness and are often more receptive to the materials presented.

Instructional Strategy

Once I had established a solid learning outcome, it was time to create a lesson that assessed whether the students successfully met the instructional goals. Based on the professor's instructions, I was to do so in the form of the reality television show *The Amazing Race*. To be honest, I had never actually watched an entire episode of the show, so I consulted the consummate stronghold of all things pop culture: Wikipedia.[5] Wikipedia may have its detractors, but when you are a librarian trying to base a lesson plan on the intricacies of a reality television program you have never really watched, there is no better source. For those who are not viewers of the program, *The Amazing Race* is a reality television game show in which teams of two individuals travel around the world and compete to be the winning pair at the end of each leg of the race or face elimination. There are clues provided throughout the race directing the teams to the next destination or requiring them to perform a task.

Once I had this knowledge under my belt, I was able to apply the basic format of the show to the class I was developing. I wrote five Route Clues that required the teams of students to *travel* to seven different locations in the library (reference, reference desk, music library, circulation desk, microfilm room, online, and the general book stacks) and find information in a variety of formats (books, articles, and audiovisual). I decided to take a student-centered constructivist approach when designing the class, and the clues I developed presented the teams with situations in which they were asked to solve problems through reliance on prior knowledge, experimentation, and trial and error. For example, students were provided with open-ended clues such as: "Locate the reference book titled, *Worldmark Encyclopedia of Cultures and Daily Life*, and use it to answer the following questions…Your next clue will be located near this set of encyclopedias." The clues were written so that the students would have to collaborate to solve problems, rather than execute a set of directives, such as: "Go to a computer, click on Internet Explorer, and go to the library's homepage. Click on the online catalog. In the search box, type *Worldmark Encyclopedia of Cultures and Daily Life*. Using the call number and your map of the library, find this book and answer the following questions…" By taking this approach, students were provided with *ill-structured*[6] situations in which multiple strategies were appropriate for tackling the problem at hand.

As the teacher, using a student-centered method placed me in the role of facilitator—the person who set the guidelines, rules, and objectives for the game, and created a semi-structured environment for the learners to explore. While I wanted the students to explore the library for themselves as much as possible, I also wanted to communicate the idea that reference librarians are available to assist them in their research. To do so in keeping with *The Amazing Race* theme, I modified the television show's Fast Forward concept. In the show, the Fast Forward allows a contestant to skip tasks during a leg of the race. In my version, each Fast

Forward located by the students allowed their team to receive assistance with a task from a librarian at the reference desk, enabling me to direct the students' learning more effectively.

By taking a constructivist approach rather than an objectivist one, I chose to make the activity more student-centered, with the participants working collaboratively in groups in order to learn what they need to know in order to solve a problem.[7] This approach meets many of the criteria that identify problem-based learning, a method that is grounded in the "learning by doing" philosophy of John Dewey.[8] This type of instruction is characterized by: (1) the role of the teacher as a facilitator of learning, (2) the responsibility of the learners to be self-directed and responsible for their own learning, and (3) the design of *ill-structured* instructional problems as the driving force for inquiry.[9] This approach is great for teaching students how to research, since it is designed to help learners construct a flexible knowledge base, and develop effective problem-solving and lifelong-learning skills.[10]

Match of Goals and Strategy

Learning outcomes should be the basis for choosing an instructional strategy, according to Mark Battersby, formerly of the Centre for Curriculum, Transfer and Technology at the Ministry of Education in British Columbia.[11] Being familiar with Gilchrist's method for writing learning outcomes and Battersby's article, I developed the curriculum for my class beginning with the learning outcome, which was "to effectively locate multiple types of information sources in a variety of formats." I then used this outcome to develop the assessment strategy: a problem-based gaming situation. For the purposes of this particular class, I feel this situated-learning method made for a more challenging and realistic game experience, in keeping with The Amazing Race theme, than if I had presented the students with a more regimented drill-and-practice assignment. This type of problem-based approach is ideal for library instruction sessions, due to its emphasis on active, transferable learning and its potential for motivating students.[12] Doing the class in the format of a game kept the intimidation factor low for the students, something I was concerned about due to the common presence of library anxiety among freshman students. It was also a good fit for the community-building goal of the overall course, since the problem-based approach is designed to help students become effective collaborators.[13]

Description of the Instruction Session: What Actually Happened?

When class began, I was definitely outside the comfort zone of my usual teaching methods, and the concomitant self-doubt kicked in. What if there isn't enough structure? What if the clues are too confusing? What if the game is too complicated, or too simple? What if they aren't able to complete the race in the allotted hour and twenty minutes? What if…? What if…? What if…? To top it off, the class was being videotaped. I hate being on camera—absolutely hate it. If the class bombed, there would be a cinematic record of my failure as a teacher. I was nervous. The camera was rolling. It was time to perform.

I began by explaining the purpose for the session, which was for the students to gain confidence in using and navigating the library for research purposes. I proceeded to let the students know that the class would be similar to the television show The Amazing Race, a program with which many of the students were familiar. After dividing the students into four teams of four, with each group representing a different country (Jamaica, Ghana, Iceland, and Japan) in keeping with the travel theme, I explained that the object of the game was to be the first team to successfully complete each of the assigned tasks and reach the Final Destination. I told the students that, similar to the television show, there would be Route Marker flags to designate the places where their teams needed to go. At each location they would need to pick up an envelope marked with a map of their representative country, which would contain a clue to their next task. I then passed out a Travel Kit to each team, which contained the following: a map of the library, an allowance of fifteen cents (needed to complete one of the tasks), the address for the library's Web site, an envelope containing the first Route Clue, a Fast Forward, and the rules of the game.

I tried to keep the rules of the game as simple as possible: if the first team to finish made any errors in completing their tasks, the second team finishing had the opportunity to win the game. Additionally, each Fast Forward could only be used once. If the students had any questions about the game, they could visit the U.S. Embassy, which was located at the library's reference desk—a centralized and realistic location for assistance. Another librarian and I acted as Diplomats, at the Embassy, and we made ourselves available to resolve any problems encountered in the logistics of the game.

For the first leg of their journey, the students were expected to locate a specific encyclopedia set and answer a few factual questions about their country. The purpose of this exercise was for the students to familiarize themselves with the location of the reference collection and the types of materials found here. The students used a variety of strategies in order to complete this task. For example, one team had a member who suggested using the online catalog, while another team used their map of the library and then browsed the shelves until they located the intended set. As a librarian, helpful in nature and disposition, it was difficult for me to keep my nose out of the problem-solving process and let the students direct their own learning. However, at this point it was becoming evident that the problem-based approach was working. Students were dialoging. They were referring to prior experiences in libraries. They were trying and failing. They were trying and succeeding. They were discovering things for themselves. They were having fun! I started to relax and have fun too.

The next Route Clue for each team was hidden near the encyclopedias and required the students to locate a specific music recording from the country their team represented. For example, one clue for Team Jamaica read, "Your team's next goal is to locate a sound recording of Bob Marley's *Exodus* in our Music Department. Your next clue will be located with this recording." I wanted the students to be aware that the library's collection of materials extends beyond books. This time the students had to use their problem-solving skills to (1) recognize that they needed to use the library's online catalog to locate sound recordings, (2) execute a successful search in the catalog, and (3) locate the Music Department in the library. Once again, the students employed a variety of strategies to complete this task, including using the Fast Forward, which permitted their team to get help from a reference librarian.

Similar to the televised Amazing Race, the next leg of the race was a Pit Stop where the students needed to locate the library's circulation desk in order to receive their next clue. At the Pit Stop, in addition to the clue, each team also received an envelope labeled, "A Possible Plot Twist." Two of the teams received envelopes that contained another Fast Forward, while the remaining two teams received envelopes containing something I called a Roadblock. The Roadblock was based on the Yield clues provided in television show, and allowed any one team to force another team to stop racing for three minutes. The students loved this twist in the game, and found pleasure in the ability to Roadblock their classmates at crucial points in the game. At this point, things were getting more competitive, and the presence of a Reality Television Hostess, played by a senior from the Theater Department, fueled the dramatic tension. Our Hostess interviewed different team members and librarians in order to instigate feuds, team rivalries, and romance. This added drama created a true reality television ambience, was a great motivator for the students, and also made for a very funny video.

Once they completed the Pit Stop, the teams were on to the next task— another format and another location. This time they were required to find a specific article about their country on microfilm. This leg of the race met with both frustration (Do the microfilm machines at your library *ever* work well?), and intrigue (The "wow, this is cool," reaction that is typically elicited from future history majors.) In contrast, the next leg of the race required the students to find an article about their country using the library's databases, a task they completed, surprisingly, with comparative ease. At last, the teams were poised to complete the final task— to locate the book about their country containing the clue that revealed the final destination. The race to the finish was on.

In the end, Team Jamaica beat Team Iceland in a surprising upset, and all the teams successfully completed their tasks and made their way to the Final Destination, a picturesque study lounge on one of the upper floors of the library. With the race at its finish, there was even some time to reflect on what the students learned. This reflection was an important part of the problem-based learning process, since it gave the students an opportunity to analyze and discuss what had been learned from their work during class, allowing the students to better understand what they know, what they learned, and how they performed.[14] As we went around the room, the students shared that they previously had not known how the call number system worked, that they had not known about the catalog, or microfilm, or the extent of our music collection. One student jokingly said that he had not known it was okay to run through the library. This statement touches on some of the most important learning aspects of the class— the library was perceived as a relaxed, friendly place, and a sense of community had been forged, both among the students and between the students and librarians. I still see many of those students studying and doing research in the library, and there is a strong sense of recognition and connection. In fact, students who weren't even in the class approached me afterwards, simply because they saw the video.

Reflection on the Instruction Session: Lessons Learned

In taking a constructivist approach to instructional design, I learned a lot about myself as a teacher and ways in which I can expand my repertoire of teaching techniques. In the following section I will share what I personally learned from this instructional process, in hopes that it will inspire others to allow for curiosity and creativity in the classroom experience, fostering an environment that allows students to experience the problematic nature of information use.[15] To that end, I will be summarizing my main points in the following way: suspend your disbelief, go outside your comfort zone, allow for organized chaos, and look for unexpected collaborations.

Suspend your Disbelief

So many times the lesson planning process is started with a negative attitude. I think we have all faced a situation where a professor makes a request for a class that is a bit different from what we are accustomed, and the immediate response is, "Are they crazy? That can't be done in fifty minutes!" You're probably tactful enough not to say this directly to the professor's face, but you do say it to one of your colleagues in the library, or, you at least think it to yourself. I know I am guilty of this, and I know I am not alone in my guilt. It's human nature. We fear trying new things, especially when we only have a week to prepare and a schedule that is already overburdened with meetings, appointments, and projects. I think it's important to get past that initial mental barrier, or at least acknowledge that it exists. In my process, once I consciously get past the negativity and accept that I will be trying something new, it's time to tackle the next step…

Go Outside your Comfort Zone

I'll admit it. I have always been a passive learner. I like lectures, photocopied handouts, and outlines with roman numerals. I do not like role-playing, brainstorming, and sharing my thoughts with the class. However, I do have the sense to realize that while I might enjoy sitting through a fifty minute lecture on the subtle nuances of the library's catalog— many, many people probably will not. Even though I sometimes find it difficult to comprehend how students can learn in styles different from my own, I know that they can, and do, all the time. I have been in possession of this knowledge since my days in library school, but there are still times when I fall into the same old rut of lecture, database demonstration, and hands-on practice. I know that while I may learn in one way, it's probably not always the best way, or the only way, to approach teaching a class. Last summer I attended the ACRL's Information Literacy Immersion Program, which provides instruction librarians with the opportunity to work intensively for four-and-a-half days on all aspects of information literacy.[16] My experience in the program really impressed upon me the need to vary my instructional approach to accommodate a variety of learners and to take more risks in the classroom. The following semester it was time to loosen the reins, mix up my repertoire, and take some chances. This leads to my next point: allow for organized chaos.

Allow for Organized Chaos

I really like structure and organization. No surprises here— I am a librarian. I am comforted by classes which are predictable. However, I have come to realize that in order to be a great teacher, rather than merely a good one, I have to allow for the unexpected. Taking a student-directed approach to teaching requires flexibility, confidence in your abilities as a professional, and the ability to exude calm under pressure. Those organizational talents really come in handy too, since you can't have a truly student-directed class that is educationally meaningful without a skilled professional pulling the strings behind the scenes. In fact, several of the students who attended the Amazing Library Race class actually commented on the organization of the game and the attention to detail that went in to the clues. I have to admit that the class took a lot of preparation, energy, and hard work, and it was wonderful to have that work recognized by the students. However, I can only take a portion of the credit for the success of the lesson. I had lots of help. Sometimes it is possible to accomplish a desired objective on your own, and sometimes your vision may require enlisting the help of other experts, or being open to others enlisting you. So…

Look for Unexpected Collaborations

Designing the Amazing Library Race, entailed collaborating with the professor for the course, who served as director, producer, and visionary on the project; a senior theater student, who acted as the hostess of the show; a visual design major, who edited the episode; and three librarians, who assisted the students with their research and who additionally were roped into acting on the video. The culmination of this hard work, talent, and collaboration resulted in drawing the attention of campus administrators who are using the class as a model activity for student engagement. So, not only did I discover my colleagues' hidden acting skills as a result of teaching this class, I also have been asked to be involved in a campus-wide initiative to overhaul the college's Freshman Experience Program. While taking on a class of this scale may involve some extra work and coordination, the exposure could result in some very positive public relations for your library's instruction program and for the library.

Application to Other Instructional Settings

I feel that the instructional approach I have described here is most appropriate in educational situations where students "Don't know what they don't know." In taking a problem-based approach, an important part of the learning cycle is when the students identify their knowledge deficiencies in relation to the problems with which they are presented.[17] From a library standpoint, I think this approach is very useful for teaching skills with which students probably have some prior experience, such as locating a book in a the library. For example, a student may assume that they know how to find a book in your institution's library, because they knew how to find a book in their high school's library. However, the student may not know that they don't understand the arrangement of your library, because your collection uses Library of Congress rather than the Dewey Decimal System with which they are familiar. Completing a problem-based activity would help this student identify where his/her knowledge deficiency lies. It is also a useful approach for classes without formal research assignments, such as sessions conducted during orientation and some freshman introductory courses. Whatever the instructional situation, this strategy will definitely keep your students engaged and motivated— so get ready to tell your next class to put their running shoes on!

Notes

1. Association of College and Research Libraries, *Information Literacy Standards for Higher Education* (Chicago: Association of College and Research Libraries, 2000). Available online from http://www.ala.org/ala/acrl/acrlstandards/informationliteracycompetency.htm.

2. Constance A. Mellon, "Library Anxiety: A Grounded Theory and Its Development," *College and Research Libraries* 47 (1986): 161.

3. Anna Van Scoyoc, "Reducing Library Anxiety in First-Year Students," *Reference & User Services Quarterly* 42 (2003): 337.

4. Deborah Gilchrist, "Improving Student Experience: Assessment as Learning" (lecture, Institute for Information Literacy, Association of College and Research Libraries, Boston, MA, 2006), 10.

5. *Wikipedia, The Free Encyclopedia*, Available online from http://www.wikipedia.org.

6. Cindy E. Hmelo-Silver, "Problem-Based Learning: What and How Do Students Learn?" *Educational Psychology Review* 16 (2004): 237.

7. Ibid., 236.

8. John R. Savery, "Overview of Problem-based Learning: Definitions and Distinctions," *The Interdisciplinary Journal of Problem-based Learning* 1 (2006): 16.

9. Ibid., 15.

10. Hmelo-Silver, "Problem-Based Learning," 236.

11. Mark Battersby, "So, What's a Learning Outcome Anyway?" (Education Resources Information Center, 1999, ED 430611): 9.

12. Hmelo-Silver, "Problem-Based Learning," 236.

13. Ibid., 241.

14. Savery, "Overview of Problem-based Learning," 14.

15. Randy Burke Hensley, "Curiosity and Creativity as Attributes of Information Literacy," *Information Literacy and Instruction* 44 (2004): 32.

16. Information Literacy Advisory Committee, "Institute for Information Literacy Immersion Program," Association of College and Research Libraries, Available online from http://www.ala.org/ala/acrl/acrlissues/acrlinfolit/professactivity/iil/immersion/immersionprograms.cfm. [Accessed 12 September, 2007].

17. Hmelo-Silver, "Problem-Based Learning," 236.

Teaching Resources
The Amazing Race: Library Edition

Object of the Game
Be the first team to reach the "Final Destination" and successfully complete each of the tasks assigned. Each of the "Route Clues" you receive will provide you with instruction on what you will need to bring to the final destination as proof of your completion of each of the challenges.

Contents of Your "Travel Kit"
Being familiar with the contents of your kit is essential to being able to successfully complete all the tasks. Your travel kit should contain the following:
1. Map of the library
2. Cash allowance (you will need this to complete one of the tasks)
3. URL for the Library's Web site
4. Your first "Route Clue"
5. A "Fast Forward" pass

Rules of the Game
1. If you have any questions about the game, you can visit the "U.S. Embassy." The Embassy will be located at the library's reference desk, and its diplomats will be available to resolve any problems you encounter.
2. Each Fast Forward pass you receive will allow you to receive help with a task from a librarian. Each Fast Forward pass you receive can only be used once.
3. In order to win, you will need to be the first group to reach the Final Destination and have completed all the tasks correctly. If the first team to finish has made any errors, the second team to finish has the opportunity to win the game etc.

What You Will Learn in the Process
At the end of this process you should feel confident using several research tools in order to locate multiple types of information sources in a variety of formats.

Sample Route Clues
Route Clue One
Locate the reference book titled, *Worldmark Encyclopedia of Cultures and Daily Life*, and use it to answer the following questions about your team's country. Your next clue will be located near this set of encyclopedias.

1. What day do the Jamaican people celebrate Independence Day?
2. How do you say "fabulous" in the language spoken by Rastafarians?
3. What types of information are the books in the library's reference collection useful for locating?

You will need to bring your answers to the "Final Destination."

Route Clue Two

Your team's next goal is to locate a sound recording of Bob Marley's *Exodus* in our music library. Your next clue will be located with this recording.

In order to win the game, you will need to bring the sound recording with you to the "Final Destination."

Route Clue Three

For your next challenge you will need to find the following **New York Times** article in the library's microfilm collection:

Earthquake in Jamaica. Published: July 12, 1888. Page 8.

Your next clue will be located nearby.

In order to win the game, you will need to bring the article with you to the "Final Destination."

Route Clue Four

For your next challenge you will need to go to the library's Web site and use one of the library's databases to retrieve an article about your country. The article's title *must* contain the name of your country

Name of the database used: _____

Once you have printed your article, present it to the U.S. Embassy in order to receive your next clue.

In order to win the game, you will need to know the name of the database you used to access the article AND you will need to bring a print out of the article with you to the "Final Destination."

Route Clue Five

For your final task you will need to locate a book of fiction set in Jamaica. The book you are looking for will bring you to tears, and it was written by a jewel of an author. It was published in 1997. If you are successful, this book will lead you to the "Final Destination."

In order to win the game, you will need to bring this book to the "Final Destination.

Pit Stop

Go to the library's circulation desk in order to receive your next clue.

Roadblock

The Roadblock gives you the power to delay one of the opposing teams for three minutes. You can use this pass at any time. To do so, send one of your team members to the U.S. Embassy with this pass. The embassy will dispatch a "Customs Agent" to enforce the Roadblock.

Fast Forward

Save time by getting a librarian to help with a task of your choosing. Ask for help at the library's reference desk.

This pass is good for help on only one task.

CHAPTER 15

Electronic Portfolios as a Means of Authentic Assessment

William Jefferson and Eloise M. Long

Authors' abstract: The use of portfolios as documentation of professional growth and competence has been well established in many professions. In an effort to provide our students with a vehicle for collection and presentation of this documentation, we offered a course in which participants developed and published an electronic portfolio that referenced content and academic standards, and incorporated multimedia and relevant linkages. This course was taught in a traditional computer lab, but the class had a non-traditional composition; it was made up of both graduate and undergraduate students. In this chapter we will focus on the development, presentation, and evaluation of the course.

Editors' notes: Will and Ellie emphasize the authentic experiences which students can gain during the process of learning. These authors use student portfolios to track the actual learning experiences encountered during a course that they co-teach. They encourage the students to push themselves, by including a self-reflective assignment which asks (1) What? (2) So what? and (3) Now what? (Doug's students sometimes are heard mumbling these questions when he teaches a class. "What is he trying to say?" "So what in the world am I doing here?" and "Now what am I going to do, there are still forty-five minutes left to go?")

Introduction

In recent years the use of portfolios has become commonplace in schools and universities to reflect a trend toward "authentic assessment." Wiggins defined authentic assessment as having four common characteristics: (a) the real-life dimension, or true representation of performance in the field; (b) the evaluation of performance against well-articulated standards, which are openly expressed to students; (c) an element of self-assessment, which serves to help students develop the capacity to evaluate their own work; and (d) the expectation that students present their work publicly and orally.[1]

Clearly, an authentic assessment tool should be multi-dimensional and comprehensive; it must be judgment based. Personal research by Brown[2] and Heath[3] points to the portfolio as a tool that could be used to focus on performance and abilities as applied to an individual's field of practice.

In spring 1996 the Council for Teacher Education at Kutztown University passed a recommendation that portfolio development be integrated into all undergraduate professional educational programs. Print portfolios have been a mainstay in assessing the competencies of pre-service educators. At the clinical field experience level, evaluations are supported by evidence included in portfolios that can include teacher work, classroom observations, awards, grants, or other honors, record of books read, videos, Web sites, newsletters, blogs, etc.[4]

The advent of simplified Web-publishing tools and easy-to-use social software *Weblications*, such as PBWiki and Blogger, gives students an electronic alternative to the print portfolio. Research conducted by Dysthe and Engelsen[5] suggests that using an electronic portfolio allows students to gain access to a collection of shared documents and learn from each other. Phelps and Dillard[6] concur and write that a shared ePortfolio improves interaction between the teacher and student and provides a vehicle to display the student's best work.

For these reasons, the course Electronic Portfolios for Librarians and Educators was created and delivered. Currently, the course is offered as an elective for undergraduate and graduate education students, library science majors, and graduate students enrolled in the Instructional Technology Specialist program. In this chapter, we describe the three-credit hour course and its potential application in an information literacy context.

Instructional Goals

Our formal goals for the course are designed to support the Pennsylvania Department of Education (PDE) standards and empower students to:

1. Develop an electronic portfolio highlighting the knowledge they acquired through their Library Science and Instructional Technology coursework.

2. Collect concrete *Library 2.0* evidence to share with prospective employers.

3. Hone skills with MS Office automation tools and learn unique uses for traditional tools.

4. Acquire additional hands-on experience with Web and multimedia technologies.

5. Demonstrate an understanding of real-world challenges and experiences of working K-12 educators and librarians.

6. Work cooperatively in a dynamic group setting and assume a leadership role in the classroom.

7. Reflect on concepts learned and discuss applications of these concepts in a library/educational setting.

In addition to serving as an excellent tool for organizing a student's work, the electronic portfolio helps to organize a student's thinking. A key element of our ePortfolio course was the mandatory reflection paper for each course assignment. As students developed artifacts for their portfolios, they wrote a short paper reflecting on what they accomplished, what they might do differently in the future, and how the exercise could be applied in their current teaching situation or future career as an educator. This activity is consistent with the thinking of Van Wagenen and Hibbard, who suggest that three questions be considered: (1) *What?* (2) *So what?* and (3) *Now what? What* includes a summary that identifies the artifact, while *So what* includes a reflection on what was learned from the experience.[7] *Now what* documents ideas for further learning or changes to be tested.

Instructional Strategy

The official definition of a *portfolio*, according to Campbell, Cignetti, Melenyzer, Nettles and Wyman, emphasizes the organization of the document and its ability to validate professional growth and competence.[8] Although this definition can apply to either print or electronic versions of a portfolio, it is no longer effective to rely on just words to describe our work. We respond to the old proverb, "A picture is worth a thousand words," and heed the words of Kimeldorf and Hagy as they suggest that portfolios "…are a visual medium, the vehicle of NOW."[9]

In the planning phase of the course, we discussed the design of the portfolio shell. Two options seemed obvious. We could teach the students how to develop a CD-ROM-based portfolio or a Web-based portfolio. While CD-ROM-based portfolio development would have been easier to teach, we felt a Web portfolio would be more beneficial to our students for a number of reasons. Most of our students are planning careers as K-12 classroom educators or librarians. Demonstrated abilities with Web development and Web publishing would give our students a competitive advantage when seeking employment. Web portfolios require students to learn more than just Web site development and publishing. Students also learn more subtle skills such as user interface design, creation of platform-neutral artifacts, and video optimization techniques for Web delivery; therefore, our choice was clear—Web-based portfolios would become our course standard.

Artifacts that our students created included interactive games that were designed to help K-12 students learn a variety of information literacy concepts, i.e. the Dewey Decimal system, research strategies, and accessing and using electronic resources.

Examples of this student work and a sample of our ePortfolio template can be accessed online at http://www.kutztown.edu/library/instructional/portfolio_student_ePortfolio.htm. The process of creating electronic portfolios and the resultant products and reflections demonstrate the success our students achieved in meeting the goals and strategies of the course.

Match of Goals and Strategy

We measured student success in the following ways. The practical, real-life dimension was articulated using traditional tools such as Word, Excel and PowerPoint. The graduate students used subject matter derived from their current classroom situation, while undergraduates used material from their field experiences to create educational games, i.e., self-scoring quizzes, Jeopardy-type review games, non-linear learning activities, and multi-path storybooks. The students also created effective animated online tutorials using Wink, a freeware Flash development tool for the PC. In some cases, the final products were used in the K-12 classroom or public library situation and evaluated for their effectiveness.

Secondly, we discussed the expectations and standards for each project. Consistent with our constructivist beliefs, we allowed students to meet the standards by accessing prior knowledge and adjusting to their own learning styles. In this manner, we accommodated those who had considerable experience with the various technologies. For example, rather than using our standard ePortfolio Web template, one student created an animated interactive Web portfolio using Flash.

Thirdly, students assessed their work, reflecting on the immediate quality of the project itself and on potential improvements or uses for the project in the future. Barton and Collins stressed the importance of such documentation to transform documents into evidence and assist portfolio developers in articulating their thoughts.[10] The artifact and reflective paper allowed us, the professors, to evaluate the quality of the project as a whole, rather than judging the technical aspects or completeness of each artifact in isolation.

Finally, we addressed the importance of including an exhibition aspect in the portfolio process. In this way, ownership of learning was directed to the student. The course capstone activity was the presentation of the completed electronic portfolio. Each student delivered a fifteen-minute presentation highlighting the various projects that were created during the semester.

Description of the Instruction Session: What Actually Happened?

This was an interesting course for a number of reasons. Since the class was comprised of both undergraduate and graduate students, differentiated assignments were necessary. We used the Blackboard Course Management System (CMS) to facilitate this aspect of our instruction. For most assignments, our graduate students were required to develop more complex artifacts than were expected of our undergraduates. Class discussions also were led by the graduate students, who selected appropriate journal articles and posted "Questions to Ponder" in the CMS discussion forums. Undergraduate students prepared for class by reading the articles and preparing to discuss the "Focus" items posted on the discussion board.

The mixed undergraduate/graduate class environment worked reasonably well. Undergraduate students were able to interact with and learn from the graduate students, many of whom were practicing K-12 educators. This gave the undergraduates an opportunity to ask the inevitable "What is it really like in the classroom?" questions and gain perspectives external to those of their professors.

Final student presentations were delivered in the classroom with both professors and peers commenting on the presentation and contributing to the summative assessment. It was evident from the presentations that the majority of our students had gained confidence in their ability to use the Web medium effectively.

Some students used their portfolios in interview situations. One undergraduate student attributed her success in obtaining her first library job to the Web skills she acquired in the Electronic Portfolio class. Several of our graduate students commented that they were immediately able to apply the tools and techniques learned in our class.

Reflection on the Instruction Session: Lessons Learned

While fine-tuning always occurs after a first effort, we were relatively pleased with our Electronic Portfolio course design. Certainly, the combined section of graduate and undergraduate students was interesting. Undergraduate students had the opportunity to learn from two professors and a cadre of working K-12 educators.

We can also see potential advantages in separating the graduate and undergraduate students. As interest and enrollment in the portfolio course grows, we may do exactly that. A major challenge in teaching technology classes is effectively responding to the wide diversity in computer literacy among the students. This problem is amplified when graduate and undergraduate students attend the same class.

With separate instruction for undergraduate and graduate students, greater differentiation in instruction and tool selection could occur. For instance, with undergraduate students it would be reasonable to use an open source Web tool such as PBWiki as the foundation for their ePortfolio while full-fledged Web development with Dreamweaver would be appropriate and desirable for graduate students. Ideally, we believe that graduate students should also have more latitude to customize assignments. When our students produced a newsletter or instructional module that they were able to use in their K-12 classrooms, that assignment had far more meaning for them than a more generalized group learning activity.

In future offerings of this course, greater effort will be made to articulate the value of the assigned reflective activities. While our students generally produced fine reflections, it did take some time for several students to understand that reflective writing assignments really were required and they were important in their own right. The reflective assignments helped students think more deeply about their work while shifting their focus beyond immediate grade concerns.

While the Blackboard CMS worked well for this course, we would like future courses to have even stronger assignment mapping to PDE, International Society for Technology in Education (ISTE), or Association for Educational Communications and Technology (AECT) standards. This could be accomplished using Blackboard, but might be better facilitated using a purpose-built tool such as Taskstream that allows both uploading of student artifacts and mapping of assignments to specific educational standards.

A clear *win* in this course was the use of standard office automation tools for novel purposes. It is not difficult for one to imagine the collective groan of twenty-five students when the inevitable PowerPoint assignment is given. However, when future librarians learned how to produce a non-linear PowerPoint and began to realize the potential for the PowerPoint to be used as a storytelling tool, the grimaces turned to smiles.

Application to Other Instructional Settings

Electronic portfolio assignments are ideal for helping a student to organize work and demonstrate knowledge acquisition. The portfolio provides a framework that encourages students to develop the abilities needed to become independent, self-directed learners. Educators at the University of South Africa (Unisa) found portfolio assessment to be valuable for a Module in Research Information Skills.[11] The module was developed in concert with the need of master's students to write a thesis. In the module, each student was expected to submit two assignments which were assessed and feedback was given. The students revised their work and then submitted the final portfolio. The portfolio demonstrated the necessary skills for effective retrieval, evaluation, organization, and the use of information for research.

The University of Connecticut incorporated information literacy into its General Education guidelines.[12] The one-credit course required students to do the research for a twenty-page paper. The resulting portfolio included eight sections: Statement of Topic, Concept Map, Research Questions, Research Log, Research Strategy Worksheet, Selection of Online Sources, Annotated Bibliography, and Reflection on the Semester.

The State University of New York system included information literacy in a series of general education mandates.[13] The three-credit general education course, "Oral Communication and Information Literacy," was co-taught by the Communication Department and the Library. The library had three weeks during the semester to teach information literacy skills. The resulting Paper Trail was an annotated portfolio of the research process.

To integrate portfolio assessment in a one-hour or one-credit course the following approaches may prove useful.

Scenario One: Present the students with a general, but narrowly defined research thesis statement. Have the students choose three terms that could be used to search an electronic database on this topic. Direct each student to develop a list of synonyms for each of the identified search terms. Ask each student to try various search term combinations in the database to see which combinations of terms yield the most relevant search results. Ask each student to add their best queries (their search terms and Boolean logic scheme) to a Wiki page so their approach can be shared with and discussed by the class.

Ask the students to work independently and repeat this process with a thesis statement relevant to a research assignment of their own. Have the students publish their synonym lists, best search queries, a brief listing of suitable articles, and a short reflection statement in their electronic portfolio so their work can be reviewed by the professor who assigned the research project.

Scenario Two: Present the class with a broad, ill-defined research thesis statement. Have the class refine the statement into several workable possibilities. Have one student serve as the recorder and write each revision out on a whiteboard or blackboard. Ask each student to write a reflection in their electronic portfolio describing what was wrong with the original thesis statement and what was improved through each successive revision of the statement.

Scenario Three: Ask students to develop working definitions of the following terms: Abstract, Scholarly, Peer-Reviewed, Primary Source, Periodical, AND, OR, and NOT. Have the students develop a query for a full-text, primary source, scholarly document using at least two of the Boolean operators listed. Have the students document the query in their online portfolios by explaining what functions the Boolean operators serve in the query.

By assigning practical work like this, one discovers that development and delivery of an authentic assessment portfolio places the student into the role of both creator and teacher. There is an adage that states "you *really* know something when you can teach it". Electronic Portfolio projects beg to be presented. Any opportunity for the student to present before faculty and peers is an opportunity to build confidence and improve public speaking and presentation skills.

Although the ePortfolio course we offered was a semester-long, three-credit course, our assignments could be broken down into modules that would be appropriate for one or more information literacy class sessions. No matter how you structure your ePortfolio sessions, collaboration with the classroom instructor is essential to validate the authentic assessment process. This collaboration includes identification of information literacy skills to be acquired, the processes and products used to demonstrate competency, reflection and feedback, and, finally, presentation of the artifacts by the students.

We share our best wishes to you in your efforts to integrate authentic assessment and electronic portfolio work into your information literacy instruction. Through our classroom instruction and research, we have found ePortfolio assignments to be effective as a teaching and learning tool and an approach that appeals to our students. We hope this chapter inspires you to consider adding ePortfolio assignments to your future instruction.

Notes

1. Grant Wiggins, "Teaching to the (Authentic) Test," *Educational Leadership* 46 (1989): 41.

2. C. A. Brown, "Planning Portfolios: Authentic Assessment for Library Professionals," *School Library Media Research* 5 (2002).

3. M. Heath. "Electronic Portfolios for Reflective Self-Assessment," *Teacher Librarian* 30 (2002): 19-23.

4. Eloise M. Long, "The Promise of Portfolios: Organizing for Success," *Learning and Media* 48 (2006): 9-10.

5. Olga Dysthe & Knut Steinar Engelsen, "Portfolios and Assessment in Teacher Education in Norway: A Theory-based Discussion of Different Models in Two Sites," *Assessment & Evaluation in Higher Education* 29 (2004): 239-58.

6. S.F. Phelps and K.R. Diller, "Transforming the Library: Applying Multiple Assessment Methodologies to Library Instruction and Planning" (paper. International Evidence Based Library & Information Practice Conference, Chapel Hill-Durham, NC May 6-11, 2007)

7. Linda Van Wagenen & K. Michael Hibbard, "Building Teacher Portfolios," *Educational Leadership* 55 (1998): 26.

8. D. Campbell, P. Cignetti, B. Melenyzer, D. Nettles, and R. Wyman, *How to Develop a Professional Portfolio: A Manual for Teachers* (Boston: Pearson, 2004).

9. Martin Kimeldorf and Barbara Hagy, "Expanding the Definition and Use of Career Portfolios," Quintessential Careers. Available from http://www.quintcareers.com/career_portfolios.html. [Accessed 7 September 2007].

10. J. Barton and A. Collins, "Portfolios in Teacher Education," *Journal of Teacher Education* 44 (1993): 200-9.

11. Ina Fourie and Daleen van Niekerk, "Using Portfolio Assessment in a Module in Research Information Skills," *Education for Information* 17 (1999): 333-52.

12. Shikha Sharma, "From Chaos to Clarity: Using the Research Portfolio to Teach and Assess Information Literacy Skills," *The Journal of Academic Librarianship* 33 (2007): 127-35.

13. Jennifer Nutefall, "Paper Trail: One Method of Information Literacy Assessment," *Research Strategies* 20 (2005): 89-98.

Teaching Resources

URLs to many of the tools discussed in this article and instructional resources we have developed at Kutztown University are provided in the tables below:

Project	Tool	Website
Social Software	Blogger	http://www.blogger.com
Social Software	PBWiki	http://pbwiki.com/
PDF Creation	Acrobat	http://www.adobe.com/products/acrobat
Web Development	Nvu	http://www.nvu.com
Web Publishing	Fetch	http://www.fetchsoftworks.com
Flash Development	Wink	http://www.debugmode.com/wink
Video Editing	iMovie	http://www.apple.com/software
Course Management	Blackboard	http://www.blackboard.com
Course Management	Taskstream	https://www.taskstream.com/pub/

Kutztown University's Learning Technologies Center "Quick Start" Guides	
Acrobat	http://www.kutztown.edu/library/instructional/quickstarts/adobe_acrobat_pdf_format_quick_start.pdf
Nvu	http://www.kutztown.edu/library/instructional/quickstarts/nvu/NVU_Quick_Start.pdf
iMovie	http://www.kutztown.edu/library/instructional/quickstarts/imovie_podcasting/2_iMovie_quick_start.pdf
Blackboard	http://www.kutztown.edu/library/instructional/quickstarts/blackboard/blackboard_quick_start_students.pdf

CHAPTER 16

Picture This: A Snapshot of How Technology Motivates Student Research

Li Zhu and Kathleen Zakri

Authors' abstract: In this chapter we describe a project-based strategy that provides motivation for students to engage in learning how to use the computer and practicing research techniques. To enhance student curiosity and commitment to the learning process, Windows XP Movie Maker provides a creative platform for presentation of research findings based on research topics selected by students. In scaffolding student learning and expanding the breadth of teaching information literacy skills via creative methodologies, "Picture This: Research and Digital Expression," an outcomes-based project, provides opportunity for students to enjoy the learning experience.

Editors' notes: Li and Kathleen provide Li's students with an authentic learning experience which becomes the basis for dialogue regarding research skills. Their students use movie-making software to create a presentation based on their individual research... all future Coppolla's and Spielberg's are encouraged to attend...

Introduction

An open-topic research project can be a powerful motivator to some students; to others, even the phrase, *open-topic*, can be daunting and debilitating. With this in mind, how can instructors help give shape to student work? Whether the topic is My Dream Vacation or an exposition on North American Songbirds, students quickly discover that there is a difference between settling on a broad topic and knowing what to *do* with that topic.

This chapter describes the implementation of a project-based instructional strategy, which addresses the above-named challenges in a constructive, nontraditional way: namely, by substituting the traditional *term paper* genre with that of the *movie*. Specifically, students used Windows Movie Maker to present their research findings on such topics as Women of the Civil War, Cars of the 1950s, and Global Warming. Ultimately, this technology seems to have positively affected student motivation while aiding in the delivery of information literacy objectives.

Instructional Goals

Kathleen Zakri, Dean of Instruction, and Li Zhu, Head Librarian and Information Literacy faculty have worked together to include Introduction to Information Literacy and Research (LIBS100) in its General Education requirements for associate degree programs. LIBS100, a three-credit course taught by Zhu within a series of career-related courses referred to as the Career Core, provides students an opportunity to learn basic research and technical skills while building information literacy competencies essential for personal and professional success. However, since students enrolled in LIBS100 may lack basic computer skills, teaching students how to use the computer is a necessary instructional component. Hence, Picture This: Research and Digital Expression, an outcomes-based project which supports Bloom's Taxonomy Cognitive Domain, is introduced during the beginning of the course to motivate students to acquire computer skills while practicing research techniques.

Picture This supports the instructional goal to provide students an opportunity to develop basic knowledge and skills related to fundamental computer operations that include Windows operating system, file management, and document production as well as application of common computer software. In addition, the project supports the instructional goal to provide students opportunity to identify research techniques for electronic, print, and Internet resources. The instructional goals clearly indicate the complexity in teaching information literacy skills while motivating students to achieve the instructional objectives for the project. Accordingly, upon successful completion of the learning activity, students will:

1. Demonstrate familiarity with the campus network system, exhibiting the ability to create and manage computer files

2. Locate and apply Microsoft Windows XP Movie Maker's menu and tool bar functions to create multi-media movies based on research topics selected by students

3. Exhibit understanding of the general research process, demonstrating ability to select a research topic, formulate research questions, utilize search tools, gather information, and select, evaluate, analyze, and synthesize information using a movie platform

4. Display understanding of APA style, demonstrating ability to identify citation elements and proper citation for electronic, print, and multi-media resources, as well as to establish awareness of multi-media copyright and plagiarism infringement.

To scaffold student learning and expand the breadth of teaching, the instructional objectives for Picture This provide the foundation for other projects assigned in LIBS100, enhancing the connection between the research process and the concept of information literacy. In addition, the instructional objectives support the Association of College and Research Libraries (ACRL) *Information Literacy Competency Standards for Higher Education* for "it enables learners to master content and extend their investigations, become more self-directed, and assume greater control over their own learning."[1]

Instructional Strategy

In order to ensure the project-based instructional strategy effectively fulfills intended instructional goals and objectives, methods such as student-centered instruction, interactive, guided lectures, and use of the metaphor employed in the Picture This project sustain student learning.

Student-centered instruction presents opportunities for students to take ownership of new learning from the selection of a research topic relevant to student interest through the presentation of research findings. To enhance curiosity and commitment in academic and career-related research, in lieu of presenting research findings in a Word document, a multi-media approach, (in this case, the creation of a movie using Windows XP Movie Maker) provides another venue for demonstrating student research findings. Results from student evaluations regarding Picture This indicate that students regard the software to be user-friendly and fun to use. Furthermore, the learning experience provides opportunity to apply creativity when presenting findings from the research process.

Visual, kinesthetic, and tactile modalities of instruction support the student-centered, hands-on learning environment. For example, students are required to research the Internet for images, graphics, and photographs, as well as to find complementary music from multiple sources (e.g., from CDs, the Internet, and students' original music) to create a movie. To augment student success, visual aids such as a projector connected to the campus network system augment interactive, guided lectures that include explanation of the project and rubric, a demonstration regarding how to use Windows XP Movie Maker, and samples of former students' movies.

In addition, when the interactive, guided lecture is coupled with the use of metaphors, the connection between understanding theoretical concepts of information literacy and applying the concepts becomes more apparent to students. While scaffolding computer and information literacy teaching and student learning, the employment of a *party planning* metaphor captures students' interest and ultimately leads to a basic comprehension of the research process.

Prior to the introduction of Picture This, students discover how conducting research is similar to organizing a party, the process of which can be broken down into steps. Step 1: Deciding on a party theme sets the initial parameters for party planning, just as selecting a topic determines the breadth and depth of the proposed research. Step 2: Determining materials needed to support the party's theme is a necessary task, just as identifying information is needed to support the research question. Step 3: Establishing where and how to find the party materials is essential to successful planning, just as accessing and finding information is critical to providing evidence to support a hypothesis statement. Step 4: Ascertaining the best places to purchase party materials contributes to planning a quality event, just as selecting and evaluating information enhances the validity of the research findings. Step 5: After careful scrutiny, sorting and grouping essential party materials as well as eliminating non-essential materials enhances continuity with the party theme and presentation, just as analyzing and synthesizing the most important information as well as eliminating unnecessary, invalid, or extraneous information is essential to the presentation of the research findings.

The party planning metaphor provides students with a connection between theoretical concepts regarding the research process and the application of the concepts through utilization of prior knowledge as well as prepares students for beginning a journey in utilizing information literacy skills for research and for lifelong learning.

Match of Goals and Strategy

Librarian, Li Zhu, writes, "I designed Picture This: Research and Digital Expression, an introductory, major assessment, to motivate students in developing information and computer literacy skills needed for academic and professional success. As illustrated in table 1, my instructional goals and strategies are grounded in constructivism."

TABLE 1		
The Constructivism Connection for Picture This: Research and Digital Expression		
Constructivist Theory Learning Environments[2]	Instructional Goals for Picture This	Instructional Strategies for Picture This
New learning depends on prior knowledge and experience	Build upon basic computer literacy skills to understand the process for conducting authentic research	Pre-work (use of file management, Internet, selection of research topic and supportive resources) Party Planning Metaphor
New ideas transpire as learners reflect on experiences and adapt ideas to accommodate each new experience	Continue to scaffold learning with introduction of Windows XP Movie Maker to motivate students to take a new approach in application of the research process	Interactive, guided lectures, (e.g., comparison and contrast of two movie samples) Facilitation (e.g., discovery and exploration of Windows XP Movie Maker) Omelet Metaphor Classroom assessment techniques
New learning involves active engagement and significant problem-solving and critical thinking actions	Motivate students to use creative and critical thinking skills to apply technology in conducting authentic research	Individual creation of movies using Windows XP Movie Maker Facilitation Mode Personalized attention
Significant learning transpires via evaluation of former ideas and drawing new conclusions via learning by doing	Continue to scaffold learning via connection between computer and information literacy with conducting authentic research Motivate students to have a heightened awareness of copyright and plagiarism infringement	Cooperative Learning Peer Review Presentation of research findings Evaluation (e.g., use of rubric criterion for student evaluation of research findings and presentation and consequences of multi-media copyright and plagiarism infringement) Student Reflection

In addition to melding instructional goals and strategies with constructivism, Picture This embodies Zhu's philosophy of teaching LIBS100. "I believe that the three main components include how to use a computer effectively, how to conduct research, and how to use information ethically. I view myself as an architect who creates blueprints for teaching LIBS100 that provide an incremental plan for new learning while building upon students' prior knowledge and skills."

Description of the Instruction Session: What Actually Happened?

The General Education curriculum is the means by which Bryant & Stratton College meets its institutional student learning outcome: "... to develop lifelong learning competencies in all students through the development of information literacy skills that assist students to formulate essential questions, research and apply the answers, and communicate the results within the dynamic communities of college, career, and life."[3] The journey begins in LIBS100 where first-term students, traditional and non-traditional adult learners, enrolled in associate degree programs are required to earn three credits in information literacy. Hence, the rationale for the Picture This project is to motivate students who possess varied levels of computer literacy and research experience to use a computer to both conduct research and learn the research process, and to use information ethically for the research project. To complete the requirements for the project, students must (1) create multi-media movies for their own research topics, (2) engage in authentic research, and (3) learn how to use Windows XP Movie Maker to present research findings in a creative format.

A computer lab that houses twenty PCs with access to Microsoft Office and Windows XP Movie Maker, a computer workstation, and a projector connected to the campus network is the starting point for the journey that lasts approximately three weeks and encompasses the preparation and production for Picture This until completion of the learning activity.

Preparation as well as identification of prior knowledge and skills is integral to how effective and meaningful the learning experience becomes for students. Therefore, prior to the in-class Windows XP Movie Maker demonstration, students are asked to utilize basic knowledge and skills gained from individual exploration combined with previous instruction from LIBS100 regarding file management as well as selection of images from the web with complementary music to (1) select a research topic and (2) identify information needed for individual movies. Pre-work is purposely designed and scheduled prior to an in-class demonstration regarding how to use Windows XP Movie Maker to provide continued opportunity for scaffolding knowledge and skills related to computer literacy as well as information literacy.

Via an interactive, guided lecture and demonstration of Windows XP Movie Maker, students commit to and take ownership of the learning process. At the beginning of the project, students learn the rationale for, and the importance of, the research project for LIBS100 as well as the creative format selection and production of the research findings, and receive detailed information regarding the basic project requirements. Next, a compare and contrast instructional approach enables students to view two sample movies. The first movie sample, created in

Windows XP Movie Maker, is reminiscent of a homemade family movie and does not adhere to the standards for crediting intellectual property rights. In contrast, the other movie sample, also created in Windows XP Movie Maker, includes proper recognition of intellectual property rights reflected by appropriate APA citation for all sources. From the demonstration and discussion, students have opportunity to become familiar with Window XP Movie Maker, discover the value of using the software, and understand how to use information ethically. Most importantly, the compare and contrast instructional approach provides opportunity for students to realize the need to analyze, evaluate, and synthesize research findings as well as for LIBS100 faculty to reinforce "citing bibliographic reference in proper style and constructing a reference list in research papers and assignments"[4] which is one of the course outcomes listed on the standardized syllabus.

The lesson continues with a PowerPoint presentation that provides additional information regarding the research project's content, structure, and format as well as a review of an accompanying rubric, which explains the assessment criteria. Additionally, in support of a student-centered instructional strategy, students also learn how they can use the rubric criteria to evaluate their final research findings and presentation. Likewise, a re-examination of the party planning metaphor builds on prior teaching and learning to enhance student confidence and comfort level with the research process.

Students next experience an in-class tutorial regarding basic Windows XP Movie Maker functions. To enhance a visually-supported and methodical explanation, the employment of an *omelet* metaphor captures students' interest and provides the motivation to explore how to use Windows XP Movie Maker software and create a movie that presents research findings.

During the interactive, guided demonstration, students discover how the process for presenting research findings in a movie format is similar to the step-wise process of making an omelet. Step 1: Gathering the varied ingredients is the first step in following a recipe on how to make an omelet, just as gathering videos, pictures, and music is the first step in following the Picture This rubric on how to make a movie. Step 2: Working at the kitchen counter, measuring wet and dry ingredients ensures accuracy and accessibility of all ingredients for making an omelet, just as working in Windows XP Movie Maker's Collection area, importing videos, pictures, and music (already labeled, sorted, and, organized), ensures accessibility of all files for making a movie. Step 3: Gradually adding ingredients to an oiled, preheated pan that is resting on a front stove burner marks the beginning of the process for cooking an omelet, just as dragging and dropping each file, one at a time, to Windows XP Movie Maker's Storyboard feature, marks the beginning of the process for making a movie. Step 4: Adding extra ingredients (e.g., broccoli and tomatoes) not listed in the recipe enhances the texture and taste of the omelet, just as using the Edit Movie function to add extra effects (e.g., transitions and animation) not required in the rubric enhances the presentation of the research findings. Step 5: Transferring the omelet from the pan to a serving plate is the final step in the process, just as using the Finish Movie function and saving the enhanced version of the research findings to a computer or CD is the final, irreversible step in using Windows XP Movie Maker's software.

To provide students opportunity to practice what they have learned about Windows XP Movie Maker, the instructional methodology transitions from an interactive, guided lecture with metaphor approach to a facilitation mode where students use their pre-work (i.e. selection of a research topic and identification of information needed for individual movies) and begin to create their movies.

The facilitation mode, an essential instructional strategy when teaching computer and information literacy skills, allows LIBS100 faculty to connect with students one-on-one to encourage discovery, creativity, critical thinking, problem solving and motivation that is needed to participate fully in a meaningful and successful learning experience. For LIBS100 faculty, providing facilitation supports student success as well as the College's mission to deliver "outcomes-based education and training through a flexible, contemporary curriculum in a personalized environment."[5]

In support of the facilitation mode and classroom assessment techniques (CATs), the instructor should evaluate all aspects of the research process as well as communicate successes and challenges using Windows XP Movie Maker.[6] In like manner, the use of CATs allows the LIBS100 faculty to address students' concerns and motivate them to continue to build upon critical and creative thinking skills.

Subsequent lessons provide additional instructional support via interactive, guided lectures and facilitation. Through these lectures, students receive (1) supplemental resources and materials that provide additional tips on how to use Windows XP Movie Maker, (2) sample APA citations, (3) an activity supporting how to avoid infringement of multi-media copyright and intellectual property rights, and (4) additional online tutorials for using the Windows XP Movie Maker software. During these lessons when LIBS100 faculty transition from the interactive, guided lecture mode to the facilitation mode, students benefit from personalized attention. In the facilitation mode, LIBS100 faculty continue to provide students opportunity to take ownership of the new learning as well as motivate them to enjoy the process by encouraging discovery, creativity, and persistence in using the software as a platform for research findings and participating in a cooperative learning environment that includes peer review. In addition, LIBS100 faculty provide students opportunity to seek individual assistance after class, and if needed, students may request tutor assistance from the Learning Lab. Most importantly, during large group or one-on-one instruction, LIBS100 faculty provide students opportunity to realize the connection between the research process used in the project and in all future research projects for program-related and General Education courses as well as to appreciate how these projects provide opportunity to develop "...basic lifelong learning skills for long-term career success."[7]

In celebration of the learning experience, students present their research findings by showing their final Window XP Movie Maker project where dialog regarding successes, challenges, and opportunities is encouraged. Since students have the freedom to select a topic of their choice, many students conduct research on topics related to personal as well as professional interests, experiences, and life-changing events. Moreover, even though the project requires basic rather than comprehensive research, first-term students receive a solid understanding of the fundamental research elements and begin to develop information literacy competencies that support how the College defines its lifelong learning vision.[8]

Reflection on the Instruction Session: Lessons Learned

We have found that in order to motivate first-term, traditional and non-traditional adult learners, we must design and implement instruction that captures student attention from the onset of the term, that motivates student persistence during the term, and that provides student satisfaction at the end of the term.

Based on her experience in China, Zhu first selected Microsoft Office Power-Point as a tool to capture students' attention and motivate them to learn how to use a computer effectively, conduct research, and use information ethically. She states, "During 2005, my PowerPoint project proved successful and not only captured student interest but also heightened student confidence level and skills. However, in 2006, I found that many of our students from the new cohort were already familiar with PowerPoint software. Hence, instead of motivating and challenging students, the project created apathy among students."

"I continued to search for an alternative approach to capture student interest and motivate them to complete LIBS100 successfully. In December 2006, I received an inspiration for using Windows XP Movie Maker from a personal, family situation. When I learned of my grandfather's illness, in lieu of traveling to China to visit, my husband and I created a family video using Windows XP Moving Maker. The experience gave me the inspiration to use the software for the 2007 student cohort who were taking LIBS100 and resulted in us designing and implementing Picture This: Research and Digital Expression, an initial research project that could be easily completed in the first few weeks of the term."

In general, we believe that using a creative, technical platform provides the opportunity to motivate students to take ownership of the research process. For example, during the spring 2007 semester, we administered a LIBS100 Assessment and Teaching Strategies Survey in Zhu's five classes; findings indicated that thirty-five out of seventy students identified Picture This as their favorite LIBS 100 project. However, we approach the findings with caution for we have also found that taking an innovative approach to research may also frustrate students who lack patience, confidence, or computer literacy skills.

Application to Other Instructional Settings

We believe that technology is a vehicle that provides an opportunity to motivate students to conduct research while using a creative platform to present research findings. However, Windows XP Movie Maker is not the only technology that has the potential to motivate students to conduct research, nor is making a movie the only platform for creatively presenting research findings. We strongly advocate that faculty and librarians explore other available technology (e.g., Microsoft's

PowerPoint, PowerPoint Producer 2003, or Sharepoint Designer 2007) as well as other platforms for presenting research findings that may sustain instructional goals and strategies, enhance the design and implementation of hands-on learning activities, and support information literacy across the curriculum.

Notes

1. Association of College and Research Libraries, *Information Literacy Competency Standards for Higher Education* (Chicago: Association of College and Research Libraries, 2000). Available online from http://www.ala.org/ala/acrl/acrlstandards/information-literacycompetency.cfm

2. Ruth V. Small, *Designing Digital Literacy Programs with IM-PACT: Information Motivation, Purpose, Audience, Content, and Technique* (New York: Neal-Schuman Publishers, 2005), 14.

3. "Bryant & Stratton College 2007 Self-Study" (unpublished document, Bryant & Stratton College, Buffalo, NY, 2007), 146.

4. "Bryant & Stratton College Information Literacy and Research (LIBS100) Course Syllabus" (syllabus, Bryant & Stratton College, Buffalo, NY, 2007).

5. Bryant & Stratton College. *Bryant & Stratton College Official Catalog* (Buffalo, NY: Bryant & Stratton College, 2007), 3.

6. Thomas A. Angelo and K. Patricia Cross, *Classroom Assessment Techniques* (San Francisco, CA: Jossey-Bass, 1993), 154.

7. "Bryant & Stratton College Student Success" (brochure, Bryant & Stratton College, Buffalo, NY, 2007).

8. "Bryant & Stratton College Student Success Model," in "Bryant & Stratton College 2007 Self-Study" (unpublished document, Bryant & Stratton College, Buffalo, NY 2007), Exhibit X.

9. Small, *Designing Digital Literacy Programs with IM-PACT*, 42.

Teaching Resources

Introduction to Information Literacy (LIBS100) Course Outcomes Support Bloom's Taxonomy

Cognitive Domain

Zhu's LIBS100 Instructional Goals Based on Bloom's Taxonomy Cognitive Domain[9]		
How to use a computer effectively	**How to conduct research**	**How to use information ethically**
• Demonstrate familiarity with the computer network system and understand how to connect to the campus network and the Internet. • Know how to use computer communication tools to deliver information, such as e-mail and online chat. • Demonstrate familiarity with online search tools and understand how they work. • Be familiar with using some common application software and demonstrate ability to use the software to create research reports. • Demonstrate the ability to discover the new functions of the software and the ability to select the appropriate software for the research report.	• Understand the basic research process. • Demonstrate the ability to define a worthwhile research topic. • Demonstrate how to determine the information needed for the research project. • Demonstrate how to find the information needed for the research project. • Demonstrate the ability to select and evaluate the information resources. • Demonstrate the ability to analyze and synthesize the information for the research project. • Demonstrate the ability to transfer research skills to other research projects.	• Demonstrate the awareness of using information ethically, such as copyright issues and plagiarism infringement. • Understand the general rules regarding the citation of sources. • Demonstrate the ability to identify the basic citation elements, such as author, date of the publication, for different types of information sources. • Demonstrate the ability to understand in-text citation and the References List. • Demonstrate the ability to create detailed citation for the research report, such as how to format the entire research paper in APA format. • Demonstrate the ability to transfer the knowledge learned from using APA citation style to using other citation styles.

Picture This: Research and Digital Expression Project Rubric

Picture This: Research and Digital Expression Project Rubric Required Elements	Excellent 10-9.0	Good 8.9-8.0	Fair 7.9 -7.0	Poor 6.9 & below	*Total Points*
Selection of an original, meaningful research topic that is related to a personal or professional interest (10 points)					
Creation of an interesting title and sub-title that captured the identified audience's attention (10 points)					
Selection of appropriate, inspiring, humorous and informative content that does not include violent or graphic images or music (10 points)					
Selection of a minimum of 8 quality images that may include scanned pictures, digital photos, or digital videos (10 points)					
Identification, selection and use of a minimum of 2 quality pictures, images or videos from the Internet, scanned pictures or images from print sources, or any non-published digital images or videos (10 points)					
Selection and insertion of appropriate, non-offensive music from CDs, default music stored on a computer in the Music folder, the Internet or students' original music that complements the text and images (10 points)					
Creation of text with corresponding images that includes an introduction, body and conclusion and presents a well-written blend of original ideas with research findings, without infringement of plagiarism (10 points)					
Appropriate utilization of APA style and correct citation for all sources (10 points)					

Picture This: Research and Digital Expression Project Rubric Required Elements	Excellent 10-9.0	Good 8.9-8.0	Fair 7.9 -7.0	Poor 6.9 & below	Total Points
Demonstration of the ability to create and save movie project file in the designated folder (10 points)					
Submission of project on designated due date (10 points)					
Sub Total of Points without Extra Credit					
Extra credit: Utilization of special effects available in Movie Maker or saving movie to a CD (10 points)					
Final Total Points					
Project Grade (A=100-90 points, B=89-80 points, C=79-70 points and F= 69 and below					

Bringing Them into the Community: Innovative Library Instructional Strategies for International and ESL Students

John Hickok

Author's abstract: U.S. universities are experiencing high numbers of international students, and even higher numbers of incoming ESL (English-as-a-Second-Language) students. Although academic libraries often do not have special outreach efforts for these students, they face unique challenges that warrant such effort. In this chapter I describe reaching and teaching ESL students through three instructional strategies: Inviting (going to them via clubs and classes), Involving (providing contextually-rich experiential learning sessions), and Interfacing (improving one-on-one communication). The underlying pedagogical philosophy of these strategies is experienced-based learning, as formulated by the developmental psychologist Vygotsky.

Editors' notes: John has created a Student-Centered program for a group of students for whom English is not their first language. By engaging them in various encounters, he assists these students to feel comfortable in the completely unfamiliar U.S. academic library environment. John uses an excellent example of such confusion when he mentions gubflah. He writes, "Congratulations! You have just won a brand new gubflah!" (What the heck is a gubflah? ~Doug.) (Sounds like the name of a rock band ~Ryan.)

Introduction

The number of international and ESL (English as a Second Language) students in higher education is growing and growing rapidly. There are currently a half-million international students in the U.S.,[1] and over ten million K-12 children—where English is a second language at home—approaching college age.[2] These students arrive at universities with special challenges, different from homegrown English-speaking students. Yet very few academic libraries offer specialized outreach or instruction to these students, to help them integrate into the academic community. By this, I mean learning the research expectations the U.S. academic culture places on them, and knowing how to successfully meet those expectations. This chapter will model how one academic library—the California State University Fullerton (CSUF) Pollak Library—*is* offering such specialized outreach and instruction.

Before beginning, however, a brief mention of the challenges that international and ESL students face is appropriate. One is a cultural challenge. During 2005-2006 I spent a year living in Asia on a research grant to study libraries there. I visited over two hundred libraries in all fifteen countries of East and Southeast

Asia. My observations verified that the library experience children in different Asian countries have can vastly differ from that which children growing up in the U.S. have. Some examples follow. A U.S. child will typically grow up accustomed to open stacks and circulating books while a child from an Asian country may not. A U.S. child will likely be taught—via U.S. culture—that librarians are helpful information experts, while a child in an Asian country may experience librarians as merely unskilled workers. A U.S. child may have a likely chance of growing up with a school library of supplemental reading books, while a child from an Asian country might experience a school library (if he or she has one at all) as mostly just a study hall or textbook repository. Thus, when students from another country arrive in the U.S. with their experience (or schema, to use an educational term) of what a library/librarian is all about, and then encounter a U.S. library/librarian that is vastly different from their lifelong experience, it yields a cultural disconnect and a challenge to overcome.

Library literature in the past decade confirms this situation. Liu, for example, found that international students faced challenges in using U.S. academic libraries due to unfamiliarity with open shelves, classification, and other common features.[3] Liao, Finn, and Lu found that opting for the Internet, rather than available library electronic resources, was higher among international students, due to their unfamiliarity with such resources.[4] And Jackson noted that international students desired more orientation and training in unfamiliar services such as interlibrary loan and reference appointments.[5] Obviously, it would be erroneous to generalize *all* libraries' conditions abroad as the same, or *all* international students as the same. A student growing up using the Taipei, Taiwan Public Library (TPL), for instance, would likely feel comfortable in a U.S. library, due to the TPL's adoption of many U.S. library characteristics.

Another challenge is the language barrier. Although international students may have met the minimum English proficiency requirement to enter the university—e.g., a passing score on the Test of English as a Foreign Language (TOEFL)—they may still struggle with English vocabulary. For example, while *magazines, newspapers, and journals* may be recognizable, the term *periodicals* may be entirely unfamiliar. Add to this some cultural-communication issues—such as the habit of smiling/nodding/agreeing to be polite even when not understanding, as is common in some cultures—and the challenge of understanding unfamiliar words or explanations becomes even greater. As one author, writing about international students in libraries, noted, minimum proficiency in English is "far from a guarantee of cultural understanding or good communication."[6] For ESL students who have grown up in the U.S., there is the advantage of having already likely experienced school or public libraries. However, even with this advantage, the extra challenges of unfamiliar vocabulary, misspellings in computer searches, or mixing languages (Spanglish, Chinglish, etc.) can make understanding the library more difficult. One researcher in this area noted that when ESL students appear reluctant to respond in a reference or instruction setting, it may be due to the extra internal translating time they are having to employ.[7]

Instructional Goals

At CSUF's Pollak Library, instruction is a high priority. Serving a campus of thirty-six thousand students, the library conducts over six hundred librarian-taught sessions—for nearly eighteen thousand students—annually. A growing percentage of those thirty-six thousand students are international and ESL students. Reaching those students, in particular, has become a priority, due to the extra challenges these students face in understanding libraries. The library's mission statement affirms this commitment to offering specialized services for the campus' cultural diversity.[8]

Instructional Strategy

The traditional Library Instruction (LI) lecture/demo presents several obstacles for international and ESL students. First, the *pace* of these LI sessions can be intimidating. Sometimes in an effort to cover as much as possible in a fifty-minute time frame, librarians end up speeding through concepts. Often, international and ESL students cannot keep up. Second, the *content* of a traditional LI session includes a substantial amount of jargon, which tends to overwhelm international and ESL students. LIs are packed with specialized vocabulary—*ILL, Circulation, Call numbers*, etc.—and without context or understanding, the terms become meaningless. To demonstrate this, imagine hearing this sentence: "Congratulations! You have just won a brand new *gubflah*! Take this coupon to any retail location where *gubflahs* are sold to redeem it; you'll be glad you did!" Are you excited about your new *gubflah*? Perhaps, but more likely, you don't know whether to be excited or indifferent, in that you have no idea what *gubflah* means! And third, the *instruction style* raises difficulties for students who do not readily connect with the material. The lecture/demo style is passive, un-involving, and fails to bring in *experiential context* into the learning.

In a departure from the traditional LI lecture/demo, three innovative strategies have been developed in the CSUF Pollak Library; these can be summarized as The Three I's: Inviting, Involving, and Interfacing.

Inviting

Inviting involves *going to* international and ESL students, not just waiting for them to come to the library on their own. How is this done? By going to venues where they congregate: student cultural clubs (e.g., the Chinese Students Association, the Thai Club, etc.), activities hosted by the International Office, ESL classes, and more. Our intent, of course, is not to just show up unplanned, but to go to these venues with a presentation on *their* culture, and the library's relationship to it. Studies repeatedly show that students learn new concepts better in a context that is more interesting, essential, or familiar to them. For instance, a student might be eager to learn databases that track sports stats or stock quotes, but indifferent about learning similar databases for academic purposes. Thus, an outreach visit to an international or ESL group has to be in the context of something interesting/familiar to them, like their home country. The purpose of the visit to these students is not to begin teaching library skills; it is to acknowledge their country/culture, and introduce the library as a bridge. This could take the form of a brochure with materials the library has about their country/culture or in their language; or it could take the form of a lively, musical PowerPoint show, filled with slides of their country (Compiled from where? From library materials, of course.) The purpose of the Invite strategy is to give students a *reason* to come to the library, and introduce the library as a bridge between their culture/experience and U.S. culture/experience. After our initial visits with international and ESL student groups, follow-up sessions, actually in the library, can be scheduled via the club presidents, ESL instructors, etc. By working with these leaders, we gain better interest from students. Working with club presidents, for example, our session may be billed as "The Library: A Bridge between Your Culture and U.S. Culture;" working with ESL teachers, our session may go as "Introducing the Library: The Information Hotspot for Completing your Assignments."

Involving

Involving is the next strategy. It calls for moving away from a direct instruction style and adopting more experiential instruction. This strategy entails having students participate by going to the open shelves, rather than just being told about them; having students actually look up books on their country, rather than just seeing a demo about it; having students collaboratively assemble a correct APA citation, rather than just be given a handout about it; and all the while, comparing what they are experiencing with their own schema—their home context—of libraries.

Experiential instruction draws from student-centered learning (Constructivist) pedagogy, and in particular, the ideas of Russian psychologist Lev Vygotsky. Vygotsky taught that children learn by being immersed in their societal environment and by observing, participating, and interacting in experiences.[9] For example, where Behaviorism would teach children to stack blocks via repetitive drills and commands, Vygotsky's experiential learning would have children immersed in a room of other children stacking blocks, where they would interact and work together. Vygotsky's concepts are important in the field of teaching ESL, as well, in that language is more effectively learned by being immersed in an experiential environment in which social interaction leads to individualized learning.[10] During these sessions of immersing students in the library environment, instructors should continuously point out similarities and differences between libraries in their countries and the U.S. library they are in. A side-by-side comparison list can even be used. This brings *their* background and experience into the picture, so they have some basis, or experiential context, in which to compare and relate what they're hearing and seeing.

This was easy for me to do for international students from Asia as I lived in Asia for a year studying their libraries. For those without such direct knowledge of libraries abroad, you can make efforts to learn—query the students themselves, consult visiting foreign scholars, talk to faculty and U.S. students who have lived abroad, and study the most recent library literature on different countries—for example, Robert Stueart's 2007 book on international library comparisons.[11]

Interfacing

Finally, Interfacing refers to a better way of interacting with these international and ESL students. In a traditional lecture, the librarian/instructor is the authoritative modeler. Often, this translates to one-way communication: the librarian imparts, the students receive. Interfacing involves more two-way communication, such as soliciting information about their libraries *first*, then sharing information, such as similarities or differences. It involves *scaffolding*, a term used by Khami-Stein and Stein—a Library and TESOL (Teachers of English to Speakers of Other Languages) research team—to denote gradually introducing new information built upon already known information.[12] For example, simply saying "After you find books, take them to Circulation" may be incomprehensible input. Students may have no idea what you mean by *Circulation* (Is it the door turnstiles? Is it the air vent?) Rather, saying "After you find books and you want to take them home, or check them out of the library, take them to the Check-out, or *Circulation* Desk" is more comprehensible. This simple rewording provides them the term check out, which is more easily understood, and also the newer term of circulation.[13]

Match of Goals and Strategy

The strategy of The Three I's described in this chapter is an innovative approach for an academic library serving international and ESL students. The strategy matches the goals of reaching out to these target populations well. This strategy is not intended to be a replacement for other library instruction efforts—such as library instruction sessions for specific courses, in which international and ESL students may be present—but rather, a supplemental effort.

Description of the Instruction Session: What Actually Happened?

Inviting

During the 2006-2007 school year, the strategy of The Three I's was implemented at the CSUF Pollak Library. First, for Inviting, I attended the campus's annual club week promotion (outdoor booths of all the student cultural clubs). I introduced myself to club presidents, told them of my interest and experience in their countries, and then promoted the wonderful resources on their countries in the library. I gave them a library brochure about their country (e.g., hotlist of books, databases, videos, etc. relating to their country) and offered to make a short, lively presentation to their club at some future time. The results were encouraging: 90 percent responded in the affirmative. Club presidents were impressed to see someone so interested in their culture. Similarly, I approached the ESL department and ESL instructors one-on-one. I said "if you have many students from Asia in your class, I have a lively, ten-minute PowerPoint show about their countries I would like to bring in." In my case, the targeted students were from Asian countries. Your own targeted students, and preparation, may be for students from other countries/cultures: Latin America/Latino, Middle East, Africa, etc.

Later, at different times during the year, I then made my presentations at *their* club locations or classrooms. Having actually traveled to Asia and taken photos of libraries there, I was able to show those as part of my lively presentation. I had fun with this! This was not a dry, academic lecture. And it was not an instruction session, per se, either, but rather, a session to merely generate interest. I brought refreshments too: bags of popcorn and gallon jugs of fruit punch—rather inexpensive, so typically within consideration of a library's budget. I had music from their countries playing in the background as they arrived as well—some from the library's music collection, others from online sites recommended by the club president. I then enthusiastically talked of my visit to their countries and libraries, plus the great resources the library had—noted on a brochure I handed out.

Involving

Second, for Involving, I planned follow-up sessions—in the library this time—with the various groups. During these sessions I made an effort to bring in the context of their specific culture.

FIGURE 1. Brochure Created For the Thai Club

Library Materials all about THAILAND

In the CSUF library

☑ Books about Thailand!
☑ Videos about Thailand!
☑ Articles about Thailand!
☑ Maps of Thailand!

Come check them out!

Two column comparison sheets between their country/culture and the CSUF library—of different library features/services—were handed out. They talked

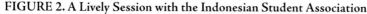

FIGURE 2. A Lively Session with the Indonesian Student Association

together collaboratively in filling out their column. Following that, I did *not* begin lecturing on the other column, for them to dutifully fill-in the blanks. Instead, we headed around the library, to *experience* the library. The word *tour* is an automatic turn-off to some librarians, because it conjures up images of traipsing crowds, low retention results (i.e., absorb now, forget later), and something not academic enough to devote librarian time to. But that is only one way of thinking of tours. For international and ESL students, tours are experiential learning. They allow for *not just writing down* that "bound journals look like books but they're not," but for actually seeing them, handling them, and commenting on them with their friends. The students are actually seeing the library in action. Thus, during this tour, they see and experience actual circulation transactions, open-shelf browsing, and reference exchanges. This last item, in particular, is so important for international students to experience. Many international students have an impression of librarians as unhelpful or untrained; or, equally problematic, have a cultural tradition of "don't bother the person working." Both of these can be overcome by having them witness and experience friendly, helpful, and impressive reference exchanges.

FIGURE 3. Two Column Comparison Sheets between Their Country/ Culture and the CSUF Library

Comparison of your home country (university) library and CSUF's library

Home library [ ] CSUF library

Shelves
1. Open for browsing?
2. How are the books arranged?

Checking out books
1. How do you check out books?
2. How many can you take? (& for how long?)

Reference help
1. How friendly/helpful are the librarians?
2. When & where is help available?

Magazines/Newspapers/Journals
1. Where are they? Are there many?
2. Can you photocopy them? Take them home?

Library catalog
1. Is the catalog electronic (online)?
2. Is it accessible outside the library?
3. How do you look up a book?

Databases
1. What kind of article databases are there?
2. Are they accessible outside the library?
3. How do you look up an article?

Following the experiential tour, I then continued the session with hands-on experiencing of electronic resources (online catalog, databases, etc.) I conducted sample searches—particularly for items on their country—in almost a role-play scenario, as if I were them. Students once again compared, on their comparison columns, their own background/experience of electronic resources, to what they were witnessing. In the case of the ESL classes, they had an assignment from their teacher to find specific resources, so the peer collaboration—all of them comparing what searches worked, what searches didn't—was abuzz with activity. The depth of actual learning from this experience (actually having that "ah ha!" moment) was—as I observed—far greater than what would have resulted from a traditional library lecture only.

Interfacing

Finally, I employed the many suggestions of Interfacing while meeting with the students. As an ESL instructor myself, I have gotten in the habit of doing these almost automatically, for example, defining new terms immediately within sentences. When mentioning databases, for instance, I routinely say "...the databases, *which are electronic collections of articles*, are..." For librarians seeking to enhance their interfacing with international and ESL students, I would suggest inviting ESL instructors for an in-service meeting. They would be helpful in explaining common communication hurdles of international and ESL students (e.g., understanding idioms, pronouncing an *r* versus an *l*, etc.) and offering more suggestions for interfacing with them.

Reflection on the Instruction session: Lessons Learned

Implementing The Three I's strategy was a professional delight. I work with international and ESL students all the time anyway, but to do specific outreach to bridge their background experience of libraries with a U.S. library was a joy. Hearing a student remark about a search feature of the online catalog, "Oh, I get it now! This is similar to a button on my university's catalog back home!" made every minute preparing it worth it.

This is not to say, however, that this is an easy task. For one, it is time intensive, and I had to squeeze preparing it in between regular library duties. Thus, I would recommend attempting a team approach, where others can help prepare the country/culture-specific brochures. Another issue is follow-up/post-assessment. I did not create plans for any follow-up visits, or develop any assessment tool to measure learning from this strategy. Informally, of course, I noted results, such as the "Ah ha!" expressions on students' faces. But "Ah ha's" are not exactly quantifiable data. So a recommendation to myself, and others using experiential learning, would be to compare the ESL student's knowledge level at the end of these sessions with that of other students.

Application to Other Instructional Settings

The Three I's strategy falls in the area of supplemental/outreach instruction. It would be difficult to apply this to regular course-specific library instruction sessions, since they would have mixed students—both U.S. and international—with the U.S. students not needing the whole comparative-column experience. However, The Three I's strategy *would* be applicable to any programmatic settings involving international and ESL students. For example, if a university requires all new international students to take an English 100 course, or something similar, where a library segment is included, the strategies of The Three I's could be used.

Notes

1. IIE: Institute of International Education, "Open Doors 2005: Report on International Educational Exchange, International Student & Total U.S. Enrollment." Available online from http://opendoors.iienetwork.org/?p=69692. [Accessed 4 September 2007].

2. NCES: National Center for Education Statistics, "The Condition of Education: Participation in Education: Elementary/Secondary Education: Table 6-2. Number and Percentage of Children Ages 5–17 Who Spoke a Language Other Than English at Home and Who Spoke English With Difficulty, by Selected Characteristics: 2005." Available online from http://nces.ed.gov/programs/coe/2007/section1/table.asp?tableID=754. [Accessed 4 September 2007].

3. Ziming Liu, "Difficulties and Characteristics of Students from Developing Countries in Using American Libraries," *College and Research Libraries* 54 (January 1993): 25-31.

4. Yan Liao, Mary Finn, and Jun Lu, "Information-Seeking Behavior of International Graduate Students vs. American Graduate Students: A User Study at Virginia Tech 2005," *College & Research Libraries* 68 (January 2007): 5-25.

5. Pamela A. Jackson, "Incoming International Students and the Library: A Survey," *Reference Services Review* 33 (February 2005): 197-209.

6. Yoshi Hendricks, "The Japanese as Library Patrons," *College & Research Libraries News* 52 (April 1991): 221-25.

7. Miiam Conteh-Morgan, "Connecting the Dots: Limited English Proficiency, Second Language Learning Theories, and Information Literacy Instruction," *The Journal of Academic Librarianship* 4 (July 2002): 191-96.

8. California State University Fullerton, Pollak Library, *Vision/Mission Statement*. Available online from http://www.library.fullerton.edu/content/AdministrationUnit/General/ LibraryMission.htm. [Accessed 17 September 2007].

9. Lev Vygotsky, *Mind in Society: The Development of Higher Psychological Processes* (Cambridge, MA: Harvard University Press, 1978), 79-91.

10. Patricia A. Richard-Amato, *Making it Happen: Interaction in the Second Language Classroom, From Theory to Practice* (White Plains, NY: Longman, 1996), 38-41.

11. Robert D. Stueart, *International Librarianship: A Basic Guide to Global Knowledge Access* (Lanham, MD: Scarecrow, 2007).

12. Lia D. Kamhi-Stein and Alan P. Stein, "Teaching Information Competency as a Third Language: A New Model for Library Instruction," *Reference & User Services Quarterly* 38 (1998): 173-79.

13. Library literature has an ample supply of additional works on interfacing with international and ESL students. This sampling includes Sarkodie-Mensah, on listening more to them and utilizing writing; Liestman, on avoiding jargon/slang and using examples/analogies; De Souza, on asking better/more focused questions; and Curry and Copeman on not rushing interaction to a premature closure: Kwasi Sarkodie-Mensah, "Dealing with International Students in a Multicultural Era," *Journal of Academic Librarianship* 18 (September 1992): 214-216; Daniel Liestman, "Implementing Library Instruction for International Students," *PNLA Quarterly* 56 (Winter 1992): 11-14; Yvonne De Souza, "Reference Work with International Students: Making the Most Use of the Neutral Question," *Reference Services Review* 24 (1996): 41-8; Deborah Copeman and Ann Curry, "Reference Service to International Students: A Field Stimulation Research Study," *The Journal of Academic Librarianship* 31 (2005): 409-20.

CHAPTER 18

Zines! Librarians and Faculty Engaging Students in Creative Scholarship

Amanda Hornby, Suzan Parker, and Kari Lerum

Authors' abstract: Zines have been recognized by cultural scholars as unique products of knowledge that give voice to marginalized populations and issues. In this chapter we introduce a collaboratively-developed assignment in which students were asked to create a zine in Meanings and Realities of Inequality, an upper-division interdisciplinary course at the University of Washington Bothell. The zine assignment asked students to research, explore, and reflect upon an aspect of social inequality in their community. The assignment required a variety of creative methods—such as interviews, collage, library research, cartoons, poetry and photography—in order to move beyond intellectual abstraction to grapple with the concrete reality of inequality in the community. Students shared and articulated their reflections in a public forum, thus reinforcing their role as producers of knowledge within a broad community context. Creating zines provided the students a useful scaffold in their research process as they worked on their more traditional final research product, a ten-page research paper.

Editors' notes: This chapter is the only chapter included which uses Critical pedagogy as a primary strategy. Amanda, Suzan, and Kari use a project-related assignment to help students to reflect upon an aspect of social injustice, such as the plight of inner-city schools. Students then create zines to illustrate these difficult issues. If you'd like to subscribe, you can contact the authors directly... but hurry, we hear that the postal rate will be increasing soon...

Introduction

Zines have been increasingly recognized by cultural scholars as unique knowledge products that give voice to marginalized populations and issues.[1] Short for magazine or fanzine, a zine is a self-published work written from a personal point of view. The content is any subject the creator cares about, the distribution tends to be small, and the readership tends to be local. Zine authors, or zinesters, are motivated by a desire for self-expression, not profit. Zinesters may work alone but sometimes work collaboratively, and they often consciously resist glossy high-tech mediums, opting instead for tools that illuminate their handmade creation process. As such, zine formats frequently include hand-writing and drawings alongside typeset and photocopied images. Zines have historical roots going back to early American political pamphlets, as well as to underground punk fanzines of the 1960s and 1970s.[2] In the 1980s and 1990s, zine publishing became more prevalent among some youth subcultures in the United States and elsewhere, including third-wave feminists of the Riot Grrrl movement, whose writing, art, and music often centered on the personal politics of body image, sexuality, feminism, abuse and sexual assault.[3]

This chapter describes an assignment in which students were asked to create and share their own zine in Meanings and Realities of Inequality, an upper-division course in the Interdisciplinary Arts and Sciences program at the University of Washington Bothell. In this course, librarians collaborated with the faculty member to design an assignment and series of instruction sessions that would support students with the resources and skills needed to create successful zines. Through this collaborative effort, we found that zines offered students a creative and personal means to research and write about challenging social issues. The emotional and cognitive processes of producing zines enabled students to develop a more complex understanding of a given social problem. The medium of the zine provided a creative entrée into students' final research papers.

Instructional Goals

Our primary goal for the zine assignment was to facilitate students' emotional and creative engagement with some aspect of social inequality. Creative, emotional, and artistic expression is a worthy goal in and of itself, and we specifically wanted to uphold this as an important moment distinct from the work of writing a critical academic analysis. In our previous experience with evaluating undergraduates' writing, we have observed that students will often either distance themselves too far from the topic as a way of appearing objective, or will become too immersed in their own subjective position to adequately assess alternative perspectives. By creating zines, students would have a safe and uncensored space to explore and develop their personal commitments to the topic, enabling a multi-dimensional understanding of a social inequality. Through this reflective process, we expected that students would find it easier to later critically identify their own position as one of many possible.

We intended for this assignment to highlight the differences in style and purpose between scholarly and non-scholarly writing. Zines are different in flavor and tone from periodicals of academic or corporate publishing: being personally published, having collaborative or blurred authorship, and having a community-oriented nature. The point is not that one or the other is better, but rather to develop in students a consciousness that these genres can serve very different, but important purposes. It was our hope that creating zines would validate students' personal engagement in a social issue by providing a low-stakes space for exploration, and thereby improve the quality and depth of their questions and approaches to the scholarly research for their final project.

Our other learning goals for the assignment highlighted and evaluated the practices and politics of knowledge production. Through the zine assignment, we wanted students to experience themselves as producers of knowledge rather than merely passive receivers to be *banked* with knowledge by the faculty and librarians.[4] It was our hope that the assignment would facilitate recognition that students have the potential to impact the larger community of knowledge and would come to recognize their own relationship to structures of power.

Instructional strategy

Students were asked to create a zine about an aspect of social inequality of their choosing. Zines were to include personal reflections, and a variety of evidence on the topic, such as poetry, photos, and journal articles. Some students supplemented their research with service learning projects to help inform the content of their zines. This provided a vehicle for them to report on what they experienced and learned to a wider community. The instruction sessions were structured as workshops in which students, the faculty, and librarians collaborated together. The first zine workshop helped to explain the zine assignment and the current and historical contexts of zines, which was followed-up by an instruction session on social science research sources to prepare students for the final ten-page research paper. The zine assignment and workshops culminated in a two-hour in-class zine-swap where students read and shared each other's zines.

Within academia, zines have been studied primarily for their historical and sociological significance. Although zines offer a window into out-of-school adolescent literacies, a review of the literature reveals a scarcity of material related to the potential use of zines as a discursive practice within a scholarly context.[5] Added to that is the prevalent view within the zine community about the inauthenticity of zines being appropriated as a pedagogical method within the institution of academia.[6] As an example, in an interview with three adolescent zinesters, author Guzzetti's suggestion for using zines in the classroom is met with skepticism and dismissed as an example of "zine-likeness," at best.

Hodgson defines zines as "texts that exist as overt and self-conscious sites of active resistance against culturally prescribed categories and identities".[7] This echoes McLaren's view of culture as a "field of struggle in which the production, legitimation, and circulation of particular forms of knowledge and experience are central areas of conflict linked to class struggle."[8] Through zine-making, authors are consciously rejecting institutionally endorsed channels for producing knowledge, including academic research. Therefore, the challenge for educators is to maintain the authenticity of the zine purpose and ethic as we ask students to create zines outside their subcultural context.

Duncombe states that the strength of zines "lies not in what they say they will do, but in what they actually are. They are politics by example."[9] Critical pedagogy asks students to move beyond abstraction and to become immersed in the social and political realm in a genuine way that connects beyond the classroom and into the community.[10] We hoped that through the zine assignment, students would make connections to the wider communities and issues in question, and that their zines would have an impact beyond the classroom. One way this was accomplished was through a display of student zines in the Library. Students and faculty certainly do not expect to see student work in an academic library—a place they equate with vetted and approved scholarship. The zine display allowed students to see themselves represented as valued producers of knowledge, and served to legitimatize their own voices as well as the reality of the inequalities they were describing.

Although there are currently very few zine collections in public or academic libraries, the literature reveals an increasing interest in collecting zines as a way to reach out to underserved populations, particularly adolescents. In alignment with the American Library Association's *Library Bill of Rights*, zine collections expand the diversity of the collection, as well as the library's patron base.[11] Bartel, who writes about implementing a zine collection at the Salt Lake City Public Library, makes the case that "all the voices that describe and examine the human condition must be represented in order to preserve our culture, our freedoms, and our ability to learn and choose intelligently."[12] The literature shows evidence that librarians who venture into zine territory must struggle not only with the decision of what merits inclusion in the collection, but also with how best to provide access to them. It is our hope to also draw attention to the potential of zines as a unique teaching tool with the potential to help students develop their research skills.

In developing the zine assignment, we assumed that:

+ Students are active co-constructors of knowledge.
+ Zines provide a space for unheard voices to be heard.
+ Students need to engage with social inequalities of marginalized populations (including those they experience themselves).
+ We all learn from each other—the field of teaching includes students; the field of learning includes faculty and librarians.
+ Reading each other's stories is transformative.
+ Higher education can and should make the world a better place.

Match of Goals and Strategy

We found that the medium of the zine was perfectly matched to the course content focusing on social justice issues and social inequalities. Bell states that "the act of producing cultural products serves to incorporate and introduce new ideas into public discussion" and brings a particular community together to explore ideas and issues.[13] In keeping with the zine assignment goals, the strategy librarians and faculty employed in the instruction sessions was to present the workshops collaboratively, to validate zines as an authentic medium of expression, and to incorporate students' voices and experiences into the workshops and assignment.

Description of the Instruction Session: What Actually Happened?
Lesson Plan

To ensure successful instruction in the Meanings and Realities of Inequality course, the three of us worked intensively to integrate the course content with the zine assignment, critical thinking, research resources and strategies, and students as creators of knowledge. We created a series of successive, targeted library instruction sessions throughout the ten-week academic quarter. The lesson plan for the zine assignment included three components: (1) a presentation and discussion introducing students to zines; (2) a social sciences research workshop; and (3) a zine-swap and evaluation session.

Introduction to Zines Discussion

The goals of the zine workshop were to introduce students to the zine assignment, to provide an overview of zines, and to validate this unique medium of expression. The zine assignment required students to research, explore, reflect upon, and articulate an aspect of social inequality in their community. The final research paper was also introduced, and its goals included the fact that students would first explore their research topic through a zine. The students' zines were to include a variety of research on the topic, such as ethnographic observations, collage, statistics, library research, illustrations, and handwritten and typewritten entries. Students were asked to target the zine to a broad audience, including the faculty, classmates, others inside and outside the academic community. The class discussed their own experiences with zines, and we supplemented the discussion by defining zines and describing their history and their social and political context. Emphasizing students as creators of knowledge—not just consumers of it—the workshop provided space for student input, inquiry, and the sharing of personal experiences with zines and issues of social inequality. We also created an extensive in-class handout and online class research guide to ensure that students had support and access to a robust set of resources that would help them make zines, understand what zines are, and help them to find zines locally. The discussion and collaboration between students, faculty, and librarians continued beyond the introductory workshop and into subsequent class discussions and individual research consultations.

Social Science Research Workshop

The zine assignment provided students with a useful scaffold in their research process as they worked on exploring their zine's social issue through traditional academic research methods. To facilitate their scholarly work, we held a two-hour research session on academic social science resources during the fourth week of the quarter. In this follow-up instruction session, librarians guided students through generating research questions about social inequality based on the initial informal writing and research they were doing for their zines. This led to a lively discussion about the differences between scholarly research writing and zines, underscoring the importance of evidence and citation within academic research. Students voiced their preference for creating zines over writing research papers, but also noted that they felt more prepared to tackle their final ten-page research paper. Librarians then introduced tools for finding relevant social science research sources—such as subject indexes, databases, and scholarly encyclopedias. Students were given hands-on time in the Library's computer lab during the second hour of class to find relevant scholarly sources, and space to discuss and compare scholarly sources with the non-scholarly sources used in their zines.

Zine-Swap

The two-hour long zine-sharing exercise was held during the eighth week of the academic quarter. As a capstone to the zine assignment and instruction sessions, we held a two-hour in-class peer-to-peer zine-swap where students read, evaluated, and traded zines. Peer review, personal reflection, and a spirit of classroom community were encouraged. Structured somewhat like a poster session, the zine-swap had students walk around the room to read each others' zines and to provide verbal peer-evaluations based on criteria faculty provided. Students had created three copies of their zines and the class (and the excited librarians and faculty) enjoyed reading their classmates' zines. We were thrilled to find students had thoughtfully investigated a wide range of social inequalities, including: racial discrimination, funding inequities between public schools, homelessness, domestic violence, civil marriage rights for same sex couples, human rights in Darfur, and media depictions of women and body image. The workshop differed from traditional peer-review or poster sessions in that students traded zines and even reported giving zines to their families as gifts (imagine students swapping research papers with such enthusiasm!).

Assessment

The students' completed zines provided us with a unique product to assess the success of the zine assignment and workshops. By evaluating the students' zines, we were able to assess their understanding of the topic, their excitement and passion for the issue, and the manner in which they engaged with different types of sources. The completed zines provided evidence of students' ability to express themselves and to articulate their views on a social inequality, as the following examples from student work reveal.

Student Mary Meyer created a spiral-bound, hand-drawn zine, formatted primarily as a comic strip, on the topic of inequalities in education. Through a dramatic narrative of pictures and words, she explained her emerging understanding of this issue:

> "One day I thought, 'Hey, maybe I should be a teacher!'.... So I read *Savage Inequalities* by Jonathan Kozol. I had NO IDEA that some kids have classes in closets. Some kids run thru puddles of toxic waste at recess. And some kids have textbooks that tell them someday we'll send a man to the moon! And that most of these kids are... kids of color. WHY? I could not understand. WHY?"[14]

Through borrowed poetry and images, students such as Jennifer Gaudinier tackled tough aspects of social inequality. By quoting from poems, and researching advocacy events in the community, Gaudinier exemplifies the assignment's emphasis on connecting with the community and informal research in her zine on advocacy for sex workers.[15]

These examples from student zines are evidence of their personal creativity, initial exploration of research resources, and reflective writing. Bartel states that,

FIGURE 1. "Hey! Maybe I Should Be A Teacher!"

FIGURE 2. "These Are Amazing Inspirational Women"

"the idea that everyone can make a difference, that every opinion or experience counts, that individuals have power, is at the core of zine culture."[16] Our students' zines clearly demonstrate this principle.

Reflection on the Instruction Session: Lessons Learned

The zine assignment and workshops engaged students in the research process and actively included them in the instruction sessions. We found that students became personally invested in research topics related to social inequality by first exploring these issues through their zines. The instruction sessions engendered lively classroom discussion and increased student engagement in the research process. The faculty reported that the zine assignment increased the quality of students' final research papers. The zines were successful in providing new points of connection between students, the campus, their families, and the community. By co-creating the zine assignment and co-facilitating the workshops, we were also successful at establishing a high level of faculty and librarian collaboration. The final success story was the popularity of the Library's student zine display, which inspired faculty to think about unique research assignments and garnered interest from the campus literary journal.

A challenge inherent in this assignment was how to authentically reproduce the zine purpose and ethic in a higher education setting. Additionally, because zines are driven by self-expression, many students wrote about very personal experiences relating to their aspect of social inequality. Although self-disclosure of personal information was not a problem for our class, issues of student privacy can come into play. Another challenge with the assignment and our instruction was that some students were not familiar with zines or how to create them. A challenge for the faculty was how to grade and evaluate the zines without losing the zine spirit of creativity and collaboration. After consultation with the students, assignment evaluation was based on criteria that specifically addressed zines' unique format and content, including: creativity, variety of content, cohesiveness of message, and overall appearance. The faculty member and students filled out evaluation forms for each of the zines, but the faculty member was responsible for synthesizing and translating these comments into the final grade. Some students indicated that they wanted us to articulate these formal grading criteria earlier in the process; others said that they were happy that their creativity had not been prematurely constrained.

Application to Other Instructional Settings

Zines can provide a valuable opportunity for faculty and librarians to collaborate. The zine assignment and zine workshop outlined in this chapter can be adapted and applied to a variety of such collaborative instructional settings:

- English as a Second Language course: students can use zines to write about their experiences informally in English, and create zines with images, poetry, objects, and personal pictures from their own culture.
- Composition and/or Creative Writing course: through personal zines, students can write journal entries, engage in creative writing or informal writing on a variety of topics, and hold peer-review sessions through zine-swap workshop.

+ History course: students can study zines as primary sources; students can also create a zine written from the perspective of a historical figure, or particular historical time period.

+ Communication Studies course: students can engage in media literacy by examining an issue—such as the depiction of men or women in advertising—through visual artifacts and personal writing; zines could also be explored as a non-commercial medium of expression.

+ Natural or Environmental Science course: zines can be used to informally write about empirical research or class experiments, to creatively research environmental issues, the use of scrap or recycled paper and objects can be part of the zine assignment.

+ Women Studies course: students can read and research zines created by Third Wave Feminist zinesters; students can use their own zines as a vehicle for educating each other about key issues in Women Studies.

+ First-year experience course: the zine assignment can connect with youth/teen culture; zine-swap workshop can be used to build classroom community.

+ Older returning students: writing for zines can validate their personal stories and be used to connect to scholarly literature through an experience-based issue/topic.

We found that zines offered students a creative and personal means to research and address challenging social issues. The highly engaging process of producing zines enables students to develop a more complex understanding of a given social problem. Zines allow the treatment of a social issue to be moved outside the normal venue of the classroom discussion.

Notes

1. Stephen Duncombe, *Notes from Underground: Zines and the Politics of Alternative Culture.* (New York: Verso, 1997).
2. Julie Bartel, *From A to Zine: Building a Winning Zine Collection in Your Library* (Chicago: American Library Association, 2004).
3. Kristen Schilt, "'I'll Resist with Every Inch and Every Breath': Girls and Zine Making as a Form of Resistance." *Youth & Society* 35 (Sept, 2003): 71-97.
4. Paulo Freire, "Pedagogy of the Oppressed," in *The Critical Pedagogy Reader*, ed. Antonia Darder, et al (New York: RoutledgeFalmer, 2003), 57-68.
5. Barbara J. Guzzetti and Margaret Gamboa, "Zines for Social Justice: Adolescent Girls Writing on their Own," *Reading Research Quarterly* 39 (2004): 408-36; Michele Knobel and Colin Lankshear, "Cut, Paste, Publish: The Production and Consumption of Zines," *Adolescent Literacies in a Digital World*, ed. Donna Alvermann (New York: Peter Lang, 2002), 164-85; Judith Williamson, "Engaging Resistant Writers Through Zines in the Classroom." *The Zine & E-Zine Resource Guide.* Available online from http://www.zinebook.com/resource/engagingwriters.html. [Accessed 1 August 2007].
6. Barbara J. Guzzetti, S. Campbell, C. Duke, and J. Irving, "Understanding Adolescent Literacies: A Conversation with Three Zinesters," *Reading Online* 7 (2003).
7. K. Hodgson, S. Moore, and T. R. Biebrich. "Zines, Women and Culture: Autobiography through Self-Publication." *Canadian Folklore* 19, (1997): 123–35.

8. Peter McLaren, *Life in Schools: An Introduction to Critical Pedagogy in the Foundations of Education.* (Boston: Pearson/Allyn and Bacon, 2007).

9. Duncombe, *Notes from Underground.*

10. Joan Wink, *Critical Pedagogy: Notes from the Real World* (Boston: Pearson/Allyn & Bacon, 2005).

11. American Library Association. "Library Bill of Rights." Available online from http://www.ala.org/ala/oif/statementspols/statementsif/librarybillrights.htm. [Accessed 1 August 2007].

12. Bartel, *From A to Zine.*

13. Brandi Leigh-Ann Bell, "Riding the Third Wave: Women-Produced Zines and Feminisms," *Resources for Feminist Research/Documentation Sur La Recherche Feministe* 29 (fall, 2002): 187-98.

14. Zine excerpt reproduced with permission from Mary Meyer.

15. Zine excerpt reproduced with permission from Jennifer Gaudinier.

16. Bartel, *From A to Zine.*

Teaching Resources

Bibliography of Resources

This bibliography provides several academic studies of zines, as well as the integration of zines into teaching. We also recommend the following resources on how to create zines, and how to start a zine collection in public or academic libraries:

+ Barnard College Zine Library. Available online from http://www.barnard.edu/library/zines.

+ Mark Todd and Esther P. Watson, Whatcha Mean, *What's a Zine?: The Art of Making Zines and Mini Comics.* (Boston: Houghton Mifflin, 2006).

+ Alex Wrekk, *Stolen Sharpie Revolution: A DIY Zine Resource.* (Portland, OR: Microcosm, 2003).

+ ZineWiki. Available online from http://zinewiki.com.

Contributors

Editors

Douglas Cook, DEd, is Distance Librarian and Professor at Shippensburg University of Pennsylvania. He received his MLS from the University of Maryland and his doctorate from the Pennsylvania State University. He was the 2005/06 Chair of the ACRL Education and Behavioral Sciences Section (EBSS). He has recently been elected as a Member-at-large of the Governing Board of the Associated College Libraries of Central Pennsylvania (ACLCP), a regional academic library professional development organization. He has had three book chapters published including "Creating Connections: A Review of the Literature" in *The Collaborative Imperative: Librarians and Faculty Working Together in the Information Universe,* eds. Richard Raspa and Dane Ward (Chicago: ACRL. 2000). With Tasha Cooper, he edited the book, *Teaching Information Literacy Skills to Social Science Students and Practioners (Chicago: ACRL. 2006).* When he is not out taking his Garmin GPS unit and his Sony digital camera for a walk in the woods he may be contacted by e-mail at dlcook@ship.edu.

Ryan L. Sittler is the Instructional Technology/Information Literacy Librarian and Assistant Professor at California University of Pennsylvania. He received his MSLS from Clarion University of Pennsylvania, and is on the verge of completing his MSIT at Bloomsburg University of Pennsylvania. Additionally, he received the H.W. Wilson Scholarship in 2005. Ryan co-authored his most recent publication with Chantana Charoenpanitkul, "Undergraduate Social Work Students and Government Documents: An Integrated Approach to Contextual Learning," in *Teaching Information Literacy Skills to Social Science Students and Practitioners (Chicago: ACRL. 2006).* His previous publication, "Distance Education and Computer-based Services: The Opportunities and Challenges for Small Academic Libraries" appeared in the spring 2005 issue of *Bookmobile and Outreach Services.* A born writer, Ryan has been the Berks County, PA Poet Laureate since 2002. When he isn't teaching students how to find information or use new technology, he may be found trying to beat his own high score on Guitar Hero III or playing poker against some rather famous individuals (one time, it was Montel Williams – true story!) He may be contacted by email at sittler@cup.edu.

Authors

Susan Avery is the Coordinator of Instructional Services in the Undergraduate Library and Assistant Professor of Library Administration at the University of Illinois at Urbana-Champaign. She received an MILS from the University of Michigan, a master of music from the University of Minnesota, and a bachelor of science in music education from St. Cloud (MN) State University. Her research and writing interests focus on creating meaningful instruction for first-year students, faculty/librarian collaboration, and training of those participating in library instruction. She has presented at LOEX, ACRL, ALA, and regional conferences, and has published in numerous publications. She may be contacted by e-mail at skavery@uiuc.edu.

Christine Bombaro is a Collection, Research, and Instructional Services Librarian and Coordinator of Information Literacy at Dickinson College in Carlisle, PA. She earned her BA in history and a secondary teaching certification from Dickinson College. She received her MLS from Drexel University, where her research focused on providing effective library service to patrons whose native language is not English. Her professional accomplishments include archiving the personal papers of Arthur M. Schlesinger, Jr. for the John F. Kennedy Memorial Library in Boston. Prior to joining Dickinson College, Christine was a software trainer for the Supreme Court of Pennsylvania. She is extremely grateful to her colleagues at Dickinson College for their unwavering and unconditional support of "The Seven Deadly Sins of Plagiarism." She may be contacted by e-mail at bombaroc@dickinson.edu.

Debbie Crumb is the Library Instruction Coordinator at Renton Technical College. Her undergraduate degree is in Spanish from Central Washington State University and her MLS is from the University of Hawaii. She has thirty years of experience as a librarian and library administrator in academic, state, and public libraries. She has won the outstanding librarian, faculty or staff member award at each of the past three libraries she has worked. Debbie may be contacted by e-mail at dcrumb@rtc.edu.

Linda Davies is the Science and Biomedical Sciences Librarian in Cardiff University. She has a degree in zoology and librarianship, and a postgraduate certificate in education (Post 16) both from the University of Wales. Linda has twenty-five years experience as a librarian in school, public, and academic libraries and has been teaching information skills in university libraries for twenty years. She is currently joint leader of the RFID (Radio Frequency Identification) Self Service Project for the University Library Service. She may be contacted by e-mail at DaviesL10@Cardiff.ac.uk.

Carl DiNardo is a Reference and Instruction Librarian at Lock Haven University of Pennsylvania. He holds a BS in turfgrass science from the Pennsylvania State University and a MSLS from Clarion University of Pennsylvania. Presently, his research interests include reference and instruction methods vis-à-vis current and emerging technologies and promotion of library services in the academic setting. He may be contacted by e-mail at codinardo@gmail.com.

Dawn Eckenrode is a Reference and Instruction Librarian at SUNY Fredonia.

She received an MLIS from the University of Texas at Austin in 2002 and a BS in journalism from Ohio University. Over the course of her career, she has taught library instruction classes for a wide variety of subject areas in both community college and university settings. Her interests include library outreach initiatives, as well as innovative approaches to library instruction that actively engage students in the research process. She may be contacted by e-mail at Dawn.Eckenrode@fredonia.edu.

Lyda Ellis is an Instruction Librarian and Assistant Professor at the James A. Michener Library of the University of Northern Colorado. She earned her MLIS from the School of Library and Information Studies at the University of Alabama. She also holds an MA in history from the University of Alabama and a BA from Meredith College. She teaches a credit-bearing research course titled "LIB 150: Introduction to Undergraduate Research" which is taught both traditionally and online. Additionally, she offers library instruction for Northern Colorado's Center for International Education and the Center for Honors, Scholars, & Leadership. She works as the Student-Athlete Liaison and she is the subject specialist for criminal justice. She may be contacted by e-mail at lyda.ellis@unco.edu.

Susan M. Frey is a Reference/Instruction Librarian at Indiana State University. She holds a BA in art history from SUNY Stony Brook, an MS in library science from Long Island University, and an MLS in liberal studies from Indiana University. She has presented nationally for such organizations as SLA, LOEX, and the Popular Culture Association, and is published in journals such as *Reference Services Review* and *Collection Building*. She also reviews for *Choice* and *Reference Reviews*. Susan has recently been invited to join the Library & Information Services editorial board of MERLOT. Her professional interests center on teaching and learning, educational technology, and information and society. She is currently studying the image of the librarian in Cold War spy novels. She may be contacted by e-mail at sfrey@isugw.indstate.edu.

Renata Gibson is Instructor/Public Services Librarian at Northwest Vista College. She earned her MSIS from the University of Texas at Austin and her BA in art history from the University of California at Davis. She is interested in how active learning and new social software technology can make students more information literate. She may be contacted by e-mail at rgibson13@mail.accd.edu.

Jim Hahn is Orientation Services Librarian at the Undergraduate Library of the University of Illinois at Urbana-Champaign. He received an MS in library and information science and an AB in history from the University of Illinois at Urbana – Champaign. His research and writing interests include mobile learning and first-year and transfer student success. He is a book reviewer for *Library Journal* and has published in *Library Mosaics*. He may be contacted by e-mail at jimhahn@uiuc.edu.

John Hickok is the Coordinator of Library Instruction at California State University Fullerton (CSUF), and an adjunct instructor for the ESL and TESOL departments at CSUF. He holds an MLIS from UCLA (1995) and a master's in TESOL from California State University L.A. (2001). His research and writing interest is in library instruction and information literacy of international and ESL students. He has spoken on this topic at many international library and educational conferences, and during 2005-2006, visited all fifteen countries of East and Southeast Asia to research their library instruction and information literacy efforts. John is the CSUF chapter president of Phi Beta Delta, the international scholar's society, and is a member of ALA's International Relations Round Table. He may be contacted by e-mail at jhickok@fullerton.edu.

Amanda Hornby is the Reference and Instruction and the Media and Technology Studies Librarian at the University of Washington Bothell/Cascadia Community College Campus Library. She earned her MLIS from the Information School at the University of Washington, and holds a BA in English literature from Lewis and Clark College. She recently presented on the use of new media in library instruction at ALA conferences in Seattle and Washington, D.C. Her research and writing interests include new media and human rights films. She may be contacted by e-mail at ahornby@uwb.edu.

William Jefferson is Assistant Professor and Library Learning Technologies Center Coordinator at Kutztown University. In that capacity, he is responsible for delivering educational technology training to the Kutztown faculty community. He also teaches graduate and undergraduate microcomputer and electronic portfolio courses in the College of Education's Instructional Technology program. He holds an MS in educational technology from Lehigh University and an MS in library science from Clarion University of Pennsylvania. He also works part-time as a Reference Librarian and Computer Specialist at Nazareth Memorial Public Library in Nazareth, PA. Avocationally, he enjoys golf and spending time with his wife Jeanette. He may be contacted by e-mail at wjeffers@kutztown.edu.

Anna Montgomery Johnson is a faculty librarian at Mt. Hood Community College in Gresham, OR, where she coordinates reference services and the library instruction program. Anna received an MS from the Simmons College Graduate School of Library and Information Science. She earned a BA in English literature from the College of William and Mary, where she was awarded the G. Glenwood Clark fiction prize by the Society of Alumni. As a veteran short story writer and new librarian, Anna is making her first contribution to library literature by writing about storytelling. She may be contacted by e-mail at anna.johnson@mhcc.edu.

Kari Lerum, PhD, is Assistant Professor in the Interdisciplinary Arts and Sciences program at the University of Washington Bothell, where she teaches courses in inequality, sexual politics, research methods, feminist theory, global health, and social justice. She earned her MA and PhD in sociology from the University of Washington Seattle, and her BA from Pacific Lutheran University. Her research focuses on the intersections of sexuality, culture, institutions, and power. Past publications include ethnographic research on sex work and other forms of service work; her current research focuses on sexuality education for children and adults on the local/domestic front, and HIV/AIDS activism for sex workers on the global scale. She may be contacted by e-mail at klerum@uwb.edu.

Eloise M. Long, EdD, is Associate Professor and the chair of the Department of Library Science and Instructional Technology at Kutztown University. In addition to chair responsibilities, she teaches library science and technology courses and supervises clinical field experience students. She received a EdD in educational leadership from Immaculata University, a certificate of advanced study in technology from Chestnut Hill College, and a MLS from Kutztown University. She served as an elementary school librarian in Wilson (West Lawn) and Parkland school districts. She is a member of the Board of Directors of the American Association of School Librarians (AASL). She may be contacted by e-mail at long@kutztown.edu.

Kathleen Lowe is Associate Professor and Reference and Instruction Librarian at the University of Montevallo, Montevallo, AL. She received a BA in history from The Ohio State University and an MLS from the University of Alabama. She joined the faculty at Montevallo in 1996. She attended the first ACRL Information Literacy Immersion Institute in 1999 in Plattsburg, NY. Her research interests include teaching, collaboration in the academy, and the history of women in Alabama particularly the role that the University of Montevallo played in women's education. She co-authored "Launching a Learning Community in a Small Liberal Arts University" with Dr. Glenda Weathers, which was selected by the ALA's Instruction Round Table as one of the "LIRTs Top Twenty" library instruction articles of 2004. She may be contacted by e-mail at lowek@montevallo.edu.

Julie Maginn is Assistant Professor and Access Services Librarian at Raritan Valley Community College in New Jersey. She holds a BA in history from Rutgers University, an MLIS from the School of Communication, Information and Library Studies at Rutgers University and is in the process of working toward an MA in leadership and public administration from Centenary College. She has been the editor of the New Jersey Library Association's College and University Section/ACRL New Jersey Chapter newsletter since 2006. When not trying to improve her library instruction sessions, she enjoys watching B horror movies, checking the weather... and of course, playing games. She may be contacted by e-mail at jmaginn@raritanval.edu.

Judy McMillan is Instructor and Public Services Librarian at Northwest Vista College. She served on the Program Planning Committee for the 2007 Texas Library Association Annual Conference and has held leadership positions in various professional library organizations. Judy is an advocate of active learning in library instruction. Her most recent publication is "Faculty Outreach: A Win-Win Proposition," *Reference Librarian* 82 (2003). She may be contacted by e-mail at jmcmillan@mail.accd.edu.

Nigel Morgan is a Subject Librarian at the Science and Biomedical Sciences libraries at Cardiff University, Wales. He has a degree in English literature and a postgraduate diploma in librarianship (both from the University of Wales) and is a Fellow of the United Kingdom's Higher Education Academy. He is interested in all aspects of information literacy teaching and always tries to bring a sense of fun and the unexpected to his library instruction classes. He regularly presents at events and conferences throughout the UK and has also presented at ALA and LOEX of the West. He may be contacted by e-mail at MorganNJ@Cardiff.ac.uk.

Eric Palo is Director of the Library at Renton Technical College. Before that he was a library department head at the University of North Carolina – Chapel Hill and has worked in academic and public libraries in three states. He received an undergraduate degree in history and a MLIB from the University of Washington. He has won awards for being an outstanding faculty member, graduating first in his class from an army non-commissioned officer's academy, for service to his high school, and for best child's costume in the 1955 Kemano British Columbia May Day Parade. Eric may be contacted by e-mail at epalo@rtc.edu.

Suzan Parker is the Reference and Instruction, and the Social Sciences Librarian at the University of Washington Bothell/Cascadia Community College Campus Library. She earned her MLIS from the Information School at the University of Washington, and holds a BA in literature from Reed College. Her previous publications have focused on visual literacy and faculty/librarian collaboration in instruction. She has presented on visual literacy at ALA, using cultural artifacts as a pathway to information literacy at LOEX of the West, and on the developmental and contextual nature of information literacy at the League for Innovation in the Community College. She is currently co-chairing the ACRL Intellectual Freedom Committee and is interested in ways to increase awareness around intellectual and academic freedom issues affecting college and university libraries. She may be contacted by e-mail at sparker@uwb.edu.

Linda Reeves is Assistant Professor and Public Services Librarian at Northwest Vista College, a fast-growing community college in San Antonio. As a former college English teacher and a graduate of ACRL's Information Literacy Immersion workshop, Linda believes in the importance of the instructional role of librarians in helping students become information-literate lifelong learners. She received an MLIS from the University of Texas at Austin and a BA and MA in English from Ball State University. Her recent publications include "If Online Education is a Shifting Playing Field, What Position Should Community College Librarians Play?" (with Celita DeArmond) in *It's All About Student Learning: Managing Community and Other College Libraries in the 21st Century*, eds. David R. Dowell and Gerard B. McCabe (Westport, CN: Libraries Unlimited, 2006); and "Trying it On For Size: Piloting Synchronous Online Reference with Elluminate vClass," *Internet Reference Services Quarterly* 10 (Fall 2005). She may be contacted by e-mail at lreeves3@mail.accd.edu.

Karla M. Schmit is an Education and Behavioral Sciences Librarian and Assistant Director of the Pennsylvania Center for the Book at The Pennsylvania State University. She holds an MLIS from the University of Southern Mississippi. She has a BS in elementary education and a master's of science degree in reading education from Minnesota State University, Moorhead. She is currently a doctoral candidate in curriculum and instruction at The Pennsylvania State University. Her research focus is primarily the critical study of children's literature. She is exploring the social constructs and situated literacy practices that teacher education students bring to the discussion of children's literature. In 1998, she was awarded the Frederic G. Melcher Scholarship by the ALA Library Service to Children. She may be contacted by e-mail at kms454@psu.edu.

Kathleen Zakri is Dean of Instruction at Bryant and Stratton College's Syracuse North Campus. She received a master's degree in adult education from Elmira College. Her campus responsibilities include ensuring faculty and librarians provide outcomes-based learning that meets rigorous standards, supports information literacy, and encourages lifelong learning. For the College, with the System Director of Library Services, she co-chaired a sub-committee for Information Literacy across the Curriculum. With Li Zhu, she assisted in the creation and facilitation of "Fishing in the Deep Waters of the Internet: Ways to Cast a Wider Net" for a regional faculty in-service sponsored by the College's Faculty Development Committee. As a freelance writer, she has had short stories, poetry, and articles featured in local and national publications. She may be contacted by e-mail at kmzakri@bryantstratton.edu.

Li Zhu is Head Librarian and Information Literacy faculty at Bryant and Stratton College's Syracuse North campus and is the recipient of the 2007 Bryant and Stratton College's Information Literacy Instruction Award. Her responsibilities include instruction of a three-credit information literacy course, collection development, cataloging and reference, and campus library Web portal development. She received an MLIS degree from Syracuse University. She received a master's degree in education with a concentration in geography teaching methodology, textbooks, and curriculum design from Northeast China Normal University, China and Nanjing Normal University, China. Prior to her library profession, she was an associate professor at South China Normal University where she taught geography instructional methodologies. She authored *Population, Resource ,and Environment* (China: The Peoples Education Press, 2001) a senior high school textbook used nationwide in China. She may be contacted by e-mail at lzhu@bryantstratton.edu.